The

RAINFOREST™

The Secret to Building the Next
Silicon Valley

By Victor W. Hwang and Greg Horowitt

PUBLISHED BY REGENWALD
LOS ALTOS HILLS, CALIFORNIA, U.S.A.

Published by Regenwald
Los Altos Hills, California, U.S.A.

Cover and book design by Bill Rogers

Printed in the United States of America

ISBN-13: 978-0615586724

Library of Congress Control Number: 2012901584

Edition 1.02 May 22, 2012 (orig. published on February 21, 2012)

For Anders and Augustine, whose generation will inherit the Rainforest.

"And on the other hand, if I convey to my men my love for sailing on the sea—and each of them is so inclined because of an urge in his heart—then you will soon see them diversify according to their many particular abilities. This one will weave sails. The other will fell a tree with the flash of his axe. The other, still, will forge nails. And there will be someone somewhere who will observe the stars so as to learn how to helm.

"However, in the end, all will be one. Creating the ship isn't about weaving the sails, forging the nails, reading the stars, but rather imparting a taste for the sea, which is unifying. And in this light, there is no longer conflict, but in community there is love."

—Antoine de Saint-Exupéry, *Citadelle* (1948)

Contents

Introduction: Our Journey

We knocked on the door and were ushered into a waiting area. At first glance, there was nothing remarkable about the room. It was a typical office in an emerging city. This one happened to house a national institute charged with leading innovation development for the country. We have been to many of these institutes around the world, and they all look about the same.

But then we saw the wall.

What someone decides to put on a wall is revealing. Walls are aspirational. College students often decorate their walls with admired musicians, sports cars, or celebrities. Large companies often hang inspirational posters or modern art.

When you visit many incubators or venture capital firms in Silicon Valley, you see something unique to that world. You see trophies, but not brass cups or blue ribbons. Instead, the trophies are the names of the successful startup companies the firm helped grow. Often, you will see logos like Google, Amazon, Cisco, and others emblazoned proudly—sometimes arrogantly—on the walls of their entrance rooms. That is what we have come to expect.

In this particular office, however, we saw something that struck us as bizarre. Right above the place where visitors sit, clearly for everyone to see, were plaques we had never before seen in such a place:

What was starkly obvious at that moment was how terrible the world is at managing innovation. To date, there has been no systematic way to measure innovation, change it, or grow it. The management tool, ISO 9001, was created in the 1980s as a way to certify quality control for manufacturing processes.[1] Borrowed from a different paradigm, it was definitely the wrong tool for the job.

---

1 "Selection and Use of the ISO 9000 Family of Standards," International Organization for Standardization, accessed August 30, 2010, http://www.iso.org/iso/iso_9000_selection_and_use.htm.

For all the aspirational talk about innovation by CEOs and Presidents, society still lacks the right tools to deal with innovation. Like ISO 9001, the best management tools available are the same ones that automobile manufacturers might use to calibrate the quality of machine parts. If that is really the best management tool available for innovation, it is no wonder governments and corporations have such a hard time with it!

Why were we sitting in this room? We call this work Extreme Venture Capital—working on the fringes of the world's venture economy to fund the growth and development of promising startup companies. This work takes us from places as developed as Japan, Taiwan, Scandinavia, and New Zealand, to still emerging regions such as Mexico, Egypt, Kazakhstan, Colombia, Saudi Arabia, and the Palestinian Territories.

We are atypical venture capitalists. Our practice consists of two interconnected halves. On one side, we do what many venture capitalists do—we identify and invest in highly selective technology startup companies, and try to help them grow quickly and profitably, forming close partnerships with our entrepreneurs. Frequently, we work with scientists who are building companies from scratch based on their university research. Our chosen startups span a range of sectors from software to hardware, from biomedicine to bio-agriculture, from renewable resources to clean water.

On the other side, we take the insights gleaned from our hands-on experience and apply them to global development by working with governments to develop venture funds, startup incubators, and technology policy in emerging markets. We have a rare set of proficiencies at this intersection of private venture and public policy. We have advised dozens of institutions, such as the World Bank, the U.S. Agency for International Development, and numerous foreign governments. We have mentored thousands of entrepreneurs and innovators in over 30 countries. This has given us a special vantage point from which to observe some of the most interesting emerging companies in the world. We have managed organizations—Larta Institute, CONNECT, and Global CONNECT—that are considered thought leaders in this field. Today, we run T2 Venture Capital, which is headquartered in Silicon Valley and has offices in San Diego, North Carolina, Washington, D.C., and Dubai, among other places.

Over decades of combined experience, we have developed a unique field of expertise—*the analysis and fostering of innovation systems.* In so doing, we have discovered that the development of entire innovation systems differs profoundly from the conventional wisdom for encouraging innovation at the scale of individuals or small teams.

A New Theory of Everything

This book is different than what you might expect. This is not actually a book on how to innovate an idea or a product. It is rather a book about the nature of innovation. To be more precise, it is about the nature of complex innovation systems—whether they are in Silicon Valley, a large corporation, or anywhere else—and how we can foster the development of those systems. We believe that society, up to now, has failed to explain how such systems behave.

This gap in knowledge is significant because innovation is increasingly treated like the salvation for the world's economic future. Hundreds of books, tens of thousands of articles, and probably millions of Tweets have been scribed about how to "do" innovative actions one idea at a time. Very little has been written about how to "cause" innovation on a systemic level. Despite enormous public investments globally, only a few regions like Silicon Valley have become enduring *innovation ecosystems*— human networks that generate extraordinary creativity and output on a sustainable basis.

What is the nature of such innovation ecosystems, and how can we deliberately build them? In this book, we propose a radical "theory of everything" to explain the workings of innovation ecosystems. We call our model for such a system *the Rainforest*. It is an ambitious undertaking, and we probably don't get everything perfect. But we believe that by weaving together our personal observations with what we know about human nature, evolutionary biology, economic cooperation, and social systems, we can offer a new and more productive way of thinking about innovation. As a result, we can bridge together micro observations and macro theory. This book does not stop at theory: we give you practical tools to enhance innovation.

We believe in capitalism, but also see its limitations. Despite the successes of capitalism, there is still much of the world, including much of the United States, that has not experienced its full benefits. We wanted to write this book because we kept asking the question "Why?" Why do some regions boom while others sleep? Why do the best efforts of CEOs and prime ministers to spur innovation fail far more often than succeed? Why do some businesses stay at the cutting edge while others stagnate? Why does policymaking seem so disconnected from the real entrepreneurial process? Why are the practical tools of economic policy, government programs, and corporate venturing so limited when it comes to fostering innovation?

By constructing a new bottom-up explanation for human behavior in innovation ecosystems, we are challenging some basic assumptions that economists have held for over a century. In proposing this theory, we are influenced by several breakthrough ideas in academia, including insights on sociobiology from Harvard, economic transactions from the University of Chicago, and design theory from Stanford. We have drawn from a spectrum of human thought: economics, political science, legal theory, business, sociology, psychology, design research, biology, chemistry, neuroscience, physics, and mathematics. Our goal is to present a horizontal theory that stretches across many fields of knowledge. Out of necessity, we have had to simplify our coverage of many disciplines, but we are confident they all contribute to a consistent thesis.

The Rainforest model serves as an "antidiscipline" to the study of neoclassical economics. Harvard biologist E.O. Wilson describes an antidiscipline as the "adversary relation that often exists when fields of study at adjacent levels of organization first begin to interact".[2] For example, chemistry might be considered the antidiscipline of Newtonian physics, because the study of atoms at the basis of chemistry often leads chemists to believe that the fundamental laws of chemistry can be used to help explain the phenomena that physicists observe. In this book, we start with a different set of atoms—human beings—to explain why certain communities can generate so much innovation while most others fail. As we argue in this book, it is a question that the field of economics has largely failed to answer.

Our ideas might be considered a subset of the field of complexity economics, the study of complex economic systems.[3] However, we differ generally from complexity economists in our emphasis on practical observation and application. Our unique work has allowed us to observe what actually happens in real life, and so we endeavor to explain what we see in order to give people practical tools to navigate the real world.

The idea of the Rainforest is derived from our work with governments and policymakers, but we believe that the conclusions we draw from this work can be of great value in the field of business management. For instance, our Rainforest Recipe serves as a complement to the work of W. Edwards Deming and the practice of Total Quality Management (TQM) in large corporations. The challenge for colossal and often slow-moving bureaucracies to catalyze innovation is not limited to governments.

2 Edward O. Wilson, *On Human Nature* (Cambridge: Harvard University Press, 1978), 7.

3 For more information about complexity economics, see e.g., Eric Beinhocker, *The Origin of Wealth: Evolution, Complexity, and the Radical Remaking of Economics* (Boston: Harvard Business Press, 2006); W. Brian Arthur, *The Nature of Technology: What it Is and How it Evolves* (New York: The Free Press, 2009). A quote from Brian Arthur: "The movement that started complexity looks in the other direction. It's asking, how do things assemble themselves? How do patterns emerge from these interacting elements? Complexity is looking at interacting elements and asking how they form patterns and how the patterns unfold." (excerpted from "Coming from Your Inner Self, Conversation with W. Brian Arthur, Xerox PARC," Excerpt, by Joseph Jaworski, Gary Jusela, C. Otto Scharmer, April 16, 1999), http://web.archive.org/web/20080724094936/http://www.dialogonleadership.org/Arthur-1999.html. Archived from the original on 7-24-2008 (accessed on 8-25-2011).

Abstract of the Rainforest Model

Whereas neoclassical economists believe that macroeconomic output is determined by inputs—such as labor, land, capital, and (some argue) technology—such a theory fails to describe the behavior of real-life innovation ecosystems. To explain the differences between highly productive systems like Silicon Valley and most other places in the world, what is most important are not the *ingredients* of economic production, but the *recipe*—how the ingredients are combined together. Human systems become more productive the faster that the key ingredients of innovation—talent, ideas, and capital—are allowed to flow throughout the system.

In the real world, however, human nature gets in the way. Our brains are instinctively tribal. We are designed to trust people closer to us and to distrust those further from us. Ironically, the greatest economic value is created in transactions between people who are the most different from one another. Human nature, with its innate prejudices, creates enormous transaction costs in society. Thus, what we think of as free markets are actually not that free. They are still constrained by invisible transaction costs caused by social barriers based on geographical distance, lack of trust, differences in language and culture, and inefficient social networks.

Rainforests like Silicon Valley are able to overcome these transaction costs through a distinct set of social behaviors. These social behaviors correspond to the mechanisms that are necessary to maximize the free flow of talent, ideas, and capital in a human network. These behaviors, however, require that individuals rise above short-term selfishness and focus on long-term mutual gain. The Rainforest theory therefore contradicts the notion that economic productivity is highest when the rational pursuit of selfish motives is greatest. The key factors driving the strength of human innovation ecosystems are: diversity of talents, trust across social barriers, motivations that rise above short-term rationality, and social norms that promote rapid, "promiscuous" collaboration and experimentation among individuals. This is the culture of the Rainforest.

We propose various tools for designing, building, and sustaining Rainforests. People learn culture not from top-down instruction, but through actual practice, role modeling, peer-to-peer interaction with diverse partners, feedback mechanisms that penalize bad behavior, and making social contracts explicit. Leaders who can bridge between social networks to bind greater communities together for common action are essential to building and maintaining Rainforests. Public subsidies of venture capital are ineffective when fund managers are not culturally attuned to foster symbiotic relationships between investors and investees. Public attempts to foster innovation that do not focus on changing human behavior are doomed to fail. To build Rainforests, we must transform culture.

The Rainforest model is more than a metaphor. Innovation ecosystems are not merely *like* biological systems; they *are* biological systems. Talent, ideas, and capital are the nutrients moving through this biological system. Measuring the velocity of such nutrients can provide us the tools with which to measure the health of an innovation ecosystem by observing dynamic activity over time, rather than static points in time. When particular social behaviors allow the movement of talent, ideas, and capital to be even freer— as they are in Rainforests—we find that human networks can generate extraordinary patterns of self-organization.

The Rainforest model explains the largely invisible mechanisms that underlie innovation ecosystems like Silicon Valley. It is not *creative destruction* alone that is sufficient. Far more important is *creative reassembly*, the ability of humans to combine and recombine into ever-increasing patterns of efficiency and productivity.

How to Read This Book

To follow this book, imagine you are riding in a fast-moving vehicle that can soar in the heavens one second, but then zoom rapidly down to Earth the next, so closely at times that you can see the movement of individual atoms. It is as if you had a magical microscope that could operate at any level of magnification you could imagine.

We start Chapter 1 high in the sky. We view the entire Rainforest at the macro level, as an airplane might see a blanket of green from high above. We introduce you to the basic concept of the Rainforest. In Chapter 2, we show how conventional theories of economics and innovation fail to explain what we see happening today in thriving Rainforests. Then, in Chapter 3, our magnification increases. We zoom in to examine the interactions of individual atoms, cells, and species of animals and plants. We look at the unusual behavior of certain people in innovation systems and how their activities affect the inner workings of Rainforests. In Chapter 4, our microscope gets even closer. We explore human nature, examining how we are wired, and how it affects the ways in which we innovate.

In Chapter 5, we start to zoom out again. We describe the unwritten social rules that are working invisibly in Rainforests. In Chapter 6, we provide a recipe and tools for creating Rainforests and address why conventional recipes for innovation have failed. In Chapter 7, we explain the role of capital in Rainforests and why it differs from ordinary views on capital. As we close the book, our microscope zooms back out, even further than before. In Chapter 8, we fly above the treetops, and look again at the Rainforest from high overhead. We examine new ways to measure innovation that are radically different from those used in the past. However, given what we have learned from being close up, we see the ocean of treetops in the canopy of the Rainforest in a fundamentally different way. And in Chapter 9 and the Epilogue, we fly to the heavens.

Chapter One: What is the Rainforest?

The Mystery of Innovation

> *Basil Exposition:*   *A lot's happened since you were frozen. The Cold War's over!*
>
> *Austin Powers:*   *Well! Finally, those capitalist pigs will pay for their crimes, eh? Eh, comrades? Eh?*
>
> *Basil Exposition:*   *Austin... we won.*
>
> *Austin Powers:*   *Oh, groovy! Smashing! Yea, capitalism!*
>
> — **Austin Powers: International Man of Mystery**[1]

---

1   *Austin Powers: International Man of Mystery*, directed by Jay Roach (Los Angeles: Mike Myers, et al, 1997). Excerpt granted courtesy of New Line Productions, Inc.

Vodka and Physics at 25,000 Feet

It was straight out of a bad spy novel. Everyone is going to die, we thought.

It was well after midnight, and the rain outside was pounding the plane, which shook and shuddered in the heavy winds. Every so often, the windows would light up with lightning flashes. People might have gotten more airsick, but the vodka bottles flowing among many of the passengers seemed to counteract the ill effects. Vodka really is a wonder drug, it seems.

We were flying above the former Soviet Union. The plane, an old Antonov 24, was designed in 1957, before the first Boeing commercial jet ever flew. That was over five decades ago, and it felt like it. The orange-carpeted walls and disco lighting might have been the work of Austin Powers, if he was in the business of designing the interiors of old turboprop planes.

As the wind whipped the plane and the lightning flashed in our windows, it seemed that it could well be the end of us. They would find our bodies twisted among the wreckage of the orange-carpeted fuselage.

What were we doing on this plane in the first place? It was part of our work, what we call Extreme Venture Capital. We are venture capitalists based in Silicon Valley, and we are also experts in designing venture funds and growing innovation economies in new markets everywhere else.

It was a curious time and place to have a conversation about quantum mechanics. But we were. Our seatmate was Alistair Brett, a theoretical physicist who is now, like us, an advisor for the World Bank. He told us, "When I first got involved in this work, I was surprised to discover the math that economists were using." Alistair said this in his gentle manner, which seemed at odds with the radical nature of the subject. He continued, "Many of the equations used in thermodynamics are basically the same as the equations used in macroeconomics. At first, I was baffled. But then, I realized that the underlying math is the same. One field just applies the math to liquids and gases, and the other applies it to human systems."

Suddenly, high in the middle of nowhere and contemplating our demise, it all made sense. We humans tend to think of ourselves as so very important. But we are all just glorified bacteria in a petri dish, mere participants in a complex biological system we call human society. When viewed from high above, individuals become anonymous. However, our collective behavior creates discernable patterns. We behave as if we were atoms in an ocean. At a national or global level, we see only the ocean, not the atoms that make up the molecules of water. As Alistair observes, "That is why chemists and physicists can have such a hard time talking with each other."

Think of crowds at a football game. Three football fans cheering look like individual atoms. 100,000 football fans cheering in a stadium look like an ocean. Of course! Macroeconomics is about watching the rise and fall of oceans made of people. The mathematics of the movement of liquids should indeed be related to the mathematics of macro-human systems.

However, if we take that to be true, then Alistair's insight begs a huge question: what is the model to describe the systemic process of human innovation? If we can apply thermodynamics to macroeconomic behavior, why should there not be a way to describe how the simple atom-to-atom (people-to-people) interactions of human beings can have such powerful effects in communities such as Silicon Valley? In short, rather than measuring the behavior of atoms or the movement of oceans, *is there a way to watch the waves—the patterns that form as human beings come together to innovate?* And if not using traditional economics, then what?

Atoms/Molecules   Waves   Ocean

In this book, we attempt to provide an answer to this mystery of innovation. Like in any spy novel, the answer is elusive and will take many plots and subplots to reveal over time. Fortunately, we have some good clues to start the investigation. And like any new field of inquiry, the answer will require us to break some old conventions.

Therefore, with apologies to James Bond, we believe that traditional ways of describing economic behavior will possibly need to be shaken, not merely stirred.

You will have to wait until the end of the book to learn if we survived the flight from venture hell. In the meantime, we will take you on a different journey. Over the course of this book, we will travel from Silicon Valley to sub-Saharan Africa, from the Middle East to the American frontier. Along the way, we'll meet tribesmen, tradesmen, laboratory researchers, film producers, entrepreneurs, investors, and other characters in varied places around the world. We will also learn about mushrooms. But first, let us start with a simple story.

A Tale of Two Cities

It was the best of times, it was the worst of times.

In San Diego, things were booming. Despite the impact of the Great Recession, San Diego had a well-deserved reputation as a global hotspot for technological innovation. The region was a sleepy retirement and military community only 25 years ago, but now it was being hailed as one of the nation's most productive areas for the creation of new high-growth startup companies. Over 300 entrepreneurial efforts were being launched each year.[2] The city's startup companies were raising more venture capital than those of the entire Midwest.[3] People were calling the region the "wireless innovation capital of the world." Most of the world's leading biopharmaceutical companies—Merck, GlaxoSmithKline, Eli Lilly, Amgen, Biogen Idec, to name a few—had set up operations in San Diego, primarily to access the steady stream of new biomedical innovations emerging from the community. The same thing was happening in software, medical devices, energy technologies, and other sectors fueled by technological innovation. The University of California at San Diego had a similarly meteoric rise, expanding its research activities to $960 million in 2011.[4] As the surfers might say, the region was "cooking."

The explanations, it seemed, were obvious. San Diego was benefitting from policy changes that had unleashed the forces of free enterprise. Entrepreneurs could take grand ideas and turn them into realities because American society had lowered the barriers for doing so. Laws governing real estate, intellectual property, contracts, and corporations were sound and transparent, and they were easy to enforce. Taxes were low enough to keep entrepreneurs motivated. A brand new corporation could be setup in minutes and at a low cost. There were few serious artificial barriers standing in the way of building the Great American Company.

---

2 CONNECT Innovation Report, Second Quarter 2009.

3 "PricewaterhouseCoopers National Venture Capital Association MoneyTree Report," PricewaterhouseCoopers, accessed August 30, 2011, https://www.pwcmoneytree.com/MTPublic/ns/index.jsp. San Diego startups during 2001-2010 raised $11.4 billion. Midwest startups during 2001-2010 raised $10.6 billion.

4 Paul K. Mueller, "UC San Diego 2011 Research Funding Reaches Near-Record $960 Million," UC San Diego News Center, August 16, 2011, http://ucsdnews.ucsd.edu/newsrel/awards/20110816RecordFunding.asp.

Furthermore, San Diego had a tremendous network of people with deep, relevant expertise in science, technology, business, law, finance, accounting, and other key areas. This community of experts created a network of activity in which the best and brightest from around the world gravitated to the region to work with the people there, which attracted more people with complementary knowledge and skills, creating a circular, self-generating process that produced spectacular economic results. What Hollywood had done for entertainment, San Diego was doing for technology innovation.

In Chicago, however, it was the worst of times. True, there were a few unusual companies, such as the marketing wonder Groupon, but those sparks seemed like one-offs. They were not igniting the same kind of a system-wide transformation in the region that San Diego was experiencing. The experts were perplexed. Chicago had many of the same ingredients for technological innovation and entrepreneurial success. The city had almost exactly the same legal and business structures that San Diego had.

The region's educational institutions spawned a natural supply of raw talent and expertise. Two of the leading universities in the world—the University of Chicago and Northwestern University—were located a short distance from downtown, but little of their science was being translated into innovative commercial products. Nor could this lack of 'technology transfer' be attributed to disinterest on the part of the institutions. The University of Chicago—a school that counted 85 Nobel laureates as past or present teachers, students, or researchers—was actively seeking to accelerate the commercialization of its scientific discoveries.

Chicago had become one of the nation's most robust financial capitals, with massive hedge funds and the world's largest options exchange, but little of that money was flowing to entrepreneurial startups in the region. There were a number of major technology corporations already in the area—Baxter, Motorola, Alcatel Lucent, and Boeing among them—but they were not considered active participants in the commercialization of new technologies there. People had even dubbed the region the 'Silicon Prairie' to express their aspirations for it to become the American Midwest's leading hub for innovation.

Despite its infrastructure, institutions, expertise, capital, and grand aspirations, however, the metropolitan region of Chicago was seeing a trickle of technology startups compared to San Diego's flood, and those startups were having a hard time growing into sustainable companies. How do we explain the difference? The two reasons people most commonly cited to explain San Diego's success—the power of the American free enterprise system and the region's concentration of talent and expertise—could just as easily be said about Chicago, if not more so. Unfortunately, the conventional answers fail to explain the perplexing divergence of these two cities. San Diego had turned into a highly productive system of innovative activity—a Rainforest. Chicago had not.

Chicago is not alone. Today, the rest of America's industrial and agricultural heartland, not to mention the rest of the world, is essentially confronting the same challenge. Most of the world wants to be a Rainforest, but can't figure out how.

We are left with a great mystery. Like the biological riddles buried in the rainforests of the Amazon, this mystery does not easily reveal its secrets. But like scientists toiling in the jungles over many years, we believe we have uncovered some of the answers behind this puzzling mystery of innovation.

Sagan's Stew

Innovation is the story of the human race. It has made us the dominant species on Earth. The ability to collaborate—to combine disparate talents, ideas, and resources into a greater whole—has created a modern society based on mutually productive and beneficial transactions.

Innovation is still something of a mystery, however. Despite hundreds of books and thousands of papers on the subject, real-world innovation is little understood. Business school professors devote entire careers to it. Companies and governments spend billions on it.[5] Millions of people claim to practice it daily. Yet most people still don't really know what creates, fosters, or enables the process of innovation.

It is now commonplace to say that innovation drives economic growth and enables our modern standard of living. However, we know more about the birth of galaxies than we know about the systemic process that creates companies like Google or Facebook. Cosmological scientists can design carefully-planned experiments to test and confirm hypotheses about the origins of the universe—using recessional velocity, radiometric dating, background radiation, or other tools—and then make conjectures to explain what they are seeing in measurable detail. When it comes to innovation, though, social scientists are basically left to throw lots of money at problems and—like the proverbial spaghetti thrown at a wall—are left to see what sticks. We should and can do better.

---

5   See, generally, Josh Lerner, Boulevard of Broken Dreams: *Why Public Efforts to Boost Entrepreneurship and Venture Capital Have Failed—and What to Do About It* (Princeton University Press, NJ: Princeton: 2009). Comprehensive survey of efforts to stimulate innovation in a wide variety of regions, including in: Silicon Valley, Singapore, Tel Aviv, India, China, the United States, Australia, Malaysia, Britain, Norway, the European Union, France, the State of Kansas, Canada, Massachusetts, New Zealand, Finland, and numerous other countries and universities across the world.

The birth of galaxies is not unlike the birth of innovation. In 1980, millions of Americans were captivated by the public television series *Cosmos*, hosted by the astronomer Carl Sagan. After three decades, *Cosmos* is still considered the most-watched PBS series in history.

There was one especially memorable moment in the series. In the episode entitled "Blues for a Red Planet," Sagan examined the chemistry of life on earth, but he did so in a particularly striking way. He started with a huge vat of water, and then added some unusual things: four large buckets of charcoal (made of carbon), a bucket of chalk (calcium), a pail of nails (iron), a vial of liquid nitrogen, and some other seemingly random elements. All were dumped into the vat.

For a finale, Sagan took a big stick and stirred the mixture like a fairy-tale cauldron of witch's brew. He told us the things he had put in the big vat were exactly the same elements, in the same proportions, contained in a human being. But why, Sagan asked, were the elements not a human being? What was the difference between a stew of ingredients and an actual human being made of exactly the same ingredients? Sagan observed: "The essence of life is not so much the atoms and small molecules that go into us as it is the way...those molecules are put together." In other words, when you take raw elements and combine them, you need a unique recipe to turn those elements into something special, a preparation that creates something greater than the sum of its components. [6]

The same is true of innovation. Having all the right ingredients—such as those present in Chicago—will not necessarily result in successful innovation. You need to prepare those raw ingredients, combining them in just the right way, as they were in San Diego.

Unconventional Wisdom

Many people believe—and neoclassical economists have argued—that entrepreneurial innovation flourishes when governments and other public institutions take a largely hands-off approach. As capitalists and businessmen, we believed it was that straightforward, too.

We had faith in the "magic of the marketplace." We feared that intervention by public institutions could risk distorting economic incentives and burden the ability of entrepreneurs to build successful companies. After all, free market capitalism won the Cold War, much to Austin Powers' surprise at the beginning of this chapter. Capitalism has done more to relieve poverty and raise standards of living throughout the world than any international aid or

6 *The Concise Encyclopedia of Economics*, s.v. "Economic Growth," by Paul M. Romer, accessed August 30, 2011, http://www.econlib.org/library/Enc/EconomicGrowth.html. "History teaches us...that economic growth springs from better recipes, not just from more cooking."

government program.[7] If human energy can only be freed from government interference, then flashes of inspiration should follow. Networks of innovators ought to form to spur the success of startup companies. Society's role, if any, should be minimal, perhaps limited only to ensuring strong legal protections for property, training an educated workforce, and possibly investing in some cutting-edge scientific research.

Yet, what we have learned through years of working with entrepreneurs around the world is that when it comes to innovation, the unbridled free market is not as productive as conventional wisdom says it should be. We found that a recipe employing a laissez-faire approach—in short, to simply let the ingredients do their thing—is really no recipe at all. The marketplace has not worked its magic in most parts of the U.S. and the world, even where entrepreneurs are unhindered by government interference. The vast majority of the planet's venture capital and its fastest-growing startup companies are concentrated in just a few unique places.

Which begs the question: what makes these places unique? There is basically the same framework of laws governing labor, taxes, securities, contracts, and intellectual property in Indiana's Wabash Valley as there is in California's Silicon Valley. According to neoclassical economics, the barriers have been lowered, and we should step back and let innovation burst forth. The Midwest gets a large share of federal scientific research money, so one cannot really argue that there is a lack of clever people with good ideas in America's heartland. The truth, however, is that it would be much more difficult to start the "next Google" in the Wabash Valley than in Silicon Valley. The free-market theories of neoclassical economics do not provide the whole solution to this problem.

Cluster theory has also proven itself to be an inadequate explanation for the phenomenon of innovation. Economic development experts have spent years trying to develop clusters: geographic concentrations of talent, companies, suppliers, service providers, and associated businesses in a particular specialized field. While clusters are often present where entrepreneurial innovation occurs, we believe that clusters alone do not cause or even particularly facilitate innovation. Surprisingly, they can even hinder it.

We argue that the two pillars of innovation's conventional wisdom—free markets and clusters—are unable to provide comprehensive answers to the mystery of systemic innovation. *Where innovation is concerned, markets are largely inefficient.*

---

7   Fareed Zakaria, *The Post-American World* (New York: Norton, 2008), 7. "...between 2000 and 2007... income per person across the globe would rise at a faster rate (3.2 percent) than in any other period in history."

This may seem like a shocking statement to many. We did not start out believing that governments are essential to innovation, but our hands-on experiences in the field have led us to believe that public institutions have a much bigger role to play than typically thought.

In this book, we provide a new way to think about innovation, and we propose solutions that go beyond—and even contradict—conventional thinking. We are proposing a new approach to economics, one in which governments play a necessary and vital role. Public institutions can help foster a system of innovation where the raw ingredients can combine in just the right way. In so doing, these institutions can plant the seeds of the Rainforest—an ecosystem of innovation where startup companies can grow, and economies can thrive.

For the first time, we can construct a model for innovation by weaving together the latest scientific insights into the ways human beings think, act, and communicate with one another. We can use this scientific model to derive well-grounded solutions for leaders to enhance the ability of societies to innovate. We can connect the dots between seemingly disparate realms of inquiry—physics, chemistry, biology, neuroscience, psychology, sociology, economics, law, business, design research, and political science— to achieve what Harvard biologist E. O. Wilson calls *consilience*, a unity of knowledge where the evidence-based physical sciences are able to help explain and solve questions that have vexed the social sciences.[8]

A better answer to the mystery of innovation can potentially boost economies all over the world, improving the welfare of billions of human beings. On the other hand, a continued lack of understanding of systemic innovation means that many people will experience a life of economic underperformance. It also means that government leaders will continue to throw billions of dollars into poorly-planned programs that claim to spur innovation and economic growth, but end up wasting desperately needed capital.

If there is an answer to the mystery of innovation, then that answer must be more than an armchair theory. It must give leaders something to do, a plan of action to implement, so that we can actually make practical, measurable improvements in human welfare and economic performance.

---

8   See generally Edward O. Wilson, *Consilience: The Unity of Knowledge* (New York: Vintage Books, 1999).

In this book, we attempt to solve the mystery of innovation. In particular, we examine the raw ingredients of human society—people with ideas, people with talent, and people with capital—and we propose an explanation for why those raw ingredients seem to be "put together" so effectively and so frequently in certain communities to create tremendous economic wealth, but why in most places those basic ingredients do not combine effectively at all.

In other words, in terms of innovation ecosystems, most of the world still resembles Carl Sagan stirring that giant vat of water, charcoal, nails, and chalk.

Growing Weeds, Not Crops

What is the difference between a plantation and a rainforest? This is not a trick question. The differences are telling.

Plantation   Rainforest

The model of business emerging from the Industrial Revolution can be described in many ways as an *agricultural* model. Such a model is focused on controlling complex systems, using the latest technical tools to finely calibrate accuracy, precision, and productivity. The greater the degree of control, the better the output. Companies are rewarded for efficiency in production, much like farmers trying to squeeze greater crop yields out of every square foot of land using the best fertilizers, pesticides, or farming methods. Think of the archetypal image of garment workers toiling at rows of sewing machines. Or an assembly line in an automobile plant. The faster the assembly line, the more money you make. The more dependable the quality, the more customers will buy the product over and over again.

By contrast, when we think about innovation systems, the greatest productivity comes from environments that resemble not cropland but *rainforests*. In nature, a rainforest functions not because of the mere presence of raw carbon, nitrogen, hydrogen, and oxygen atoms. It thrives because of the way in which these elements mix together to create new and unexpected flora and fauna. A rainforest is an environment with special characteristics—the air, the nutrients in the soil, the temperature, for example—that encourage the creation of new species of animals and plants that are greater than the sum of their elements. A rainforest takes lifeless inorganic matter and creates systems of thriving organic matter.

Natural rainforests do not predetermine the certain evolution of new and valuable species, but they provide the right setting to foster their serendipitous evolution. In rainforests, the most promising life forms emerge in unpredictable ways from highly fertile environments. The Rainforest model we propose in this book is similar. When we think of innovation systems, we should not try to force individual innovations into existence, but we should try to design and shape the proper environment that cultivates such innovations to be born and thrive.

This paradigm shift is not easily made, because the agricultural model has dominated the way we create and perceive value in business. Think about how real businesspeople behave. In the agricultural model, one usually pulls out a weed that does not belong. If you are planting corn, you want to kill the dandelions. You would normally fire the oddball employee who chooses not to build the auto part according to predetermined, detailed specifications. In the Rainforest, however, what looks like a weed might be the most valuable new plant in the entire ecosystem. Think of companies such as Google and Facebook today—they were indistinguishable from weeds only a few years ago. The oddballs are the gamechangers in innovation systems. *In Rainforests, we want to nurture the weeds to grow.*

Thus, we discover an interesting paradox. A company that seeks to manufacture cheaper, better, more profitable laptop computers would run operations like an agricultural plantation. It would seek to control and tune all of the specific processes for producing that computer to the finest degree possible. However, a community that seeks to generate high levels of innovation throughout the whole system would do the opposite. It would run operations like a rainforest, not controlling the specific processes but instead helping to set the right environmental variables that foster the unpredictable creation of new weeds. This leads us to our first Rainforest Axiom.

....

Rainforest Axiom #1: *While plants are harvested most efficiently on farms, weeds sprout best in Rainforests.*

....

We can see an example of this paradox in the story of agriculture in America, which parallels the story of American innovation. Many of our great universities—including the University of California system, the Massachusetts Institute of Technology, and many leading academic institutions in the American heartland—were initially founded with a focus on agricultural studies. The goal was to help farmers learn how to apply technologies to boost their output. The Morrill Land-Grants Acts of 1862 and 1890 used proceeds from the sale of federal land to provide every U.S. state with funds to establish agricultural colleges. Altogether, 106 colleges were launched with the goal of increasing America's agricultural capacity. To disseminate that knowledge even further, the cooperative extension program—funded by the Smith-Lever Act of 1914—helped universities hire agents to teach those ideas to still more farmers and to take those technologies directly to the farms. It was the original model for *technology transfer*—innovation as a controlled production and distribution process from university to user.

This model has become the dominant one for sponsored innovation worldwide. Today, Fortune 500 corporations regularly support scientific research in-house or at universities in order to stay in touch with new developments, and hopefully take advantage of them. Japanese corporations work closely with governments to sponsor research they can transfer back into the corporations. U.S. federal laboratories and NASA have established a network of technology transfer centers to serve as commercialization agents, pushing government-sponsored technologies to the public. These examples are all just variations on a theme—formal, linear structures intended to take new ideas from one point and move them like an assembly line to another point.[9]

This model, however, does not resemble the way we think of innovation impacting the world today. The old model now looks increasingly like a dinosaur. Compare the formal architectures enacted by the Land-Grants Acts to the highly informal social systems that spawned startups that grew

---

9   This top-down, controlled model is typical of many failed government projects in the 20th century. James C. Scott, *Seeing Like a State: How Certain Schemes to Improve the Human Condition Have Failed* (New Haven: Yale University Press, 1999), Introduction, Kindle edition. Scott argues that "high-modernist ideology"—caused by self-confidence about human ability to master nature, create rational utopian order, and devise aesthetic geometrical plans—has led to many "fiascos" of "state-initiated social engineering." States cannot exclude the "necessary role of local knowledge and know-how."

into great companies like Google, Apple, Facebook, Twitter, Zynga, Amazon, eBay, Genentech, Sun Microsystems, and Tesla Motors. In the past, the key rate-limiter was a government's ability to teach more students or hire more agents to visit more farms and disseminate more knowledge. Today, the key rate-limiter is how quickly people and resources can be assembled together to solve problems in real-time.

In short, the key question has changed from "How efficiently can we produce more crops?" to "How quickly can we nurture the growth of good weeds?"

But what is the recipe for innovation that helps nourish the weeds? That is the question we explore in this book.

The Biology of Innovation

The foundation of the Rainforest model is the acknowledgment that humans are biological beings. Human society, therefore, is a biological system. The idea is not as strange as it might seem at first. Economist James Galbraith at the University of Texas recently stated his belief that we are moving towards "the understanding that principles that underlie biological systems are the same principles that underlie all living systems."[10]

However, humans cannot be contained in a petri dish. Our petri dish happens to be the size of our global civilization, and this particular breed of bacteria happens to wear clothes and drive cars. Despite our social networks, the billions of relationships that span continents, and our complex systems of rules to govern our relationships, we are still animals whose behavior can be studied and modeled and even predicted.

How we interact with each other is like a recipe that takes a bunch of independent atoms—human beings—and combines them into something greater than the mere sum of these atoms. Most of the time, that recipe looks quite familiar. It consists of the day-to-day interactions that make up everyday life: buying vegetables at the supermarket, making a phone call to your mother, sharing a coffee with your friend. Every once in a while, however, the recipe has an explosive effect, like an ember that bursts into a blazing fire. This is the spark of systemic innovation. Systemic innovation happens when the value we get out of a continuing series of human interactions is disproportionate to the original value of the ingredients we

---

10 *The Straddler*, "The Predators' Boneyard: A Conversation with James Kenneth Galbraith," Spring-Summer 2010 (italics added), http://www.thestraddler.com/20105/piece2.php. See also, Mark C. Suchman, "Constructed Ecologies: Toward an Institutional Ecology of Reproduction and Structuration in Emerging Organizational Communities" (Paper presented at the Workshop on Institutional Analysis at the University of Arizona, March 29-30, 1996), http://www.ssc.wisc.edu/~suchman/publications/constructed.pdf.

put into the system, not unlike a bag of fresh produce transformed into a gourmet meal. One plus one can indeed be greater than two.

How does life emerge in natural biological systems? In 1953, a biological researcher named Stanley Miller published a paper in the leading journal *Science* that revolutionized how we think of the creation of life.

> Miller had applied an electric discharge to a mixture of CH_4, NH_3, H_2O, and H_2—believed at the time to be the atmospheric composition of early Earth. Surprisingly, the products were not a *random mixture* of organic molecules, but rather a relatively small number of biochemically significant compounds such as amino acids, hydroxyl acids, and urea. With the publication of these dramatic results, the modern era in the study of the origin of life began.[11]

The upshot of his discovery: we cannot control the specific creation process of life itself, but we can ensure that the basic building blocks are present in the right type of environment. Life can emerge from a "prebiotic soup" if the basic molecules, the building blocks of life, are ready and fertile, waiting for serendipitous lightning to strike.

Innovation happens in an analogous way. Individual people are the atoms swimming in the complex biological system of human society. Innovation can be sparked to life by a particular combination of people who happen to have ideas, talent, and capital in the prebiotic soup of humanity. But those elements must be mixed in just the right way for them to find and connect with one another. When viewed from high above, humans are just particles moving around and bumping into each other. Rainforests—whether in Silicon Valley or elsewhere—are environments that encourage disconnected people to self-organize into greater forms of biological life.

---

11 "Jeffrey L. Bada and Antonio Lazcano, "Prebiotic Soup—Revisiting the Miller Experiment," *Science* 300 (2003), doi: 10.1126/science.1085145.

Science is providing new ways to understand how humans function as biological beings and as members of larger systems. The science is still largely incomplete, and there are many gaps in our knowledge yet to be filled. We cannot claim to have all the answers. However, the emerging evidence is pointing toward a paradigm shift in how we view innovation systems. By integrating the hard sciences with the social sciences, the Rainforest model connects the silos of academic disciplines to explain the process of systemic innovation. The "Tree of Knowledge" by Professor Gregg Henriques at James Madison University is a helpful framework with which to understand how this consilience of knowledge can happen:[12]

Tree of Knowledge

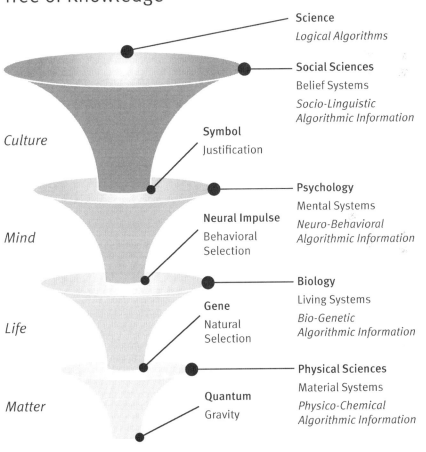

---

12 Gregg Henriques, "The Tree of Knowledge System and the Theoretical Unification of Psychology," *Review of General Psychology*, Vol. 7, No. 2 (2003), 150–182, doi: 10.1037/1089-2680.7.2.150. Permission to reprint diagram courtesy of Gregg Henriques.

The Rainforest model connects the vertical elements of this tree, linking together the physical sciences, biology, psychology, and the social sciences. A variety of academic insights are helping us to construct this new type of paradigm. For example, new understanding of the neurological processes in the human brain is providing insights into human social behavior. We are beginning to understand how people derive pleasure in the innovation process when they work together. We are also learning why the innovation process is hindered by human nature, as a result of holdover traits from our ancestral heritage as hunter-gatherers. Algorithmic insights on social systems show how certain types of human behavior, based on social norms and public goods, can lead to routinely lower transaction costs and higher economic output in given communities. Combined with our personal observations of the entrepreneurial process, we can begin to weave these strands together into a new model. Furthermore, we can devise new tools for leaders to apply this model, enabling them to make better judgments in allocating finite resources more effectively, to maximize output, and to improve economic well-being.

As author Dan Pink has stated, "There's a mismatch between what science knows and what business does."[13] The scientific knowledge that we need to understand the process of innovation is already there, but it remains in disparate pieces. We are in a position today to connect the pieces of this puzzle, constructing a model that helps us understand the underlying mechanisms and apply them for greater good.

The Bottom Line

What is the Rainforest? In biology, a natural ecosystem is formed by the interactions of a community of organisms with their environment. A Rainforest is a human ecosystem in which human creativity, business acumen, scientific discovery, investment capital, and other elements come together in a special recipe that nurtures budding ideas so they can grow into flourishing and sustainable enterprises.

---

13 Dan Pink, "Dan Pink on the Surprising Science of Motivation," filmed July 2009, TED video, 18:40, career analyst Dan Pink on the puzzle of motivation, posted August 2009, http://www.ted.com/talks/dan_pink_on_motivation.html.

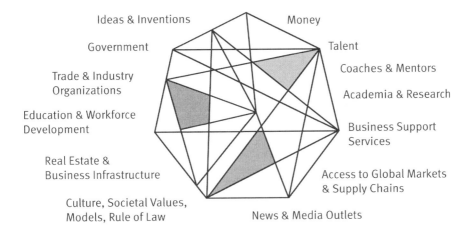

By the end of this book, we promise to give you a practical toolkit. We will reveal the invisible, underlying rules of behavior that cause people to come together in successful innovation communities. We call them the unwritten Rules of the Rainforest. We will explain these Rules and provide examples that illuminate how they function in practice. It is a surprising insight: while self-interest is natural and necessary, innovation requires a significant amount of self-sacrifice and self-restraint in order to thrive.

We will also give you the recipe and specific tools for building a Rainforest. You cannot build a natural rainforest simply by planting more trees. Instead, you provide the right environmental conditions, and then let the saplings sprout and grow on their own. Our Rainforest Recipe and Rainforest Tools provide you with a practical means to create the environmental conditions that cause innovation to flourish.

The Rainforest model helps explain the difference between a San Diego and a Chicago. Communities can have all the right elements—talented people, smart ideas, and plentiful capital—yet their results can vary dramatically. If humanity can solve this mystery of innovation and develop tools to build more Rainforests, then (to quote Charles Dickens) the future can be a far, far better place than it has ever been before.

Chapter Two:
Why Does the Rainforest Matter?

The Saga of the Anti-Google

*"I can calculate the movement of the stars,
but not the madness of men."*

– **Sir Isaac Newton, referring to his losing investment in
the South Sea Bubble**[1]

---

1   This quote is commonly attributed to Newton and is similar to a quote in *Joseph Spence, Anecdotes, Observations, and Characters of Books and Men* (orig. pub. 1820): "When Sir Isaac Newton was asked about the continuance of the rising of South Sea Stock, he answered, 'That he could not calculate the madness of the people.' —Lord Radnor"

The Anti-Google

In 1997, Professors Susan and John Gauch felt they were on the verge of something big.[2] The World Wide Web was growing quickly, and their startup company, ProFusion, had developed one of the best technologies in the world to search for information on the Web. Their technology was so good that the popular computer journal of its time—*PC Magazine*—proclaimed ProFusion as its "Editor's Choice" for the world's best meta-search engine that year.

The husband-and-wife team were professors in Computer Science and Engineering at the University of Kansas, and for years they had been at the forefront of academic research on software-based searching algorithms. In 1994, they decided to start a project—originally called Jayhawk Search—with $15,000 of university research funding. They placed the search engine on an ordinary shared university computer server. At the time, their only goal was to explore a new frontier of academic research: how to create a better search engine. Recalls Susan Gauch, "I really didn't see how anyone could make money on a free service for Web search."[3]

The company started to take off. By 1995, ProFusion was so popular that it had 300,000 users per month and had to move to its own dedicated server. In 1996, the service had over one million users per month. By 1997, it was clear they had built a world-leading invention, and at the time, commercial interest in the Web search industry was booming. Susan reminisces, "There was a time when ProFusion was better known than Google. Google actually called us to help drive traffic to them."[4]

In commercial terms, however, ProFusion was falling far behind its competitors. They had cut a few bad business deals and gotten involved with businesspeople they no longer trusted. Other companies with their own search technologies were beating ProFusion at the commercial game, even if their technologies weren't as good. Yahoo! had raised $36.8 million from investors,[5] was already selling its shares on the public markets, and was aggressively acquiring a slew of companies to rapidly expand its number of users and generate advertising revenues—companies like RocketMail (which became Yahoo! Mail), ClassicGames.com (which became Yahoo! Games), and Yoyodyne Entertainment (a direct marketing firm).

---

2 Susan Gauch, telephone interview with author, July 13, 2010. Facts from this interview are used throughout this chapter.

3 Ibid.

4 Ibid.

5 Wikipedia contributors, "History of Yahoo!," *Wikipedia, The Free Encyclopedia*, http://en.wikipedia.org/wiki/History_of_Yahoo! (accessed August 31, 2011).

In the end, ProFusion ended up getting merged into another company that did not fare any better, and the Gauches wound up with only about $100,000 for their years of effort. Susan and John probably worked for less than a minimum hourly wage by the time it was all done.

The ProFusion story is a case study in how a cutting-edge technology can end up in the dustbin of history. As Susan has concluded, "The success of an invention comes only partially from how interesting the technology is. The business side must be successful, too." [6] Susan and John never got to ring the bell at the New York Stock Exchange for the initial public offering of ProFusion. Or anything even close. ProFusion was the *Anti-Google*.

At first, the story appears simple and straightforward: great technology alone does not make a great business. It's a lesson we see played out thousands of times every day around the world. Building a better mousetrap does not necessarily mean the world will beat a path to your door. Look a little deeper, though, and the story is not so simple. The lessons are profound.

ProFusion failed because it was like a lone flower in a desert. There was no Rainforest around it. It was like an ingredient in a gourmet meal, without the rest of the gourmet meal. A great idea—the ProFusion meta-search technology—had some great technical talent behind it: the Gauches. But they did not have access to everything else needed to nurture a startup business—people who could really help them navigate the growth process, capture the loyalty of new users, develop business deals that could grow their user base, forge advertising partnerships to convert their users into revenues, hire executives who understood effective consumer marketing, and raise capital to enable them to do all these things.

ProFusion was based in Lawrence, Kansas, almost a full day's journey to any of the major regional clusters for executive talent, entrepreneurial capital, and strategic partners that understood how to build freshly minted startups into world-changing companies. Susan recalls, "Working from Kansas, we were simply not close to the industry and had a hard time being taken seriously as a company. We weren't landing those contracts. We couldn't convince large companies or investors to rely on us."[7]

The Gauches started off in their own social networks, with their own background and contacts in academia, and limited financial resources. To succeed, they had to break through the barriers created by geography, culture, and social networks. In that sense, they were not that dissimilar from pioneers in centuries past who might have had to climb over mountain

---

6 Gauch, interview.

7 Ibid.

ranges or sail across unmapped seas to trade their goods with people who lived far away in different cultures, perhaps speaking different languages. For ProFusion, the cost of crossing those mountain ranges proved to be too high.

In contrast, Yahoo! launched in 1994 from the Stanford campus, within a few minutes' drive of most of the leading venture capital managers in America and a concentration of entrepreneurial business talent with experience and expertise growing new technology startups. Yahoo!'s founders were able to access and synthesize the ideas, talents, and capital of this network.

Why do companies like ProFusion fail and those like Yahoo! succeed? It was not because Yahoo! had better technology or smarter people. The answer lies in their respective cultural environments. Yahoo! had something ProFusion did not: access to the most precious resource of all—human relationships. Yahoo! had the support of a Rainforest, while ProFusion was lost in the desert. The cost of not being in a Rainforest, the cost of having to build the right set of human relationships from scratch, was enough to kill the promising startup from Lawrence, Kansas.

Why do some places like Silicon Valley churn-out countless numbers of innovative startup companies, but places like Cairo, Egypt or Cairo, Illinois do not? It is not for lack of intelligence, hard work, technical proficiency, or money. There are smart, capable, hardworking and wealthy people all over the world. Conventional economic thinking says that the basic factors of production, such as human labor, skills, and capital resources, are sufficient to account for economic growth. Investing in these elements alone should generate economic growth.

But of course, they don't. Lawrence, Kansas was never able to replicate Silicon Valley's success despite having the basic ingredients.

There are a thousand stories in the desert. The Anti-Google is just one.

The Talent Myth

Susan and John Gauch were academic stars. Going all the way back to their college days in Ontario, the list of prizes, fellowships, and scholarships that they had been awarded are too numerous to list. They had both earned Ph.D.s in Computer Science at the University of North Carolina. They had both been published in leading academic journals dozens of times.

Smart people, however, are not enough. The world is full of smart people.

Many economists argue that governments and other public institutions should only intervene in the process of innovation where they are able to support its raw ingredients. Chief among these is talent. We invest in education and science because it strengthens human skills, one of the basic factors of production. Sometimes we invest in the teaching of entrepreneurship. And increasingly today, we even invest in creating local talent clusters, because we have a historical record that shows that clusters of highly skilled individuals seem to be present wherever successful innovation occurs.

However, the maps below show the massive disconnect between the investments we are making in higher education and the resulting outputs in innovation.[8] The American Midwest, for example (where ProFusion was located), educates a disproportionate share of graduate students in science and engineering.[9]

S&E graduate students per 1,000 individuals 25–34 years old: 2007

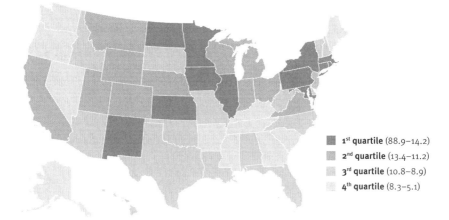

1ˢᵗ **quartile** (88.9–14.2)

2ⁿᵈ **quartile** (13.4–11.2)

3ʳᵈ **quartile** (10.8–8.9)

4ᵗʰ **quartile** (8.3–5.1)

8   National Science Foundation, "Science and Engineering Indicators 2010," Division of Science Resources Statistics, Survey of Graduate Students and Post doctorates in Science and Engineering, accessed August 30, 2011, http://www.nsf.gov/statistics/seind10/c8/c8i.htm.

9   NSF, Indicators 2010. http://www.nsf.gov/statistics/seind10/c8/c8s2o19.htm (Accessed August 31, 2011).

If we take a look at the areas where high-tech businesses actually get started, however, we end up with an entirely different map.[10] The Western United States has experienced an overwhelming preponderance of the nation's entrepreneurial activity.

Net high-technology business formations as share of all business establishments: 2006

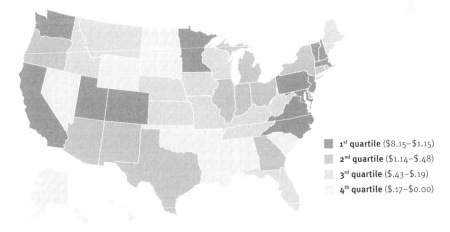

Furthermore, when we look at the amount of venture capital being invested in high-tech startup companies, we find another completely different map that seems to have little correlation with either of the previous maps.[11]

Venture capital disbursed per $1,000 of gross domestic product: 2008

10 NSF, *Indicators 2010.* http://www.nsf.gov/statistics/seind10/c8/c8s6o47.htm (Accessed August 31, 2011).

11 NSF, *Indicators 2010.* http://www.nsf.gov/statistics/seind10/c8/c8s6o50.htm (Accessed August 31, 2011).

The data indicate that regions are not necessarily getting back what they are putting in. The great majority of states that are investing significant resources in science and engineering education are not necessarily reaping the economic rewards of innovation. The presence of a cluster of smart, trained people does not mean that capital, business savvy, or any of the other elements necessary for success will naturally form to serve those entrepreneurs and enable their businesses to grow.

Indeed, any combination of ingredients will not produce the expected results unless they are combined and prepared in the right way. All the raw science and engineering talent in the world does not necessarily produce companies that can grow and thrive in the marketplace.

The Limits of Rational Choice

Imagine a scientist who has spent his entire career in one narrow field of molecular biological research. Imagine that he thinks that he has discovered the world's most promising treatment for kidney cancer. Perhaps he actually has. Now in his late middle-age, he wants to turn this discovery into a drug that real people can use.

Having spent most of his career working in a laboratory, he must figure out how to cross a vast, virtual mountain range of social barriers. He must survive an epic series of challenges involving the fragile and unpredictable dynamic of human relationships. He must contact, understand, befriend, and collaborate with a wide-ranging and disparate group of people who have expertise in business creation, management, capital-raising, intellectual property, accounting, banking, perhaps real estate, and many other disciplines. He must embark on a multi-year path to attain regulatory approval to sell his drug, with no guarantee that the path will not change tomorrow. He must differentiate himself from dozens of other scientists who came up with different treatments for kidney cancer at around the same time, some of whom might be competing against him in their own startup companies. He must develop a manufacturing process that is lean and cost-efficient, and adheres to extremely tight standards for quality control. He must gain the attention and earn the trust of doctors who must distribute his drug to real patients. He must establish a network of sales representatives, and a system for marketing initiatives. He will eventually need to negotiate and form contracts with enormous pharmaceutical companies that can help manufacture and sell the drug in larger volume. And so on. In real life, that scientist might actually have the best treatment in the world, but he would have no clue how to get it to market. He is operating in a competitive environment where a single wrong step can destroy his chance for success. As researcher Ade Mabogunje of Stanford observes, "There is a whole chain of agreements required to bring a venture into being."[12]

We work with hundreds of similar scientists every year. More often than not, these scientists are completely baffled, somewhat scared, and almost certain to make some terrible decisions at first. Scientists are only human.

People make mistakes and do dumb things all the time. However, neoclassical economic theory assumes that people act rationally to maximize their economic self-interest. Called "rational choice theory," or "rational action theory," it is a central underlying tenet of modern economic thought.[13] Rational choice theory is based on the assumption that people's actions always reflect a balanced consideration of costs and benefits in an effort to increase their personal advantage. Rational choice theory argues that the dumb things people do get cancelled out at the macro-level by the smart things other people do, so the world keeps turning and things keep getting better. However, our cancer scientist is anything but a rational choice actor. A single misstep by him could destroy his opportunity to create this drug for the rest of his life. Even if he had a magical handbook with all the information he needed, he would still make bad choices.

The world of innovation does not happen at the macro-level. Innovation is a "body contact sport."[14] It is a micro-level phenomenon. When applied to innovation, rational choice theory might make sense if you're a theorist thinking abstractly about the way the world *should* work. It does not accurately describe the way the world *actually* works. Actions cannot be condensed to a narrow set of rational impulses, but rather reflect the social and psychological complexities of real-world human interactions.

Every day at the granular level of innovation, life resembles hand-to-hand combat, not generals moving large armies on a map. People do things that are so dumb that there is no smart thing in the world that can compensate for it. Free markets do not operate in a vacuum, or in a perfect laboratory environment. They are populated by human beings who are messy and chaotic and, when they interact, create situations that are full of friction

---

12 Ade Mabogunje, personal interview with author, September 21, 2010.

13 We are admittedly oversimplifying economic models here. There are three major models—classical, neoclassical, and endogenous—but they all generally assume the rational actor model. The classical model of economics holds that productive capacity creates growth and capital increases capacity. Therefore the focus of economists is on understanding the factors of production. The neoclassical model focuses on the interplay between labor/time, capital goods, output, and investment. See, for example, the work of Robert Solow and Trevor Swan. Technology is exogenous—it allows one to create more output with fewer resources—so the policy focus is on allocation of resource choices, utility maximization, and production efficiency. In contrast, the endogenous model incorporates technology as a direct factor in economic growth. More human capital (in the form of skills and knowledge) increases output.

14 Thanks to Larta Institute's CEO, Rohit Shukla, for bringing this term into more popular use.

and impediments to cooperation. People do not always do the right thing or act in their own self-interest. Often, it is because they do not understand or are not even aware of the right thing. Sometimes it is because of emotional or psychological characteristics that do not easily fit in a neoclassical economist's orderly view of human nature.[15]

....

Rainforest Axiom #2: *Rainforests are built from the bottom up, where irrational economic behavior reigns.*

....

When it comes to innovation, the messiness, chaos, and human friction of the real world is enough to kill most opportunities before they get a shot at the marketplace. With rare exceptions, people like our cancer scientist do not stand a chance.

Freeing the Markets

By any measure, the Gauches lived in a free market in Lawrence, Kansas. They could buy things and sell things freely, as they chose. They could travel wherever they wanted. They could say whatever they desired and contract with whomever they wished. Kansas, like every other state in the nation, has a long tradition of established common law governing business contracts and property and followed federal laws on intellectual property and securities. The Gauches were the lucky beneficiaries of a functioning free market system in which to start a promising company.

However, as we learned, free markets were not enough for ProFusion. Innovative startup companies still require a unique kind of environment to thrive that free markets alone do not provide. The success of innovation requires the convergence of many disciplines and a particular kind of interaction among individuals. Innovation is a team sport that succeeds only through constant communication, iteration, and improvement.

---

15 Increasing scholarly research is challenging the explanatory usefulness of the rational actor model. See Yochai Benkler, "Law, Policy, and Cooperation," in Balleisen, Edward, and David Moss, eds. *Government and Markets: Toward a New Theory of Regulation* (Cambridge University Press, forthcoming), http://www.benkler.org/Benkler_Law%20Policy%20Cooperation%2004.pdf (accessed January 15, 2012). See also, Dan Ariely et al., "Large Stakes and Big Mistakes" (working paper No. 05-11, Research Center for Behavioral Economics and Decision-Making, Federal Reserve Bank of Boston, Boston, 2005), 19-20, http://www.bos.frb.org/economic/wp/wp2005/wp0511.pdf.; Daniel H. Pink, *Drive: The Surprising Truth about What Motivates Us* (New York: Riverhead Books, 2009). Behavioral economic research is showing that people do not respond to financial incentives as the rational actor model suggests. Richard H. Thaler, *Quasi-Rational Economics* (New York: Russell Sage Foundation, 1994).

The diagram below represents our attempt to capture a little bit of the complexity of this process.

The Innovation Funnel

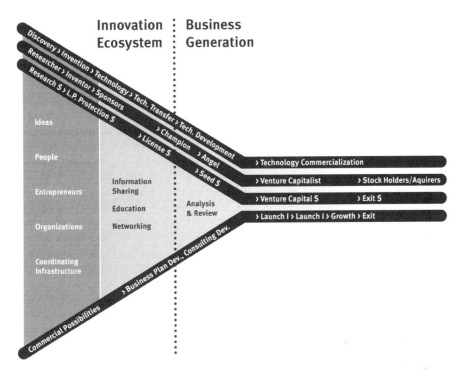

This diagram, however, can be misleading. Despite the shape of the funnel, the inputs on the left do not lead naturally to the outputs on the right. The "invisible hand," which supposedly moves resources around efficiently, does not do what we expect.[16] In most instances, the mixing of the ingredients of innovation does not happen naturally. We are not arguing against the power of free markets. On the contrary, we are arguing that...

> **Rainforest Axiom #3:** *What we typically think of as free markets are actually not that free.*

---

16 There is significant debate about the definition of the "invisible hand" and Adam Smith's original use of the term. Our usage in this book is broad and refers to the overall neoclassical economic assumption that resources in macroeconomic systems are generally allocated in efficient ways.

Of course, efficient markets require the elimination of artificial, man-made bottlenecks that restrict economic activity and prevent entrepreneurs from flourishing. Breaking through those bottlenecks, however, does not mean that the traffic will follow. An inventor who has created world-leading software or therapeutics may be free to do whatever he or she wants with it, but it is rare that they can find the right people with whom to work. Even if we get the intentional man-made barriers out of the way—government restrictions, corruption, poor law enforcement, inconsistent taxes, etc.— many unintentional barriers still remain.

Many people praise the notion of "creative destruction" in the free market. This is the term that economist Joseph Schumpeter used to describe the process in which new innovations destroy established companies.[17] In our experience, creative destruction is far from a complete answer. After all, killing companies is easy compared to growing companies. The mystery of innovation cannot be answered without understanding *creative reassembly*—how people interact in ways to generate innovation in the first place. If creative destruction causes death, then we need creative reassembly to complete the cycle of rebirth.

Free market proponents sometimes support investments in scientific research as a way to stimulate new innovation.[18] It is one of the few areas where they believe that societal intervention might be justified. It is true that scientific research is important for economic growth—human knowledge is often considered a basic factor in economic production. Scientific research, however, does not always lead to economic growth. Each $1 increase in scientific research does not necessarily result in a $1 increase in economic activity in the overall system. The research alone is not sufficient.

The story of the Anti-Google is just one example of a problem experienced in thousands of startups every day around the world. In the real world, the path from discovery to commercial product is so long, tortuous, and serendipitous that the vast majority of world-changing technologies never see the light of day. Society has a surprisingly huge backlog of scientific discoveries that are "stuck in the pipeline," stalled by the human barriers that prevent them from reaching the marketplace.

---

17 Joseph A. Schumpeter, *Capitalism, Socialism and Democracy,* 3rd ed. (New York: Harper Colophon, 1975), 84.

18 For additional information see Paul M. Romer, "Endogenous Technological Change," *Journal of Political Economy* 98 (1990): S72, http://artsci.wustl.edu/~econ502/Romer.pdf.; Paul M. Romer, "The Origins of Endogenous Growth," *Journal of Economic Perspectives* 8 (1994): 3-4, http://www.iset.ge/old/upload/Romer%201994.pdf. The endogenous growth theory seeks to develop macro-economic models from micro-economic foundations. One of the conclusions of the endogenous model is that more funding for scientific research is linked to greater economic output.

Cluster's Last Stand

The story of the Anti-Google also demonstrates the inadequacy of cluster theory to improve the situation. The institutions involved in Lawrence were doing everything by the book, applying accepted economic theories on cluster formation to stimulate innovation.

For instance, the State of Kansas actively invested in its high-tech entrepreneurs. The University of Kansas—a public institution—provided research grants to develop products for commercial application. The university promoted regional collaboration and tried to streamline the process for faculty members to create new, local spinout companies. The state was providing entrepreneurial training and even direct assistance through its chartered nonprofit, the Kansas Technology Enterprise Corporation, which gave grants to startups to help them through the early stages of development. Kansas was doing everything in accordance with the conventional playbook, following the accepted methods for enhancing the strength of its indigenous cluster to support the growth of innovative startup companies. They were following the consensus view that, to have economic growth like Silicon Valley, one must aspire to look like the cluster of Silicon Valley.

The results of these endeavors, however, were nothing like those of Silicon Valley. And the vast majority of the world looks a lot more like Kansas than California.

For one thing, politics gets in the way. Political districts are geographically defined, so government programs and incentives try to keep companies in local economic boxes. "All politics is local," is a well-known saying. Modern companies, however, cannot operate in limited geographical areas anymore. We know a number of startup companies that tried desperately to escape the constraints of their regions, unable to grow sufficiently within them. We have witnessed local economic development organizations tell startup companies to start local and stay local as long as possible. Susan Gauch remembers, "We could not convince the State of Kansas to invest in ProFusion because the state defined success as creating jobs in the State. We had goals that were global and national in scope."[19] Moreover, Web companies have flourished precisely because they are not regionally limited—they are "scalable" regardless of geography. One unintended result of cluster promotion, not just in Kansas but all over the world, is that startup companies are sometimes more likely to fail. Many companies are pushed by regional government funding to look inward geographically, when in fact they need to do the opposite to succeed. Cluster promotion often has the unexpected effect of imposing geographically-based economic sanctions on a region.

19 Gauch, interview.

The evidence is mounting that cluster promotion has failed. A recent exhaustive study in Europe declared that local and national clusters were "irrelevant for innovation."[20] The researchers—Rune Dahl Fitjar of the International Research Institute of Stavanger and Andres Rodriguez-Pose of the London School of Economics—looked at 1,604 companies in the largest cities in Norway and discovered that "global pipelines" actually determined more of a company's success than local relationships. This is exactly the opposite of what people had been expecting after decades of costly investment in innovation cluster development.

Why would we impose geographical boundaries on innovation, when in all other aspects of economics we shun boundaries and strive for freer trade? Why would we choose to imprison startups from Peoria in a domestic version of Pyongyang? How could so many smart people be so wrong for so many years?

For the past several decades, institutions and agencies have sought to create their own versions of Silicon Valley. Because regional clusters like Silicon Valley are easy to see, and have been associated with an area where entrepreneurial success has occurred, many people came to believe that clusters were essential to or even *caused* innovation to occur.[21] Just because A is observed when B takes place, however, doesn't necessarily mean that A leads to B. Creating more smoke does not cause more fire. *A cluster is a description of a phenomenon, not a prescription for policy.*

Cluster theory, as practiced by practitioners today, is largely misguided. True, clusters emerge in certain regions because it is easier to do business with people who are nearby. People who live near each other are more likely to know each other's families, go to the same schools and churches, have similar values—in short, they trust each other more. However, just because clusters happen *some* of the time does not mean that clusters should be encouraged to happen *all* of the time.

20 Rune Dahl Fitjar and Andrés Rodríguez-Pose, "When Local Interaction Does Not Suffice: Sources of Firm Innovation in Urban Norway" (working paper, IMDEA, Social Sciences Institute, Madrid, Spain, 2011), 5, http://repec.imdea.org/pdf/imdea-wp2011-05.pdf.

21 For additional information about cluster theory, see Michael E. Porter, "Clusters and the New Economics of Competition," *Harvard Business Review* 76 (1998), 85, http://www.wellbeingcluster.at/ magazin/00/artikel/28775/doc/d/porterstudie.pdf?ok=j; Michael E. Porter, *The Competitive Advantage of Nations* (New York: The Free Press, 1990); Paul R. Krugman, *Geography and Trade* (Cambridge: The MIT Press, 1991).

Times have changed. The cost of connecting with people across vast geographical distances has plummeted in a short time due to the Internet and the low cost of telecommunications. It is basically free to talk with almost anyone in the world today. The cost of travel has also fallen dramatically, due to scheduling and ticketing software that has eliminated a great deal of inefficiency from air travel. The idea that it is only cheaper and easier to do business with people nearby is not necessarily true anymore.

The "classical" startup model in Silicon Valley made more sense in a world where the costs of collaborating with people outside a particular region were higher. The model might have looked something like this diagram below, with technologies invented at Stanford University, venture capital from Sand Hill Road (the Wall Street of venture capital), legal expertise at the corner of Page Mill Road and El Camino Real (where many law firms for startups are based), and entrepreneurial talent from the local community.

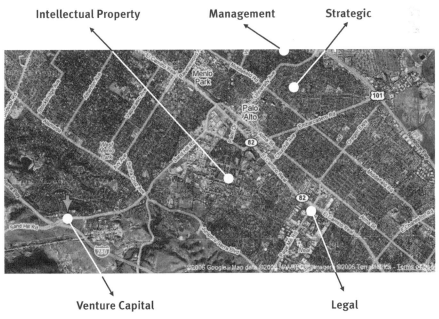

© 2006 Google Map data, © 2006 NAVTEQ Imagery, © 2006 TerraMetrics

In contrast, the startup companies we work with at T2 Venture Capital today are geographically unbounded in many ways. One of our startups, for example, includes scientists and intellectual property in New York, Australian and French entrepreneurs who immigrated to the Bay Area, investors from China and Silicon Valley, founding co-chairmen living in Florida and Minnesota, lawyers and accountants in Los Angeles, customers in Asia, and advisors and partners in other places throughout the world.

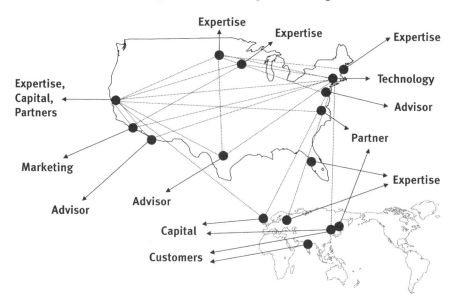

This decentralized network is an increasingly common model in the startup world, one that was exceedingly rare only a decade ago. Today, the same type of talent and capital in the "classical" Silicon Valley model must now learn to be comfortable working as part of a global network. It is the present and future of the startup business. In reality, a viable startup company today is a multi-national corporation from the day of its founding, drawing upon the right people with the right ideas, talent, and capital, wherever they happen to be located.

Like the free market model, the cluster model is insufficient when we think about innovation. It puts unnecessary limits on startup companies and artificially constrains the way we think about innovation. Rather than prescribing clustering as a solution in and of itself, we need to understand and strengthen the underlying human interactions that sometimes cause clusters, whether people are living close together or far apart.

Whereas a cluster is like the equivalent of a local town hall meeting, a Rainforest is like a conversation unconstrained by physical boundaries. A Rainforest is not about geography, but rather involves the right people regardless of geography. So, to create a Rainforest, we must retain the underlying human interactions that enabled the development of clusters—but knock down the walls.

The Unintentional Ancestry of the Rainforest

In the 1930s, a young undergraduate student named Ronald Coase wrote a little article. While pursuing his studies at the London School of Economics, he decided to visit the United States. He visited Ford, General Motors, Sears Roebuck, and Montgomery Ward, among other places, and was impressed by how well these companies were run. But he was left wondering something. His little article—"The Nature of the Firm"—took his observations and posed a simple question: why do companies exist at all?[22]

For several decades after its publication in 1937, the article received little attention. Then in the 1960s, it took off.[23] Over time, his article launched an entire field of inquiry and became one of the most cited articles in the field of economics. Coase would go on to win the Nobel Prize in 1991 for this idea and others. Today, he is one of the most influential economists in history.

Coase had noticed that, in a perfectly efficient market, we could all just do business through a bunch of separate contracts rather than tie ourselves down in formal companies. After all, setting up a company structure has its own costs and burdens. Why go through the hassle? To answer this question, Coase introduced the concept of "transaction costs." If the employees of a company had to negotiate and sign new contracts every time they wanted to conduct business with each other, he observed, the "transaction cost" of doing that would be higher than the cost of losing some freedom by working within the constraints of a single company. The benefits outweighed the costs of having people in a company together.

Coase observed that a "firm" was in fact simply a network of people who found that their costs declined when they did business together on a regular basis. In place of independent contractors, corporate structures give people an easier and cheaper way of mixing the ingredients of economic production. Groups of people tend to be more productive when their transaction costs for working together are lower.

---

22 R. H. Coase, "The Nature of the Firm: Origin," *Journal of Law, Economics, & Organization* 4(1988): 3-17; R. H. Coase, "The Nature of the Firm: Meaning," *Journal of Law, Economics, & Organization* 4(1988): 19-32; R. H. Coase, "The Nature of the Firm: Influence," *Journal of Law, Economics, & Organization* 4(1988): 33-47.

23 William M. Landes and Sonia Lahr-Pastor, "Measuring Coase's Influence" (presentation, Markets, Firms and Property Rights: A Celebration of the Research of Ronald Coase, Chicago, IL, December 4-5, 2009), http://iep.gmu.edu/CoaseConference.php.

Local clusters are no more than an extension of the Coasean model, with lower transaction costs for people who live and work close to each other.[24] Whereas a company is a group of individuals working together, a cluster is a region of individuals or companies working together. In both cases, these relationships result in lower transaction costs. And in both cases, those savings are derived from the fact that people are closer together, can communicate more easily, and trust each other more. They do not need to "re-negotiate" the terms of their transactions as often. The trust between them serves as a kind of informal contract. This is the hidden story behind many well-known economic hubs: Amsterdam, Florence, Wall Street, Detroit's motor industry, Hollywood, Silicon Valley, and Boston's Route 128, and it can be witnessed today to some degree in newer technology clusters like San Diego, Austin, and North Carolina's Research Triangle.

We believe that the Rainforest is the next step in the evolution of the Coasean framework. The Rainforest model takes the underlying insights of Coase's work and expands them—cutting across geographies, sectors, and social networks—to describe how people interact in modern networks to lower transaction costs and foster innovation. The Rainforest is a description of a virtual Coasean system that spans boundaries, enabling serendipitous reactions that lead to bursts of economic output. The Rainforest model reflects the way innovation works in the real world today.

---

24 We note the importance of the work of Professor Annalee Saxenian at the University of California at Berkeley. Her book, *Regional Advantage: Culture and Competition in Silicon Valley and Route 128* (Cambridge: Harvard University Press, 1996), is the seminal work in this field of regional thought, although she does not tie it to Ronald Coase explicitly. She analyzes the nature of entrepreneurial behavior in Silicon Valley and concludes that the traditional boundaries of a firm have been blurred: "Drawn together by the challenge of geographic and technological frontiers, the pioneers created technical culture that transcended firm and function. They developed less formal social relationships and collaborative traditions that supported experimentation. They created firms that were organized as loosely linked confederations of engineering teams. Without intending to do so, Silicon Valley's engineers and entrepreneurs were creating a more flexible industrial system, one organized around the region and its professional and technical networks than around the individual firm." Saxenian, *Regional Advantage*, 30.

We summarize the evolution of these Coasean systems—from the individual firm, to clusters, to the Rainforest—in the table below:

The Evolution of Coasean Systems

System	Units	Reason for Lowered Transaction Costs	Output of System
Firm (original Coase concept)	Employees instead of independent contractors	Reduce need for contracting; enhanced trust due to shared culture, similar goals and incentives	Corporate productivity through innovative products and/or services
Cluster	Individuals with ideas, talent, capital living close together	Physical proximity reduces geographical barriers to contracting; enhanced trust due to shared community, values, language, and culture	Small firms with ability to bring innovative products to market fast and flexibly, often starting locally
Rainforest	Individuals with ideas, talent, capital living anywhere	Modern technologies have greatly reduced geographical barriers and language barriers but need to develop norms of behavior; trust needs to be established, often from scratch, to compensate for lack of shared culture and community	Vastly greater number of small firms with ability to bring wider array of innovative products to market even faster and more flexibly worldwide

What economists call "transactions" are not limited to just commercial exchanges of goods or services. Transactions might include anything of value that one party is providing to another party, whether emotional support in tough times, looking after a neighbor's house while they are away, or a sense of communal belonging.

Thus, the Rainforest is actually a modern extension of an old idea. Ronald Coase has long argued that in order to understand the system-level economic effects of a human network, it is important to understand the actual behavior and incentives of individual actors within the system. He disdains "blackboard economics" and believes that economists tend to be too theoretical and do not pay enough attention to the details of day-to-day activity.[25] Following his line of thinking, the financial crisis of 2008 might have been preventable if economists had actually understood the specific banking transactions that were at the heart of the crisis.[26] In this book, we apply the same thinking with regard to innovation—you cannot understand the macro without understanding the micro.

The Cost of Distance

Ronald Coase is now over 100 years old. In writing this book, we were fortunate enough to connect with him.[27] He suggests today that the ideas he expressed in his original article were far from complete. The real world is far more complicated—one must deal with a range of complex social and psychological factors, personal networks, and information flows. He laments how few economists take these important issues seriously.

Firms are not strictly about *contracts* between people—more importantly, they are about *relationships* between people. That is, a company is a system that has lower internal transaction costs—not just due to the proximity of its workers or the internally organized legal and financial structures—but also due to the human ties within a company that enable people to transact business at a lower cost.

---

25 Ronald Coase, Nobel Prize Acceptance Speech (December 9, 1991). He said, "What is studied is a system which lives in the minds of economists but not on earth. I have called the result 'blackboard economics'. The firm and the market appear by name but they lack any substance."

26 Robin I. Mordfin, "A Celebration of the Mind and Work of Ronald Coase," *The Record Online* (University of Chicago Law School Alumni Magazine) (Spring 2010), http://www.law.uchicago.edu/alumni/magazine/spring10/coase.

27 Our appreciation to Professor Ning Wang at Arizona State University for serving as our facilitator in our communications with Professor Coase. For more information on recent work, see Ronald H. Coase and Ning Wang, "The Industrial Structure of Production: A Research Agenda for Innovation in an Entrepreneurial Economy" *Entrepreneurship Research Journal* 1 (2011), doi:10.2202/2157-5665.1026.

When we consider innovation, we are not focused solely on startup companies, or even companies at all. Innovation is really about the right relationships among the right people at the right time, so that innovation takes whatever outward form it needs to take, whether it is a large company, a fast-growing startup, a joint venture with a large corporation, a license agreement for intellectual property, or a nonprofit foundation. *In innovation, the superficial manifestations are secondary to the human relationships.*

So how do people work together to create these relationships with lower transaction costs? Throughout history, there have been several fundamental barriers that have kept people of diverse backgrounds from working together.

1. Geographic barriers (e.g., mountains, oceans, distance)

2. Social network failures (e.g., people belonging to different social circles)

3. Cultural and language differences (e.g., people not understanding each other)

4. Lack of trust (e.g., people fearful of working together)

These fundamental barriers hinder markets from functioning efficiently. They make free markets less free. They inhibit the creation of value.

....

Rainforest Axiom #4: *Social barriers—caused by geography, networks, culture, language, and distrust—create transaction costs that stifle valuable relationships before they can be born.*

....

The first barrier—geography—is a *physical* characteristic, while the last three are interpersonal barriers. With the increasing ease of communication and travel, it is now clear that the first one, the cost of overcoming geography, has fallen significantly and will continue to fall. Today, we can exchange documents and make Skype calls to anyone in the world at almost no cost. These changes have created a seismic shift in the way innovation is generated. Transportation and communication advances are enabling people to interact who have never had the opportunity to do so before. It is also creating a challenge: *the barriers that prevent innovators from working together are shifting from the physical to the interpersonal.*

We therefore face an interesting paradox. While greater opportunities for innovation are now possible because vast *geographical* distances are shrinking, people have not developed the skills for dealing with the vast *social* distances between diverse communities and cultures. Innovators are having a harder time building trust and collaborating across these human distances. The mountain ranges and unmapped seas that prevented human interaction in years past are being replaced by the social, cultural, and language barriers that hinder people trying to work together for the first time.

Clusters involve people who are similar. Rainforests include a wider universe of individuals who are different. When we talk about the distances between people, we are not just addressing the cultural differences between, say, Americans and Arabs. The challenge of bridging interpersonal distance is significant even within the United States. We see this in our work all the time. Scientific researchers from Lawrence, Kansas, for example, generally hang out in their own social groups. They speak the language of academia and practice its values. And they generally distrust and do not understand the motivations of perfectly decent businesspeople from Kansas City—less than an hour away.

An academic researcher and a businessman might even be the perfect theoretical partnership "on paper" if they could actually figure out how to understand, communicate with, and trust one another. According to economists, people should connect and collaborate and do business if it is in their rational interest to do so. In reality, what often happens is that inventors and entrepreneurs can sit in the same room, looking at the same presentations, hearing the same words, even having the same goals, but they still do not understand or trust each other enough to work together. We have seen this happen time and again.

Distances in Social Networks

The easiest way to demonstrate the problem of social networks in innovation is to represent them in an illustration. Let us imagine a set of inventors. They could be researchers at a university or a group of garage tinkerers. They might be represented like this:

In a perfectly efficient world, they would all know each other and would be able to freely interact with each other, like this:

However, researchers have discovered that social networks in reality are nothing like this at all. In fact, they have demonstrated what common sense tells us to be true: some people are more popular than others. In any social network, there will be hubs that connect with lots of nodes, and there will be nodes that seek to connect to others through a social hub.

We see this behavior in all types of social networks. We see it in the halls of any public high school, where certain individuals are hubs of social activity while the vast majority of individuals are not. The hub is the popular guy who organizes the parties. We see this phenomenon on the Internet, where certain Websites—think of Google, Facebook, or Twitter—become massive social hubs through which the rest of the nodes on the Web are able to find one another. We see this behavior in nature as well. As social network expert Albert-Laszlo Barabasi writes:

> ...we find that real networks are governed by two laws: *growth* and *preferential attachment*. Each network starts from a small nucleus and expands with the addition of new nodes. Then those new nodes, when deciding where to link, prefer the nodes that have more links. These laws represent a significant departure from the earlier models, which assumed a fixed number of nodes that are randomly connected to each other.[28]

---

28 Albert-Laszlo Barabasi. *Linked: How Everything Is Connected to Everything Else and What it Means for Business, Science, and Everyday Life* (New York: Plume, 2002), 86.

The worlds of inventors, investors, and entrepreneurs are no different. Only in an imaginary world would we see perfectly efficient networks *within* social groups like this:

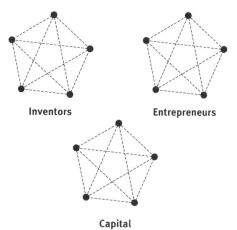

Or *between* social groups:

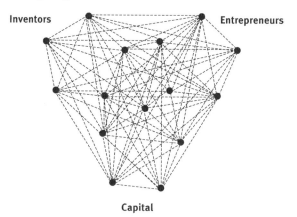

Neither of these diagrams reflects the reality of the social networks that actually underlie the innovation process. Social networks are never perfectly efficient. Certain individuals will always be more popular than others. A more realistic picture of the social networks for innovation might look more like this:

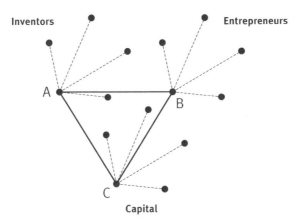

In this stylized diagram of fifteen nodes, it is only nodes A, B, and C that serve as hubs for the rest of the nodes. The other nodes can still get to each other, but they have to go through at least one of the three main hubs to do so.

Let us now pose two hypothetical situations. In the case where nodes A, B, and C are the necessary ingredients to launch a startup company, it seems like a fairly straightforward set of connections needed to bring the right pieces together. They already know each other, hopefully get along together, and can explore new collaborations if the opportunities present themselves. However, in the diagram below, where D, E, and F are the right ingredients instead of A, B, and C, we find the complexity of the situation increases significantly.

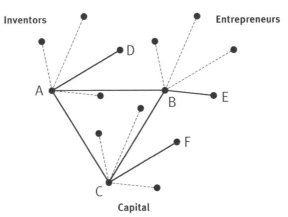

Now, instead of three connections that need to be made, there might be nine. E needs three steps to get to D; D needs three steps to get to F; and F needs three steps to get to E.

This diagram, of course, is a simplified version of reality. There can be many, many more steps to connect the right people, and the individuals traversing these networks often do not know at any given stage if they are moving in the right direction. This model doesn't even take into consideration the unpredictable nature of human interactions—phone calls or emails going unreturned for months, people who simply don't "hit it off" when they meet, those who cannot understand or trust one another, or potential partners who have trouble getting together due to scheduling conflicts—all the messy chaos of human relationships. When you take everything into consideration, you begin to understand why real-life innovation is such a complex process.

You also understand why being one of the hubs in the diagram—the A, B, or C nodes—is so lucrative. It explains why we compensate brokers so much, whether they're investment bankers, real estate agents, or marriage matchmakers. There is a high value to connecting nodes that would otherwise never meet.

It also explains why bad brokers can be so costly. They not only extract payment for their services, but by denying parties the chance to connect,they are extracting a second cost from everyone involved: the lost value of a missed opportunity. When we say the Anti-Google was in the desert, what we really mean is that it was on a distant node.

Bridge Building

If you were a naturalist trying to preserve a real rainforest in the Amazon, should you try to save one big piece of land or lots of smaller pieces of land? The answer to this question matters to innovators as much as to nature lovers.

The study of biodiversity (a term also coined by Professor E.O. Wilson)[29] has determined that biological ecosystems are much more vibrant if they are comprised of a contiguous tract of land rather than a number of smaller isolated parcels.[30] For example, a single contiguous 1,000 square-mile park

---

29 *Wikipedia's* "Biodiversity" entry. According to Wikipedia contributors, the term *biodiversity* may have been coined by W.G. Rosen in 1985 while planning the 1986 *National Forum on Biological Diversity* organized by the National Research Council (NRC). It first appeared in a publication in 1988 when E. O. Wilson used it as the title of the proceedings of that forum.

30 Jared M. Diamond, "The Island Dilemma: Lessons of Modern Biogeographic Studies for the Design of Natural Reserves," *Biological Conservation*, Vol. 7, no. 2 (1975), 129-146; and Robert H. MacArthur and E.O. Wilson, *The Theory of Island Biogeography*, Princeton University Press (1967). The Diamond article ignited what is commonly referred to as the SLOSS Debate ("single large or several small") for preserving biodiversity.

will lead to a greater number of species than two separate parks of 500 square miles each, which in turn are better than four parks covering 250 square miles each, and so on. Biologists call this phenomenon the species-area curve, and the evidence is well-documented. Connecting separate parklands produces greater biodiversity, which explains why environmental advocates often promote linking parks together—even if it means using narrow "land bridges" or "habitat corridors" to connect them. In the field of innovation, the traditional cluster model is basically the equivalent of an isolated park. In the Rainforest, individuals need to be connected using human land bridges into larger and more vibrant systems. The larger the human network, the greater the number of possible market niches and the greater the potential for diverse interactions that yield valuable results.

....

Rainforest Axiom #5: *The vibrancy of a Rainforest correlates to the number of people in a network and their ability to connect with one another.*

....

Without our human "land bridges"—like the Internet, phones, roads, and all the other communication tools we rely on today—the world would resemble lots of little Galapagos Islands pressed up against each other. There would be little interaction between groups of people. We can see this in tribal communities in Africa and the Middle East, where accent variations and cuisine differences are often distinct between communities that today are merely 20 minutes' drive away from each other.

Social barriers create transaction costs, and these costs extract energy from the system—it takes time and money to even attempt to overcome them. These costs make the difference between an entrepreneur who has to make thirty phone calls to get a crucial first deal done, versus one who can get it done with a single call. That disparity can mean life and death for a business opportunity. These barriers also destroy value by preventing valuable collaborations from happening—there is an opportunity cost to the whole system. Imagine how the story of ProFusion might have turned out differently if the Gauches had been able to partner with an experienced entrepreneur in Silicon Valley with personal ties to the people behind companies like Yahoo! or Google?

The idea of human land bridges is similar to a concept from the children's novel *A Wrinkle in Time* by Madeleine L'Engle.[31] In the story, two mysterious travelers attempt to explain to the young protagonist the concept of a "tesseract," which enables them to travel across vast expanses of time and space.

> "You see," Mrs. Whatsit said, "if a very small insect were to move from the section of skirt in Mrs. Who's right hand to that in her left, it would be quite a long walk for him if he had to walk straight across."

> Swiftly Mrs. Who brought her hands, still holding the skirt, together.

> "Now, you see," Mrs. Whatsit said, "he would be there, without that long trip. That is how we travel."

Alas, real life does not have tesseracts. Bridging social distances extracts a significant cost on young businesses, and it drags down the vibrancy of the whole system. Society has an incentive to help people bridge social distances, so they can communicate, collaborate, and build commercial enterprises. Institutions that can help entrepreneurs make those connections can lower their transaction costs and promote greater innovation throughout the system.

---

31 Madeleine L'Engle, *A Wrinkle in Time* (New York: Farrar, Straus, and Giroux, 1962). Excerpt reprinted courtesy of Crosswicks, Ltd. Images redrawn by Bill Rogers.

One way to do this is through disintermediation—directly connecting the nodes without them having to go through the hubs. This is at the heart of what companies like Google, eBay, and Craigslist do for a living. We can see the result of proactive disintermediation—what might be called a *social tesseract*—in the diagram below. The solid triangle represents disintermediation—the direct connection of nodes D, E, and F without them having to go through hubs A, B, and C.

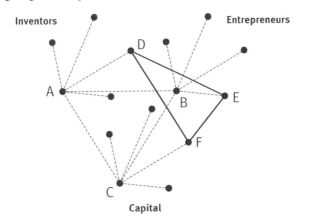

Is the concept of active disintermediation just a social-engineering pipedream? The answer is no. It is the kind of activity we have been doing in our work for years.

One of the best-known models is a program called "Springboard" at CONNECT, an organization that Greg previously managed. Promising technologists and entrepreneurs selected for the program are required to sit through a series of meetings with hand-picked experts. These highly interactive feedback sessions help the participants refine their business strategy, make connections with potential partners, and perhaps most importantly, force budding entrepreneurs to adapt to new people, new ideas, and the ever-changing dynamics of the marketplace. Springboard is, in essence, a kind of social tesseract—it shortens the distances between individuals in complex social networks. Since its inception, Springboard has graduated over 350 companies, which together have raised more than $600 million in capital and created over 25,000 jobs.

The Springboard model is not exclusive to CONNECT. Victor was the President of Larta Institute, which runs about a hundred similar sessions—both physically and virtually—throughout the country every year for startups funded by agencies like the National Science Foundation and the National Institutes of Health. Most participants in such programs do not really care about the theory behind the model. They are not thinking about how such programs overcome social network barriers to lower society's transaction costs for innovating. They only know that they are meeting useful people who are adding a lot of value.

Organizations like Larta Institute and CONNECT are based on trust. A recent international study found that the amount of trust in a nation is strongly associated with higher household income.[32] As political scientist Francis Fukuyama has argued, trust is a huge, invisible cost component in societal transactions.

> A modern society may be thought of as a series of concentric and overlapping radii of trust. These can range from friends and cliques up through NGOs and religious groups... Traditional social groups are also afflicted with an absence of what Mark Granovetter calls "weak ties," that is, heterodox individuals at the periphery of the society's various social networks who are able to move between groups and thereby become bearers of new ideas and information. Traditional societies are often segmentary, that is, they are composed of a large number of identical, self-contained social units like villages or tribes. Modern societies, by contrast, consist of a large number of overlapping social groups that permit multiple memberships and identities. Traditional societies have fewer opportunities for weak ties among the segments that make it up, and therefore pass on information, innovation, and human resources less easily.[33]

---

32 Organisation for Economic Co-Operation and Development, *Society at a Glance 2011: OECD Social Indicators* (OECD Publishing, 2011), 90.

33 Francis Fukuyama, "Social Capital, Civil Society and Development," *Third World Quarterly* 22 (2001): 8-10, http://intranet.catie.ac.cr/intranet/posgrado/Met%20Cual%20Inv%20accion/Semana%206/Fukuyama.pdf. See also, Robert Putnam, *Making Democracy Work: Civic Traditions in Modern Italy* (Princeton, N.J.: Princeton University Press, 1993). Putnam analyzed twenty regional Italian governments and determined that better government is correlated with civic engagement, political participation, and social capital.

The rate of innovation increases when people can create bridges outside of their normal circles of trust, whether across geographies, cultures, social groups, or languages. The goal of building Rainforests is to transition from a world that resembles this:

Concentric Circles of Trust

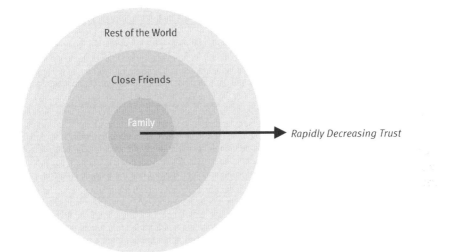

To one that more closely resembles something like this:

Overlapping Circles of Trust

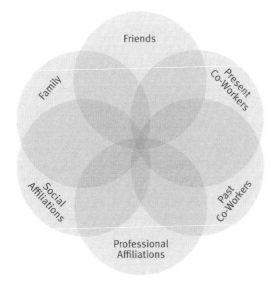

Breaking outside your circle of trust, however, often requires you to move outside your comfort zone, which is not easy for most people. There is a deep reason—beyond mere geographical distance—that people from Lawrence, Kansas cannot just hop on the next plane to Silicon Valley and start making deals.

....

> **Rainforest Axiom #6:** *High social barriers outside of close circles of family and friends are the norm in the world.*

....

While individuals or organizations that broker social trust across disparate groups can create tremendous economic value, creating that trust is extremely difficult and costly. Human beings start with a prejudice against reaching outside of their circle of trust. One must work hard to overcome the distrust that naturally occurs between people who are socially far apart.

In the next chapter, we will see how some people create these "social tesseracts," overcoming social barriers and distrust to create greater, contiguous tracts of Rainforest.

A Freer Market

Can you remember what America was like before eBay? There were millions of people who owned stuff they did not want, and there were millions of people who wanted that stuff. But they could not find each other. There used to be a lot more garage sales back then.

What is eBay but an active system that helps people overcome barriers of geography, social networks, culture, and a lack of trust to buy and sell physical products? No one would argue that there is not significant economic value created by the approximately $50 billion of merchandise transactions that happen annually on eBay through about 100 million active users.[34] It is not eBay that benefits the most—the buyers and the sellers are the primary beneficiaries.

Now, instead of the physical products exchanged on eBay, imagine a system for the exchange of invisible non-physical resources—ideas, talent, and capital. Then imagine all of the potential economic value that remains locked away today because geographical, social, cultural, language, and trust barriers hinder people from trading these resources with each other.

---

34 eBay INC. Report Strong First Quarter 2011 Results, http://files.shareholder.com/downloads/ebay/1347 843372x0x462596/0dd3fa3d-9791-4135-9f3c-30b5fb7bce7c/eBay_Q1_2011_Earnings_Release_042711_ FINAL.pdf (Accessed August 30, 2011).

When it comes to society's role in innovation, people have been asking the wrong question. In traditional market activity, the dominant historical question has justifiably been: what economic activity would happen if government just gets out of the way? In innovation, however, the question we should be asking is: what economic activity is *not* happening because of distance, cultural differences, and lack of trust, and how can social institutions help people overcome those barriers?

Therefore, we propose a new type of free market model to account for the realities of innovation. Conventional free market theory insists that innovation happens naturally when society is mostly left to itself. According to this model, intervention of any kind—such as in the form of government programs—will take resources away from the people who best know how to use them. We can call this a *passive free market* model, which reflects the belief that it is what society does *not* do that drives economic output.

Our work, however, leads us to believe in the potential value of an *active free market* model—one in which society uses targeted, cost-efficient interventions to enhance the efficiency of the market by helping people bridge social distances that currently hinder innovation.[35] Even when you remove all of the artificial constraints society might impose on innovators, the markets are still not efficient. The social barriers that exist between people create transaction costs that drag down economic productivity.

The active free market model requires us to break with conventional economic thinking. The accepted model of neoclassical economics for the past century can be depicted as inputs—traditionally land, labor, and capital—feeding into a system that generates output value. Many economists today also include a fourth input: technology. The process might be drawn like this:

Economic System

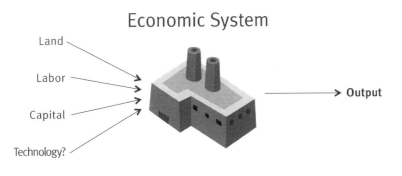

Land

Labor

Capital

Technology?

Output

35 Legal scholars have called this type of belief the Normative Coase Theorem, which prescribes that leaders should create systems of rules that minimize transaction costs. See, e.g., David M. Driesen and Shubha Ghosh, "Functions of Transaction Costs: Rethinking Transaction Cost Minimization in a World of Friction," 47 *Arizona Law Review* 61 (2005), 69.

The fundamental flaw of this model, however, is that in the real world, economic systems are made of human beings, not anonymous gears. And human beings control *all* of these factors of production. Human beings, not invisible hands, are the ones in reality who sign leases, who work hours, who invest money, and who invent ideas. If we imagine a system of four people, for example, the land might be controlled by a landlord, the labor by an engineer, the capital by an investor, and the technology by a scientist.

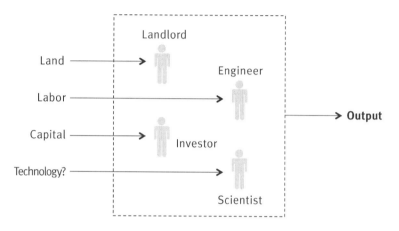

As we have discussed, real human beings are separated by a variety of social barriers, created by geography, culture, language, social networks, and lack of trust. Those social barriers can be high, and they can keep people isolated, and thus not transacting with one another.

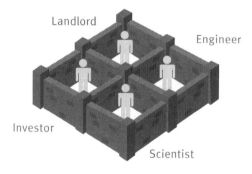

A landlord, for example, could own either one acre or one million acres, but if that landlord had zero contact with the world, the system would see little difference. The use of that land would be effectively lost to the rest of the system. The same holds true for the other inputs. An engineer can work one million hours, but if he does it standing in a closet, society would never benefit an iota from his labors. By projecting how social barriers replicate across an entire community, we can imagine how the magnified effects might proliferate.

The Rainforest model is a twist on the neoclassical one. Instead of land, labor, capital, and technology, we focus on ideas, talent, and capital. We say "ideas" instead of technology because an idea does not have to be strictly technological in order to be innovative. Think of innovations in diapers, coffee cups, and furniture design, for example. We say "talent" instead of labor because, as we show later in this book, innovation is driven by specialized talent, not just man-hours. We don't include land because natural resources like real estate, while we could not live without them, are far less important to the Rainforest than the other factors. For decades, people have confused the value of social networks in tight geographies (which can be huge) with the value of the real estate itself (which is usually a commodity).

The secret recipe of Rainforests, therefore, is about people and how they interact with one another. Social barriers that separate people with ideas, talent, and capital are like invisible "gum" in the gears of innovation systems. Passive free markets might be useful in bringing down artificially-imposed walls, but they still leave the natural social walls in place. Active free markets strive to bring down the social walls, too.

Interestingly, some in the conservative movement in the United Kingdom are already exploring these ideas. Phillip Blond, the progressive Tory thinker, was recently reported as saying that "[o]ne of the roles of Government needs to be in creating open trust networks where people do not need bureaucracy because there exists ethos and intimacy."[36]

Later in this book, we will outline ways for leaders—whether in government or in the corporate world—to support the creation of active free markets, not just passive ones.

Happily Ever After

By 2005, Susan and John Gauch had learned a few lessons. By then, they had launched their new startup company, Veatros, using a different strategy. Although the Gauches were still living in Lawrence, Kansas, they decided that Veatros needed to act globally, work with connected and trustworthy businesspeople, and link with key players in industry from the beginning. Veatros had developed a powerful technology for monitoring and tracking video. They brought in a CEO, an experienced executive who happened to be someone they could trust, and secured a first major customer in Latin America.

This time, however, they used "social tesseracts". The Gauches benefited from the assistance of organizations that helped them find new resources in other geographies, social groups, cultures, and circles of trust. The Kauffman Foundation, a two billion-dollar foundation focused on entrepreneurship, had sponsored a Larta Institute program to mentor new startups spinning out of academia, and connect them to global resources. The Gauches ended up hiring Victor, this book's co-author, to serve as their head of business strategy, with a specific focus on developing deals with major corporations and investors. As Susan recounts, "It was eye-opening to be on the West Coast. People were interested and actually understood what we were doing. There was a huge value for us in those types of personal networks."[37]

---

36 Nick Denys, "The Future of Conservative Thinking is Doing," *Platform* (blog), July 20, 2010
   http://www.platform10.org/2010/07/the-future-of-conservative-thinking-is-doing/.
37 Gauch, interview.

With the building blocks in place, all that was needed was serendipity—the lightning striking the prebiotic soup. Victor happened to be meeting with veteran venture capitalist Tim Draper, and Tim happened to suggest that his portfolio company DivX might be interested in Veatros. As chance would have it, Victor had practiced law in Los Angeles at the same law firm as the General Counsel of DivX. And DivX happened to have just made an initial public offering of its stock a few months ago, and was looking to make a small acquisition that fit with its overall strategy of building an online video library. In August 2007, DivX acquired Veatros, thereby giving the Gauches some financial security, and giving DivX a technology that could create a unique and competitive product. The Gauches had come a long way from the days of the Anti-Google. With Veatros, they were able to tap into a Rainforest of relationships, which enabled the mixing of ingredients that led to the Gauches' success.

One lesson of the Rainforest is that outcomes cannot be engineered. The Gauches could never have predicted the chain of events that led to the successful acquisition of Veatros. Dig deeper, however, and it is clear that the environment that led to that acquisition had itself been engineered. The State of Kansas had originally provided grant funds to the university, which in turn were given to Veatros, allowing the Gauches to develop their prototype. The University of Kansas, a public university, had policies in place to encourage the Gauches to license the technology and build a startup. The Kauffman Foundation was actively sponsoring activities to assist startups like Veatros that were spinning out of universities. Larta Institute, which was originally chartered by the State of California, was building networks that reached outside its own geographical boundaries. Without any of these "engineered" initiatives in place, the Veatros story would never have happened.

Serendipity itself cannot be engineered, but an environment—a Rainforest— that is conducive to serendipity can be. Fortunately, like a great Hollywood classic, the story of the Anti-Google has a happy ending.

Chapter Three: People in the Rainforest

Of Sea Cows, Otters, and Ottersons

"I discovered early in my movie work that a movie is never any better than the stupidest man connected with it. There are times when this distinction may be given to the writer or director. Most often it belongs to the producer."

— **Ben Hecht, American screenwriter sometimes referred to as the "Shakespeare of Hollywood" (1894-1964)**[1]

---

1   http://www.albany.edu/writers-inst/webpages4/filmnotes/fns03n12.html (accessed August 3, 2011), citing Ben Hecht, *A Child of the Century* (New York: Simon & Schuster, 1954).

A New Species in the Rainforest

If you struck up a conversation with Larry Bock on the street, you would almost certainly like him. Larry has an unthreatening, almost shy demeanor. He usually wears a boyish grin, and has a sense of enthusiasm and curiosity that is contagious.

If you were paying attention, you might notice that Larry does not see well. Due to a severe form of macular degeneration called Stargadt disease, he is legally blind and must read emails in 48-point font. He sees the world in pixels.

What you definitely would not realize, nor probably even believe at first, is that Larry has founded or co-founded 18 startup companies, and has been an early investor in 22 others. All told, his companies have generated a cumulative market valuation of over $40 billion. He is one of the most prolific company creators in American history that you have almost certainly never heard of. His companies have transformed the lives of millions of people, most of whom know nothing about him.

But ironically, he does not call himself an entrepreneur. Nor does he call himself a venture capitalist anymore—having given up that business many years ago—despite the fact that Ernst & Young named him a finalist for its Entrepreneur of the Year Award, and *Venture Capital Journal* called him one of America's ten most influential venture capitalists. When he was asked to deliver the commencement address at Berkeley's College of Chemistry, the school described him as a "Principal of Many High-Tech Organizations." Not exactly the most flattering or descriptive of labels. It could be worse. As Larry jokes, "My father-in-law disparagingly calls me a 'promoter.'"[2]

There probably isn't a word or phrase in the business lexicon that accurately describes what Larry has done in his career. None of the typical labels the business world uses to describe innovators—whether it's "entrepreneur," "venture capitalist," "director," "advisor," "engineer," or whatever—seem to fit Larry's role.

In this chapter, we reveal another layer to the mystery of innovation. Based on our work over the years, we have come to realize that the Rainforest is populated with a whole class of people like Larry whose titles do not really explain their jobs. They may not have achieved the same phenomenal success as Larry, but they possess some of the same traits and experiences. These people form a critical building block of the Rainforest. Without them, it is probable that many Rainforests would struggle or even die. It is certain that untold billions of dollars in economic value would never have been created, and countless people's lives would have been a lot worse off.

---

2 Larry Bock, telephone interview with author, July 25, 2011.

What exactly did Larry do, and what is the mysterious role of people like Larry Bock in the Rainforest? What do these people mean for the Rainforest as a whole? Like biologists who study the Amazonian rainforests and announce that they have discovered a new species of insect or animal, we believe that we have identified a new species of innovator. We call this species the *keystone.*

The Keystone

Larry Bock grew up in the inner city of Brooklyn, the son of a Wall Street stockbroker. From an early age, he was exposed to many of life's ups and downs. His father took his family through numerous boom and bust cycles as he invested in high technology companies. Nowadays, Larry looks upon the positive lessons from that upbringing: "I learned that even if things went really south, you could turn yourself around one year later and be back on top again. You have to be constantly reinventing yourself. Failure is just a dress rehearsal for success."

Larry dreamed of being a medical doctor, but he could not get into medical school, a personally devastating result for him at the time. Instead, he ended up becoming a lowly researcher at a new company called Genentech, where he got to observe the business of growing a biotechnology organization firsthand. He later would get an MBA and end up working at a traditional venture capital firm in California. Larry recalls, however, how he did not enjoy the venture business: "I didn't like the fact that every deal had some warts, and you started having to dissect all the bad things instead of doing the new things."[3]

Then Larry met venture capitalist Kevin Kinsella, who had an entirely different way of practicing the venture business. Kevin liked to start companies from scratch. Moreover, he was willing to mentor Larry in this valuable craft. Eventually, Kevin would help Larry start two companies, Athena Neurosciences (neurological drugs, focusing on Alzheimer's disease), and Vertex Pharmaceuticals (rational drug discovery). Athena would eventually go public and be acquired by Elan Pharmaceuticals for $625 million. Vertex Pharmaceuticals would also go public and today has a market capitalization of around $10 billion.[4]

Larry would go on to replicate this process throughout his career, in varying shapes and sizes. Today, the long roster of high-flying companies with Larry's fingerprints includes Aurora Biosciences Corporation (accelerating the drug discovery process), Illumina (genetic analysis), Argonaut Technologies (combinatorial chemistry), Caliper Technologies

---

3   Ibid.
4   As of August 31, 2011.

(lab-on-a-chip), ARIAD Pharmaceuticals (intra-cellular signal transduction), GenPharm International (transgenic animals), and Onyx Pharmaceuticals (molecular oncology), among many others.

What was the magical formula that Kevin and Larry had discovered? This formula, shockingly simple, was a radical departure from the way innovation is still done today in most of the business world. The textbook process of innovation is one that follows a linear progression, starting with basic science, to proof-of-concept, and then to market feasibility testing—all before one ever considers hiring a team, raising money, and building a company. Kevin Kinsella's process was entirely backwards, if one believed in the conventional rules. From observing Kevin, Larry observed how the firm "spent all the seed money pulling a team together rather than doing product proof-of-concept. They saw that as the fastest value creator." [5]

Larry describes it in simple terms:

> You start with a breakout field. That becomes your framework. And then you just start meeting with the world's leaders in that field. Often, these are emerging areas, so there are not a huge number of leaders in the field. I will go to one of those leaders, and I will ask them, "If I were to start a company in this field, what other five people should I involve in such a company?" And I do that successfully with every person I meet. And then pretty quickly, it always coalesces, every single time I've done it. Here are the five world leaders you need to lock up a field, and here is the compelling vision you should pursue to build that company. [6]

Larry makes the process sound easy, but there was in fact more to it. Larry was usually the first "venture capitalist" that any of these people had ever talked to, so he was able to start with a clean slate. He was not a direct academic competitor to any of the scientists with whom he spoke. Thus, he was able to start from a baseline relationship that did not trigger someone's defenses.

Moreover, Larry has a personal style that simply disarms people. He can be incredibly candid and direct, perhaps painfully so, but he usually acts in a style that seems almost humble. His personal agenda is always upfront and plain. He has an unusual ability to win people over. When necessary, he can be a good listener:

---

5 Bock, interview.
6 Ibid.

> I'm never telling them how smart I am. I'm sitting there listening to them, and I'm trying to learn from them. They open up to me more than they would open up to their academic colleagues. I was knowing stuff a year and a half before others in the field.[7]

By following this process, Larry would usually end up with a company that included, as its founding team, the entire thought leadership of a breakthrough field of science, an entrepreneur identified to run the company, a basic business strategy mapped out, and a great deal of buzz and momentum that could launch the company with high velocity.

What Larry did was to "glue" the pieces of a story together out of bunch of random fragments. It is not unlike the role of a movie producer in Hollywood. Movie producers are not the directors, they are not the actors, and they are not the financiers. Their role is to take all the ingredients of a film—the talent, the script, the money, the marketing, etc.—and turn them into a practical commercial concept. The film producer Richard Zanuck (*Jaws* and *Driving Miss Daisy*) described his job by saying, "The producer is like the conductor of an orchestra. Maybe he can't play every instrument, but he knows what every instrument should sound like."[8] A producer's job is to make 1+1+1=100. The quote by Ben Hecht at the beginning of the chapter is another way of saying that the work of a producer, for better or for worse, can make or break a film.

In the field of biology, there is an analogy to the role of someone like Larry Bock, or a Hollywood producer. It is what biologists call a *keystone species*.[9] In biological systems, whether a rainforest or an ocean, keystone species often act as central supporting hubs. They interact in so many valuable ways with so many other parts of the ecosystem that their presence has a disproportionate impact on the system. Without a keystone species, much of a rainforest's biological diversity can collapse, and many co-existing species can disappear.

One example of a keystone species that is commonly cited is the sea otter. This furry marine mammal—with an often insanely charming appearance[10]—feeds primarily on invertebrates in the North Pacific Ocean, including sea urchins, mollusks, and crustaceans. Many biologists now believe that overhunting of the sea otter by aboriginal people several hundred years ago caused an unexpected chain reaction. With a depleted

---

7 Ibid.

8 http://www.filmmakers.com/stories/Producer.htm (accessed August 1, 2011).

9 L. Scott Mills, Michael E. Soule and Daniel F. Doak, "The Keystone-Species Concept in Ecology and Conservation," *BioScience* 43 (1993): 1-4,
   http://bio.research.ucsc.edu/people/doaklab/publications/1993mills_soule_doak.pdf.

10 Otters holding hands [Video] (Uploaded March 19, 2007).
   http://www.youtube.com/watch?v=epUk3T2Kfno (Accessed August 31, 2011).

number of sea otters, the population of sea urchins grew too quickly. The expanding population of sea urchins in turn overwhelmed and destroyed the kelp beds that were the primary food of the Steller's Sea Cow, a massive creature similar to a manatee, but about twice as long, that used to thrive throughout the North Pacific. The Steller's Sea Cow became endangered in turn, and ultimately went extinct in 1768.

The sea otter is but one example of a keystone species found in the study of biological ecosystems. Other common examples include pollinators like the honeybee and hummingbirds, and fruit-dispersers like primates, squirrels, and certain birds: animals known for their critical role connecting geographic areas to form broader ecosystems. The larger the contiguous territory that is connected by these "mobile links," the greater and more stable the biodiversity of the entire system.

Keystone species are critical in the innovation Rainforest too. Individuals like Larry Bock serve as crucial hubs, encouraging a type of human biodiversity, creating an environment that gives life to numerous other species of economic actors. Keystones serve as human bridges, connecting people across social barriers to create larger contiguous systems.

When the atoms are floating independently from one another, it takes effort to pull them together and give them a concerted mission. Larry formed the invisible bonds to connect people. He opened the pathways of communication. He facilitated the kind of cooperation that overcomes social friction and allows economic transactions to occur. Entrepreneurial innovation cannot thrive without keystones like Larry Bock.

The DNA of a Keystone

What defines a keystone in the human Rainforest? Over the years, we have observed certain individuals practicing a unique manner of human interaction that is critical to the growth of entrepreneurial innovation. These interactions have the effect of lowering the cost of doing business in the Rainforest, speeding up the process of interactions in the entire system, and making it easier for people with ideas, talents, or capital to connect and collaborate with each other.

Keystones are the people missing from the story of the Anti-Google. They are the people who are usually missing, or at least too scarce, in almost all regions that that have failed at generating significant amounts of entrepreneurial innovation.

To describe the DNA of keystones in the Rainforest, we developed a framework based on our observations. Taken as a whole, this framework explains the ability of keystones to "glue together" disparate elements of the ecosystem. Our Keystone Model attempts to capture the three basic elements of what makes people like Larry tick:

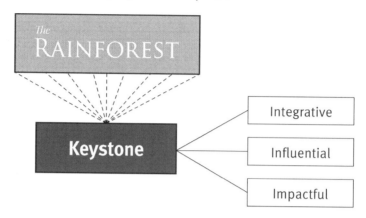

Based on this model, we can outline three attributes that are essential for an individual to be a keystone in the Rainforest:

1. **Integrative.** Keystones are people who are comfortable reaching across boundaries to bring people together. In Larry's story, he was able to bridge geographic distances and break into social groups to connect scientific researchers to each other, and to the universe of entrepreneurs, investors, and other professionals as well. Keystones have the ability to convene people who might otherwise be strangers, and encourage the best of their collaborative instincts to overcome natural distrust.

2. **Influential.** Keystones have the ability to convince people to do things that they otherwise would never do. But they never use force or coercion. They appeal to people's long-term interests and non-economic motivations, helping them rise above the easy temptation to seek short-term advantage. We saw this, for instance, in the way that Larry Bock could bring together a group of competing academics. Keystones can help people strive for higher aspirations, whether that means building a world-changing company, or saving people's lives. They often know how to appeal to deep human instincts, such as social pressure, to twist arms or create a bandwagon effect. They help establish and validate the cultural norms of a community because they have garnered enough respect to do so.

3. **Impactful.** Keystones have the ability to make things happen, not just create a lot of heat and noise. They foster real economic transactions

that create a systemic effect, not just get a few people excited for a short time. Although they do not know exactly what the final detailed results will be, they have a clear vision of the potential value they are creating through their actions. This vision can be something as big as one of Larry Bock's companies, or it can be as small as making an introduction between two people who might be able to create a valuable opportunity together.

Overall, keystones create value because they are brokers of social trust, particularly in social situations where trust is scarce.

In atomistic communities—where individuals are not bound together permanently—it makes perfect sense that there is value to be unlocked by lowering transaction costs and forging new connections. History shows that keystones are often present when people are highly individualized. We can see evidence of this on the American frontier, where pioneers were mostly on their own, but had to assemble and disassemble for practical purposes. Historian Daniel Boorstin describes the importance of certain individuals in frontier wagon caravans whose job descriptions sound remarkably similar to those of a movie producer or Larry Bock's:

> The talents most in demand were not those of the fearless lone backwoodsman, the crack shot clad in fringed buckskin; what was needed was a shrewd and effective organizer. The transients' leader had to bring a community into being and to inspire, wheedle, bride, or threaten its members to the performance of unfamiliar tasks on strange landscapes and against incalculable dangers. Flexibility, warmth, imagination, human breadth, and an encouraging voice were more in order than dignity, respectability, or nobility.[11]

While there is value in individualism, there is also significant value in the organizing of individuals. This concept of the frontier is important, and we will explore it later in the book.

There is increasing scientific evidence that validates the idea of the keystone in the Rainforest. A recent study from Professors Maryann Feldman and Ted Zoller at the University of North Carolina examines the presence of highly-networked people they call "dealmakers." A dealmaker is a proxy for what we call keystones—they are the connecting hubs of a regional network. According to Feldman and Zoller, the number of dealmakers in a community is a better predictor of the status of the regional entrepreneurial economy and more important for successful entrepreneurship than aggregate measures of regional entrepreneurial and investors networks.[12]

---

11 Daniel J. Boorstin, *The Americans: The National Experience* (New York: Vintage Books, 1965), 58-59.

12 Maryann P. Feldman and Ted Douglas Zoller, "Dealmakers in Place: Social Capital Connections in Regional Entrepreneurial Economies" (Plenary paper presented at the International Schumpeter Society Conference 2010 on Innovation, Organisation, Sustainability and Crises, Aalborg, June 21-24, 2010). http://www.schumpeter2010.dk/index.php/schumpeter/schumpeter2010/paper/viewFile/488/191.

To arrive at this conclusion, they calculated the membership of boards of directors or people employed in executive positions in startup companies in a region. They found that the San Francisco Bay Area has a vastly higher percentage of people who are involved in multiple firms. Their results: 4.5% of the actors counted in the Bay Area were involved in three or more startups, compared to 2.9% in Boston, 2.0% in San Diego, 1.7% in Seattle, 1.4% in Minneapolis, 1.2% in Austin, 0.9% in Denver, 0.9% in Salt Lake City, 0.9% in Raleigh/Durham, 0.7% in Phoenix, 0.7% in Portland, and 0.3% in Orange County (California). These numbers may not seem high in the aggregate, but they do represent huge relative differences between regions. The Bay Area has a significantly higher share of individuals who are extremely connected and contribute to the growth of multiple startup ventures. The data suggest that the number of keystones is closely tied to the overall innovative output of an economic system.

Larry Bock has now retired from his old career, the one that had no name. After so much success and decades of frenetic activity, he needed a change of pace. So, he took the same skill set and applied it to something completely different. Larry is today the founder and executive director of the largest celebration of science in the nation, the USA Science & Engineering Festival, which occurs in Washington, D.C. The purpose of this event is to inspire the next generation of young scientists by making science come to life.

We remember when Larry was just starting a small, local science festival in San Diego. We have watched as he applied the same formula that he used to build Athena Neurosciences and other companies: winning over one key person at a time, each of who in turn would lead him to several other key people, and so on. Eventually, he turned his sights on Washington to do something even bigger. Says Larry:

> When I was planning the Science Festival, people came up to me and said that they had wanted to create this science festival, too, but it would have been too hard for them to do. There was just too much competition in their worlds. If Harvard was leading, then Princeton wouldn't want to be part of it. If the National Academies were leading, then others wouldn't join. I come at it completely from the outside, not entrenched in their world, and can sit above it. I am impartial and do not have the same agenda as all the other people they know. I'm moving very fast in their universe. Within a few weeks, they see that I have met with everybody else in the area. The train is leaving this station, and they don't want to miss out on this opportunity.[13]

13 Bock, interview.

Larry has taken this simple idea of a science festival and turned it into a national event. His festival today involves dozens of Nobel Prize winners, Fortune 100 technology executives, university presidents, the White House, and crowds of kids. His first festival in 2010 drew 500,000 attendees, who participated in 1500 hands-on activities and watched 75 live performances.

Obviously, the role of the keystone—the connector of people across social boundaries—has great application beyond that of the innovation Rainforest. For Larry, it has apparently not been much of a retirement.

The Spark in San Diego

Some might hear the story of Larry Bock and think, "Well, that is interesting, but it is simply the tale of a great entrepreneur. It is a one-of-a-kind success story based on a one-of-a-kind person. You don't need to call it a new species."

True, Larry is a unique individual with special talents. What we have discovered, however, is that the basic behaviors that he exhibited are actually spread throughout the Rainforest. It just so happens that he demonstrates an extremely high concentration of them. A keystone is not merely an allocator of resources and taker of risks, as conventional economists might define the word "entrepreneur." A keystone is a connector of people. He is the glue.

There are countless other examples of keystones in the Rainforest. We will tell another story that illustrates the power of the keystone.

We opened this book by describing the dichotomy between San Diego and Chicago, but we have not yet explained why San Diego evolved so differently. They both were regions with strong ingredients: educated people, top universities, capital, and entrepreneurial talent. But for some reason, the recipe for cooking those ingredients in San Diego yielded a vastly different result than it did in Chicago. If you ask people in San Diego's technology community today what made the difference, the most common answer you will hear will be the name of one man—Bill Otterson—and the organization he helped build: CONNECT.

Bill Otterson was larger than life. He was a successful entrepreneur, and had amassed some wealth. He frequently used to say that "Everybody's going to die; they just don't know when." [14] We all say this kind of thing from time to time, of course. But for Bill, this meant something else entirely—because he was living on borrowed time.

Bill had been diagnosed with multiple myeloma, a savage form of bone marrow cancer. He was expecting to die soon. He had already decided to

14 Abi Barrow, telephone interview with author, July 28, 2011.

enjoy his remaining days to their fullest, so he stopped working, went to France with his wife, and prepared for death. However, he did not die.

So he returned, and he became a man with a mission. In 1986, Bill was hired to run a little program, which later became known as CONNECT. This program got started at the University of California at San Diego from little more than an idea. The organization was focused on the idea that improved connections between academia and business might be useful for helping entrepreneurs and the innovation process in general. Mary Walshok, the Associate Vice Chancellor of UCSD, recalls:

> We had a 1-1/3 page business plan, if you could call it that. We had a group of investors who could put in only a little bit of cash but a lot of sweat equity. The total cash was only about $80,000. Nonetheless, Bill got fired up about the idea of growing an innovation company and supporting the so-neglected entrepreneurs. He got so fired up that he came to work for no salary—we didn't have enough money.[15]

Enthusiasm, however, was not sufficient to accomplish what he did. Bill exhibited all the essential qualities of a keystone—he was integrative, influential, and impactful.

Abi Barrow, one of Bill's early program managers, remembered how Bill was an *integrator* of people:

> The important thing about Bill was that he did get everybody around the table. I don't think there was anything he did that wasn't a collaboration. His sense was that we're doing this; we'd like you to join us. It doesn't help for each of us to have our own little fiefdom. We just look stupid to the rest of the world.[16]

Today, Abi is the head of technology transfer for the University of Massachusetts, where she uses many of the techniques she learned from Bill back then. Abi believes that the culture that Bill instilled in the region has lasted long after his death in 1999: "San Diego is still pretty collaborative today," notes Abi. "It would not have been that way without him. That was his big legacy."[17]

Bill had a personal story that made him *influential* when organizing people in a common cause. He was very upfront about his cancer. When he would talk with people about CONNECT, he sometimes would hold up a tiny vial of Genentech's interferon and say something to the effect of, "This is what is keeping me alive. This is why I am doing this work. It is important that we

---

15 Mary Walshok, telephone interview with author, July 28, 2011.
16 Barrow, interview.
17 Ibid.

keep working on drugs like this to give other people the same chance to live that I have been given." In the big picture, everyone respected the fact that Bill had nothing selfish to gain by doing this hard work.

Bill was also extremely generous to other people. Mary Walshok fondly recalls how he would treat others:

> Bill always gave as much or more than he asked. Reciprocity! Bill would ask somebody for a business card or access to so and so, but as often as he would ask for help, he would give people help. He had an enormous reservoir of energy and generosity. It wasn't professional; it was personal. He would make his home available. He would pay for meals out of his own pocket.[18]

On top of that, he was a successful technology entrepreneur, which gave him significant credibility with the business community. Since businesspeople tend to respect other businesspeople, this was essential. It would have been impossible for a career university bureaucrat or a governmental civil servant to have commanded the respect that Bill received from entrepreneurs and executives. As Guy Iannuzzi, a marketing entrepreneur, said about Bill's role: "You want someone who does not need the job."[19] Bill's business accomplishments gave him extra influence in the business community.

Bill was also *impactful*—he could get people to buy into a mission that was bigger than any one person. Abi observes, "The other thing about Bill is that he thought big. He thought big so everybody could think big." [20] For instance, when the region had a shortage of engineering talent for the telecommunications companies, Bill realized that organizing the major employers to do joint recruiting would yield a larger overall impact than if each of the companies recruited on its own. The players resisted at first. They were reluctant to cooperate with their competitors. Eventually, however, due to Bill's "mile-wide grin" and his undeniable persistence convincing them of the mutual benefits, he was eventually able to organize a major, coordinated recruiting program with all the leading telecom companies in the area. Bill passed away in 1999, but the legacy of that effort is still evident today in the strong pool of engineering talent in San Diego.

Bill Otterson had all the traits of a keystone—the abilities to bring disparate people together, to exercise persuasion over them, and to give them a common agenda for mutual benefit. Like a honeybee connecting ecosystems that are miles apart, the power of a keystone is that he makes the whole so much greater than the sum of its parts.

---

18 Walshok, interview.

19 Bradley J. Fikes, "What Next For UCSD Connect? *The Godfather of San Diego's Tech Incubators is Searching (Again) for a Leader," San Diego Metropolitan Magazine* (March 2004), http://sandiegometro.archives.whsites.net/2004/mar/ucsdconnect.php.

20 Barrow, interview.

Keystone Institutions

If you spend enough time in a Rainforest—like in Silicon Valley—you begin to notice that keystones are everywhere.

They are, in fact, not such rare creatures after all. They have been lurking there all the while, but they are invisible if you don't know what to look for. A keystone does not come wearing a T-shirt with the word "KEYSTONE" emblazoned across the chest. They come in many shapes and sizes, and their business cards have all sorts of "official" titles on them. You might run into them in any number of ways. After you meet an entrepreneur at a networking reception, he might invite you to lunch or dinner with his friends who share similar interests. When you hire a lawyer, they may start referring you to trusted investors, customers, or advisors. After a chat with an engineer at a café, you are invited to join a monthly gathering of engineers who share similar pursuits. An investor who rejected the chance to fund your startup personally introduces you to five other important contacts that are a better fit for your company. These types of things happen in other places too, but in Rainforests, the velocity and quantity of such interactions are vastly greater.

....

Rainforest Axiom #7: *Rainforests depend on people who actively bridge social distances and connect disparate parties together.*

....

The world of keystones is one that is in constant motion, connecting people in the Rainforest for mutual gain and finding common ground for collective action. Keystones accelerate the process of creative reassembly.

Keystones are not just individuals—there are *keystone institutions*, as well. The story of Bill Otterson's CONNECT organization is but one example.

Rohit Shukla and his organization, Larta Institute, are another. They have designed mentoring programs for hundreds of startup companies, bridging the chasms separating entrepreneurial scientists across America, and connecting them with a global network of industry partners. A company that enters a Larta program will, over the span of a few months, find themselves integrated in a diverse community of individuals from distant places and with different backgrounds, all of whom are interested in helping bring new technologies to the market. Larta does not actually do all the hard work for the startup, but they "lead from behind" by connecting, coaching, mentoring, and grooming. The Larta team has created a keystone institution that manages, in effect, a series of bridges to connect parties for mutual benefit, nudging them into collaboration and getting them focused on real-world commercial development processes.

Professional service firms in Silicon Valley are another example of keystone institutions. Despite outward appearances, the core value of Silicon Valley Bank, for example, is not really provided by its banking services. SVB's main value is as a keystone institution. When an entrepreneur becomes a client of SVB, he or she should not be surprised to start receiving invitations to complimentary private dinners with other people who share common interests. When a venture capital firm becomes a client, they may soon be asked to showcase their portfolio companies to the rest of the Valley's investment community at an invitation-only event. People in the SVB rolodex often receive invitations to private luncheons, book talks, wine country tours, and hosted receptions. Some of the people who work there like to joke that "Silicon Valley Bank is even more fun than banking!" Almost everyone who is active in the Valley has been a beneficiary of the keystone role of SVB at some point in their careers.

Lawyers in the Rainforest also serve as important keystones. Whereas the traditional role of lawyers in America is an adversarial one—your bulldog lawyer versus my bulldog lawyer—attorneys serve a valuable role in the Rainforest as connectors and trust facilitators.[21] They might get paid by the hour, but their billing rate is often just a proxy for the greater value they provide as a keystone. Once, when we were negotiating a venture capital deal, we suddenly realized that we were using a lawyer who had at some point previously represented the startup company, three of the startup's founders, and two of the investment firms involved in the deal. In most places in the world, this might be a cause for disbarment proceedings! In the Rainforest, the parties involved typically agree to waive their objections to such perceived conflicts-of-interest because it is the accepted way of doing business, and is considered a worthwhile trade-off.

What are the common characteristics of these keystone institutions? They lower social transaction costs among people in a Rainforest by:

- Facilitating access and connections to people with ideas, talent, knowledge, capital, and opportunities by breaking down traditional hierarchies and reaching across social boundaries

- Taking actions that enable greater collaboration between individuals so they can better work on new projects and initiatives together

---

21 Lisa Bernstein, "The Silicon Valley Lawyer as Transaction Cost Engineer?" 74 *University of Oregon Law Review* 239 (1995); Mark C. Suchman, "Dealmakers and Counselors: Law Firms as Intermediaries in the Development of Silicon Valley," in M. Kenney (ed.), *Understanding Silicon Valley: The Anatomy of an Entrepreneurial Region* (Palo Alto: Stanford University Press, 2000), 71-97.

- Serving as filters for high-quality connections, which in turn helps them maintain a strong role as a respected hub in the system

- Validating and propagating cultural behaviors that are conducive for innovation

In a natural rainforest in the Amazon, the treetop canopy is where the most activity happens due to the interaction of species with intense energy from sunlight. Keystone institutions serve as "virtual canopies" in their Rainforests. Sometimes these institutions are also called "innovation intermediaries" or "boundary-spanning organizations." The fact that they are sometimes called intermediaries, however, does not mean that they stay in the middle of relationships—they connect people and then step back, letting those people develop meaningful collaborations on their own. The job of the keystone is to glue atoms together, not get stuck between them.

In contrast, many of the technology transfer centers that are typically run by universities or the federal government treat the intermediary role as a permanent one—they guard the relationships, and they always stay in the middle. We have found these models to be much less successful than those based on keystones.

Entrepreneurs

What about other participants in the Rainforest? Entrepreneurs are not the same as keystones. Entrepreneurs are like the valiant field commanders of the Rainforest, whereas keystones might be considered the connecting agents—like recruiting stations and transport networks—that bring the troops together. Many entrepreneurs are keystones, but not all are.

Much has been written about the importance of entrepreneurs, so we will not attempt to repeat what others have said countless times. But we do need to dispel a few myths about them. For the most part, this book aspires to expand the traditional narrative focusing on brave solo entrepreneurs fighting against the world, and instead look at the broader impact of the community that surrounds and supports entrepreneurs and their startups. The challenge of building Rainforests is to facilitate the growth of those supportive networks. Without those networks, entrepreneurs tend to fail at high rates.

When we observe how entrepreneurs behave at the level of Rainforests, we see them differently than at the ground level. Based on our work with thousands of entrepreneurs over the years, here are three observations that can be counter-intuitive:

- **Risk-taking.** Entrepreneurs are not risk takers per se. They are opportunity seekers. Many entrepreneurs unconsciously use what mathematicians call "probabilistic inference" to determine risk. This means that they try to use evidence from the world around them to infer the odds of success for new hypotheses. What they are doing is not seeking risk, but managing it. Good entrepreneurs are more like risk calculators than risk takers. A healthy Rainforest increases the odds of success for its field commanders.

- **Information.** Entrepreneurs must absorb knowledge and apply it differently than traditional businesspeople. They tend to be non-linear thinkers who can integrate and synthesize large amounts of information. They are able to abstract random pieces of data and assemble it in ways that are not apparent to many others. They can fill in the gaps with educated guesses. Consequently, they are attuned to "the moment," constantly looking for ways to apply their knowledge in the present and accelerate their forward momentum. Rainforests help entrepreneurs get access to better information, like field commanders who benefit from better maps or intelligence on the enemy.

- **Learning.** Theorists make bad teachers. Entrepreneurs learn best from peer and practitioner interactions, as opposed to theoretical experts who might have studied entrepreneurship but have not "done" it. Entrepreneurship assistance programs, whether in business schools or elsewhere, should focus on real-life interactions with people who can share fresh, real-world experiences. Field commanders cannot be taught solely in a classroom: they win or lose based on their ability to make good decisions in the field.

Being an entrepreneur is one of the loneliest jobs in the world. One must routinely put on a brave smile, even in the hardest of times, and remain calm, optimistic, and encouraging with customers, investors, employees, and any number of other partners and colleagues. Having access to a Rainforest of supportive, skilled people—including keystones—often means the difference between success and failure for struggling entrepreneurs.

Other Denizens of the Rainforest

There are many other participants in the Rainforest who do not receive the same glory as keystones or entrepreneurs. But like the "ordinary" flora or fauna of a Rainforest, their roles are equally vital. Successful innovation requires the labors of a vast ecosystem of executives, engineers, salespeople, advisors, consultants, venture capitalists, angel investors, accountants, landlords, lawyers, marketers, bankers, supportive friends, and countless others.

We have observed that individuals in the Rainforest act differently. They often do not seek reward in the same way as people outside the Rainforest. Economists generally assume that people are rational actors who seek to maximize their *return on investment*, whether in labor or capital. In the Rainforest, we see different behavior. Beyond their immediate self-interest, denizens of the Rainforest frequently seek a *return on involvement* from participating in and contributing to the success of innovative ventures. It is what we call the "New ROI" of the Rainforest.

Almost everyone in a Rainforest who has started a new company has witnessed the New ROI firsthand. It is the successful entrepreneur who provides you an hour full of free advice. It is the advisor who drafts up a three-page strategic plan for you, completely on his own initiative and with no expectations. It is the engineer who starts working on your software project without knowing what her actual pay is going to be.

Actors in the Rainforest pursuing the New ROI are not the "rational actors" of traditional economic theories. The reasons that people participate in the Rainforest are more nuanced than first appears. Their motivations include some economic reasons but, more importantly, they also include many non-economic ones. Among the many reasons people commonly participate in the Rainforest are:

- **Altruism.** A chance to "give back" to others. As we showed in the story of Bill Otterson, people often seek a chance to create a better world through new innovations, or sustainable job or wealth creation.

- **Adventure.** The ability to participate in new, groundbreaking technologies, ideas, and opportunities before the rest of the world does. There is an emotional rush when you realize you are seeing the "next great thing" and have a chance to play a role in its journey.

- **Challenge.** The thrill of successfully climbing a hill that others have said was impossible. Many people relish the sense of victory and accomplishment.

- **Competition.** The excitement of competing against others can get the heart pumping. Some people are wired to want to compete and win, whether in sports or in startups.

- **Connections.** The joy of networking and developing new contacts. People enjoy people. Relationships can also save time in the long run for tangible business development.

- **Friendship.** An opportunity to form new relationships with people. Relationships based on trust can also lower transaction costs for doing business later.

- **Learning.** The satisfaction of learning new things from others. The exposure to alternative perspectives and solutions. An opportunity to understand and support the development of potentially good ideas.

- **Team.** The pleasure of being part of a larger group and participating in a mission greater than oneself.

Conventionally, economists have looked at these types of motivations as nice-to-have features of life, and usually consider them to be completely distinct from business. We believe, however, that these motivations are absolutely essential to innovation. Innovating is simply too hard to do without them. When there are not enough people behaving in these "non-rational" ways, a Rainforest withers. Rainforests depend on people not behaving like rational actors.

> **Rainforest Axiom #8:** *People in Rainforests are motivated for reasons that defy traditional economic notions of "rational" behavior.*

In the next chapter, we will further explore these "extra" sources of human motivation and argue that simple economic motivation is insufficient to create the kind of innovative output we see in Rainforests.

Cataloguing the Species

In this chapter, we have tried to catalogue some of the species in the Rainforest and their behaviors. It is not unlike the way a biologist might examine a natural rainforest in the Amazon. We take an inventory of the flora and fauna and then try to discover the patterns that underlie the phenomena we observe on the surface.

The keystones of a Rainforest, like honeybees, are essential entities that support the biodiversity of the entire system. They serve as active connecting agents, so that random fragments of the Rainforest can be glued together into more valuable, larger social structures. They often do this work without direct financial benefit. Entrepreneurs are like field commanders, but they cannot thrive without the rest of the system to maximize their chances of success. Other participants in the Rainforest exhibit patterns of behavior that are rather surprising. They are frequently motivated by "return on involvement," not rational utility.

Our observations about people in the Rainforest raise puzzling questions. Traditional economic theory assumes that people acting selfishly and rationally to allocate resources should be enough to explain the creation of value. In Rainforests, we see behavior at odds with this theoretical assumption. Why should the participants in a Rainforest behave this strange way? Why is it not sufficient for everyone simply to seek their rational self-interests? What is it about human nature and innovation ecosystems that leads to these types of behaviors?

The mystery deepens. For answers, we must turn our exploration inward, to examine what happens inside the human mind.

Chapter Four: Life in the Rainforest

Part I: The Fractal Geometry of Innovation

"Did you know that the first Matrix was designed to be a perfect human world? Where none suffered, where everyone would be happy. It was a disaster. No one would accept the program...The perfect world was a dream that your primitive cerebrum kept trying to wake up from."

— **Agent Smith in the movie *The Matrix*[1]**

---

1   *The Matrix*, directed by Larry and Andy Wachowski (Los Angeles: Joel Silver, 1999). Excerpt reprinted courtesy of Peter Grossman and Larry and Andy Wachowski.

Shoulder-to-Shoulder, Yet Miles Apart

The two young women watched the same computer screen, but they were otherwise unalike. The dark-haired one was talking excitedly, waving her arms and pointing at the screen. The light-haired one was slouched next to her, arms crossed, her face almost expressionless. Together, they were trying to figure out how to solve a tricky software engineering problem. But they hardly looked at each other. They were shoulder-to-shoulder, yet miles apart.

We are watching a recorded video of these women on a monitor. At Stanford University, there is a research laboratory that videotapes these human interactions. Over the past few years, the team that runs the laboratory has simulated dozens of such interactions among innovators in the process of problem-solving. In the days following these sessions, researchers watch the videos a fraction of a second at a time, noting every facial expression made by the participants: every tic, gesture, nod, and curl of the lips.

By throwing two people together to videotape every physical nuance of their interaction, this laboratory is like a particle accelerator for the study of nonverbal human communication. The researchers are deconstructing the emotional process of human-to-human interaction into its most basic components. They are trying to observe the "big bang" of innovation at work.

These two women were participating in a simulated experiment, but the situation the Stanford researchers are trying to replicate is very real. The challenges and dynamics evoked by their experiments are continually repeated in real life, and are at the very heart of why innovation sometimes succeeds and far more often fails.

About one year after this experiment, and almost two thousand miles away, a similar scene is playing out between two grown men sitting in a fancy conference room. Only this time, the stakes are real. If you met these men on any other day, you would believe they are extremely intelligent, mature, kind, and gracious. At this moment, however, they are screaming at each other, their faces flushed red with anger.

This is no experiment. These men happen to be key members of one of our firm's startup companies. One of them is the CEO, and the other is an inventor whose technology has the potential to affect millions of people's lives. Both of them are critical to the company's success. Let us call this Company X.

We had recently learned that a similar company had gone public with a market value of about $200 million, which meant that Company X had the potential to do the same or receive an even higher valuation. There was hard evidence in this case that one plus one could actually equal a huge amount of value.

On the other hand, one minus one—that is, if they could not find a way to work together—could mean a dead-end for the millions of dollars and tens of thousands of man-hours invested, not to mention the loss to millions of potential customers who would never benefit from the product. The life or death of Company X hinged on a single relationship between two people. It was like the Stanford experiment in outward form, but the results would have real-world, substantive implications.

What is surprising to many is that this type of conflict is not unusual at all. It is, in fact, part of the routine in Silicon Valley. Fast-growing startups are like crucibles for human emotion. As Janet Crawford, an executive coach who applies behavioral science to her work with emerging companies, concurs, "Conflicts between founders and CEOs are very common issues in Valley startups. Coaches like me are often brought in to help."[2]

A single human-to-human equation can determine the success or failure of world-changing enterprises, especially in their early stages. A swarm of these equations are often the building blocks upon which products are improved, teams are built, and customers are reached. Innovation, for all the huge ripple effects it can have on the world, can always be boiled down to its most basic elements: human relationships.

The Stanford experiment with the two women is an attempt to figure out how that human-to-human equation works. It is like trying to capture Company X in a bottle. If two people getting along together or not getting along together is so important to the creation of economic value, then it is critical to understand the underlying forces behind this equation.

Understanding human behavior is the key to innovation. In this chapter, we look at the underlying social behavior of individuals in successful Rainforests—such as Silicon Valley—and come up with some surprising results. We show how human behavior that is conducive to innovation is actually not that natural—it requires us to push against fundamental characteristics of human nature and reason. We also demonstrate how people do in fact succeed despite these challenges.

Innovation takes place in the real world. The "perfect human world" that didn't work in *The Matrix* won't work in ours either. We need to understand and utilize the messy complications of the real world in order to make Rainforests thrive.

---

2 Janet Crawford, personal interview with author, November 15, 2010.

The Emerging "Science" of Innovation

In Chapter 2, we described the importance of human networks in the innovation process, and the value that can be created from collaborations across traditional social boundaries. In Chapter 3, we showed how keystones can reach across those boundaries to create value and how people are motivated by more than economic utility in Rainforests. In this chapter, we move our microscope closer and reveal yet another layer of the mystery.

What turns a human relationship into a productive collaboration? What is the chemistry of human interaction in the Rainforest that causes such interesting behaviors? At its simplest level, what makes two atoms...

...become a single pair?

Ultimately, a Rainforest must be built on a great number of pairs of atoms like this. It is the atomic basis of communities like Silicon Valley.

Before we can conceptualize a vast network of these pairings, we need to understand what makes a single one happen. We believe that there is an underlying *fractal geometry of innovation*. Benoît Mandelbrot started a minor revolution in 1982 when he argued in *The Fractal Geometry of Nature* that a single mathematical equation, repeated over and over again, could result in much of what we observe in the natural world.[3] On a simple level, this includes things like snowflakes, crystals, and snail shells. On a larger scale, it includes trees, mountains, and coastlines. Similarly, we argue that a human-to-human equation, replicated thousands or millions of times, accounts for much of what we see in vibrant Rainforests.

How does that equation work? When we break down innovation into its smallest atomic components, we find that participating in an "innovation culture" actually requires us to overcome some of our deepest instincts as human beings. We must fight two forces opposing innovation: our biology and our brains. We fight our biology because deep emotional

---

3 Benoît B. Mandelbrot, *The Fractal Geometry of Nature* (New York: W.H. Freeman, 1982). We argue that, like fractals, innovation also demonstrates self-similar aspects. The equation underlying a single relationship between two people is a microcosm of a startup company, which is a microcosm of what happens in a larger company, which is a microcosm of what happens in entire communities like Silicon Valley.

impulses, remnants of our primitive past, make human beings wary of one another. We fight our brains because innovative behavior is generally so risky and unrewarding that it does not make rational sense in most cases. As a result, when it comes to innovation systems, *the forces that push people apart are far stronger than the forces that pull people together.*

The Stanford experiment with the two women is part of an emerging wave of studies into the nature of innovation. The experiment is an attempt to precisely measure the communicative process that happens between two people working on a software programming project together. This single project, however, is just a tiny portion of a larger movement of scientists and thinkers who are defining this new field of inquiry.

Today, this "innovation science" is not so much a discrete academic discipline as it is an interdisciplinary group of researchers, thinkers, and practitioners attacking the problem from different angles—those with academic training in biology, psychology, neuroscience, mathematics, sociology, computer science, physics, economics, and other fields as well as those with practical backgrounds in company formation, business mentoring, venture capital, technology commercialization, nonprofit administration, and public sector management. Answers are still emerging, and there remain countless questions. We consider this book an initial run at stitching these fragmented answers together into a coherent theory.

Interestingly, a major creative spark for this work does not come from the traditional fields of academic study. Instead, it has been nurtured by the world of *design*. Our friend Ade Mabogunje at Stanford University might be considered a godfather of this new field of research, although he is the type of person who would probably cringe at such a title. Ade (pronounced AH-day) runs a one-of-a-kind group called the Institute for Venture Design at Stanford. Ade started a decade ago asking a question that only seems obvious enough to ask after someone like him bothered to ask it:

What is a "venture"?

We typically think of *design* as it applies to physical objects, like furniture or cell phones or kitchenware. Indeed, that is often how design teachers and researchers at Stanford and other schools apply their work. The underlying thought process used in design, however, can be applied to any human creation. It is the simple act of asking, "Why do we make things the way we do?" and "Can we make them better if we design from the bottom up?"

Given how hard we try to understand the creative process that enables us to design better chairs and automobiles, why should we not apply the same inquiry to designing better startup companies or innovative teams? After all, a piece of pottery and a new company are both human creations. They are manmade artifices—one is made by putting physical materials together, the other is created by putting human beings together.

By deconstructing the process of human collaboration, the work done in venture design research over the past decade helps explain some of the inner workings of the innovation process. The research continues today using new tools for data aggregation, new techniques for observing human interaction, and new insights from data measuring the real-time human connections occurring in real online social networks like Facebook. As Stanford researcher Mark Nelson says, "The old areas of research looked primarily at the nodes. But we have found that the real value is at the edges, not in the nodes."[4]

The inspiration behind the experiment with the two women described at the start of this chapter is a body of research attempting to explain why some couples stay married and others get divorced. Professor John Gottman, a former professor of psychology at the University of Washington, developed a method of predicting whether married couples would divorce over time. In a 14-year study, his model accurately predicted divorce 93% of the time by observing couples' behavior for merely fifteen minutes.[5] Another study detected patterns that could predict divorce of newlyweds based on just three minutes of observation.[6]

Stanford doctoral researcher Malte Jung—who has been mentored by Ade—has been applying the same techniques used by Professor Gottman to predict whether teams of innovators will succeed or fail. His primary question: can human emotions explain the success or failure of innovation?

Malte organized pairs of software engineers and gave them actual problems to solve—all the while recording their every nonverbal expression. The problems were designed to elicit high levels of emotional response in conflict situations, like physicists throwing matter together in a high-speed particle accelerator. He observed a variety of expressions, including facial muscle movements and changes in vocal tone, content, and body movement. He then categorized each expression and mapped it using a coding scheme, like physicists tracking the subatomic particles thrown off during a collision.

---

4 Mark Nelson, personal discussion with author, December 9, 2010.

5 John M. Gottman and Robert W. Levenson, "The Timing of Divorce: Predicting When a Couple Will Divorce Over a 14-Year Period," *Journal of Marriage and the Family* 62 (2000): 737, http://socrates.berkeley.edu/~ucbpl/docs/61-Timing%20of%20Divorce00.pdf.

6 Sybil Carrere and John M. Gottman, "Predicting Divorce among Newlyweds from the First Three Minutes of a Marital Conflict Discussion," *Family Process* 38 (1999): 293, doi:10.1111/j.1545-5300.1999.00293.x.

Below is a sample of some of the specific facial muscle movements observed in these experiments, drawn directly from a manual used by the Stanford researchers in Malte's team.[7] This particular scheme for facial coding was developed by researcher Paul Ekman, whose work inspired the television series *Lie to Me,* in which a detective observes facial movements to determine whether crime suspects are speaking truthfully or lying.

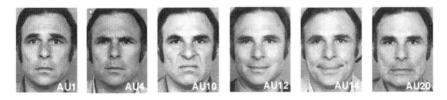

Real expressions come from combinations of these types of muscle movements. Some expressions can be positive and others negative, just as in a real-world human interaction. Hearty, joyful laughter would obviously be positive, while a nervous, restrained laugh might be negative. Other expressions are more subtle: a smirk, a squint, a sigh. The laboratory "scores" these expressions against time, assigning positive or negative points to each expression. The results can show whether a human-to-human relationship is developing positively or deteriorating negatively—what Malte calls the "Group Hedonic Balance."

An example of this work is shown below, depicting a negative pairing of people on the left ("non-regulated") and a positive pairing of people on the right ("regulated"). As time passes from left to right, teams are scored by adding points or subtracting points, based on their expressions.

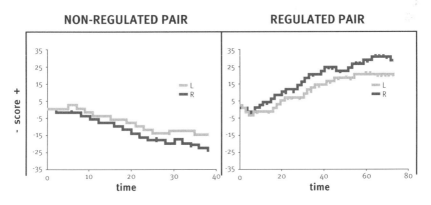

---

7   Paul Ekman, et al. *Facial Action Coding System: Manual* (Consulting Psychologists Press, 1978), as used in Malte Friedrich Jung, "SPAFF for Design Teams" (internal unpublished handbook, October 2007). Photographs reprinted courtesy of Paul Ekman, Wallace V. Friesen, and Joseph C. Hager.

Applying the Gottman husband-wife methodology to pairs of innovators, Malte ran sixteen trials of this experiment to look for correlations between the extent innovators get along and how well they perform.[8] He could qualitatively see the emotional connection—or the lack of one—happening in these experiments:

> What characterized non-regulated pairs were generally low levels of energy, with little interactivity, evidence of non-listening, and a constant presence of friction between the programmers. There was rarely any humor, or curiosity in those pairs. Regulated pairs, on the other hand, exhibited high levels of energy and interactivity, participants often laughed or told jokes, and there were ample signs that the participants were listening to each other and visibly seemed to enjoy working with each other.[9]

By just looking at the first five minutes of each interaction, he found that "the group hedonic balance significantly correlated not only with subjective performance measures but also with the objective quality of the developed software code."[10] Similarly, a larger series of experiments by Malte with 30 teams, each of three to four participants, also found significant correlation between group hedonic balance and the quality of collective output.[11] In short, *people that get along better, innovate better.*

....

Rainforest Axiom #9: *Innovation and human emotion are intertwined.*

....

It is often said that the majority of human communication is nonverbal.[12] The nonverbal signals we give each other are not just an interesting sideshow in the study of communication. Nonverbal signals indicate emotions, and emotions are at the heart of the collaborative process. We cannot understand innovation without recognizing that economic value creation is determined significantly by our emotions toward one another.

---

8 Malte Friedrich Jung, "Engineering Team Performance and Emotion: Affective Interaction Dynamics as Indicators of Design Team Performance" (PhD dissertation, Department Of Mechanical Engineering and the Committee on Graduate Studies, Stanford University, 2011), 11.

9 Jung, "Engineering Team Performance and Emotion," 23.

10 Ibid.

11 Ibid., 55.

12 Albert Mehrabian and Morton Wiener, "Decoding of Inconsistent Communications," *Journal of Personality and Social Psychology* 6 (1967), 109-114; Albert Mehrabian and Susan R. Ferris, "Influence of Attitudes from Nonverbal Communication in Two Channels," *Journal of Consulting Psychology,* 31 (1967), 248-52.

Some might argue that failed relationships are inevitable, part of the nature of human society. Conventional wisdom says that we work better with people we like, and there is nothing inherently wrong with that. Innovation still happens, as it has for thousands of years.

However, we argue that failed relationships have played a key role in hindering the development of human society. To explain why relationships matter, it helps to step back in time—about one thousand years back.

The Silk Road of Today

We are sitting in front of about fifty government officials, scientists, and businessmen staring back at us in a hotel conference room in the distant city of Almaty, Kazakhstan. In the wintertime, Kazakhstan is among the coldest places on Earth. Thankfully, we are here in late summer, when the streets are bustling with smiling people, young couples are chatting, children are playing, and fruits are ripe in the markets.

The World Bank invited us here to help develop new capital structures to invest in the commercialization of their scientific inventions. This is more of our Extreme Venture Capital.

This nation on the steppe grasslands of Central Asia has been blessed with enormous reserves of natural resources, a rich and interesting nomadic history, and a culture that has made its people resourceful, persistent, and hospitable to outsiders. We are supposed to be offering our advice on how Kazakhstan can build its own modern innovation economy, which in turn is supposed to lead to better jobs and higher standards of living there.

The refrain we hear from the Kazakhstanis, however, is the refrain we have heard in virtually every country we have visited: "How come we can't do this, too? What is the recipe?" It is at that point that we realize that Kazakhstanis already know the answer. They figured it out two thousand years ago.

Modern-day Kazakhstan was the heart of the northern route of the Silk Road, the trading pathway along which goods were exchanged between East Asia on one end and the Middle East on the other. The Tian Shan mountains, among the most inaccessible mountain ranges in the world, run roughly east and west for about 1,500 miles through the middle of Central Asia. It was along the base of these mountains that traders on camels and horseback would make the treacherous journey that took one year or more each way. They risked attacks from bandits. They faced the dangers of drought and starvation. Still, the fancy silks that the wealthy women of Rome wore two millennia ago were largely carried along these routes, one footstep at a time.

What could possibly be worth making such a difficult journey? The answer to this question is the basic process of exchange at the heart of capitalism. Imagine an Egyptian queen who desired a new silk scarf, and on the other hand, a Chinese emperor who coveted a particular kind of glass bottle. Let us also imagine that the queen has just such an extra glass bottle, and the emperor has an extra silk scarf. In each case, the person has an item they do not value as much as someone who desires it far away. It makes sense that they would exchange those items—a scarf for a bottle—which would make them both better off than if they had not made the trade.

In 1817, David Ricardo outlined the fundamental transaction that drives economic value creation in his book, *On the Principles of Political Economy and Taxation.* In the book, he argues that specialization and exchange made everybody better off. If each party specializes in what they do best, the resulting savings in labor produce enormous benefits for everyone in the system. Whereas Ricardo looked at English cloth and Portuguese wine, we use the Silk Road as our example.

An Egyptian queen's artisan might be able to make a silk scarf after years of trial-and-error, but an artisan in the palace of the Chinese emperor could do it in a few weeks. If she trades a glass for that scarf, however, then an Egyptian queen is able to obtain an object that is worth years of labor for the cost of a few weeks of someone else's labor. The same holds for the Chinese emperor who wants the Egyptian glassware.

The entire field of economics is based on this single form of transaction. We do not all make our own clothing today, for example, because it's more efficient for us to exchange money we earn for our labor to purchase the clothes produced by someone else. It would take an extraordinary amount of time for an ordinary person to replicate the workmanship, style, and quality produced by clothing manufacturers. Similarly, we do not make our own shoes, our own computers, or our own automobiles. Exchange makes us all better off because we are free to focus on the items we can produce more efficiently than others.

Innovation is simply a modern form of the Silk Road. Instead of exchanging goods, however, we exchange ideas and skills. Author Matt Ridley writes about "ideas having sex" to explain the nature of modern human economic activity:

> If culture consisted simply of learning habits from others, it would soon stagnate. For culture to turn cumulative, ideas needed to meet and mate. The 'cross-fertilisation of ideas' is a cliché, but one with unintentional fecundity. 'To create is to recombine' said the molecular biologist François Jacob. Imagine if the man who invented the railway and the man who invented the locomotive could never meet or speak to each other, even through third parties. … [T]here was a point in human pre-history when big-brained, cultural, learning people for the first time began to exchange things with each other, and that once they started doing so, culture suddenly became cumulative, and the great headlong experiment of human economic 'progress' began. Exchange is to cultural evolution as sex is to biological evolution.[13]

To explain the workings of the Rainforest, however, we need to take Ridley's idea even further. There was not, after all, only one person who "invented" all of Google. Innovation, as it exists in modern communities like Silicon Valley, is a team sport. It cannot rely on exchanges of goods or ideas solely between disparate individuals.

Therefore, we must explore new frontiers beyond the old terrain of exchange and specialization. What happens, for instance, if parties need to exchange ideas and skills that are not learned in years, but which require a lifetime to master? Or what if the ideas and skills are so extraordinary that there are only a handful of people in the entire world who possess them? What if there is only *one person* in the world with a particular skill? In such cases, it does not seem useful or even accurate to say that we are merely making exchanges to save labor. The answer to these questions requires a more complicated response than Ricardo might have envisioned—one that reveals the significant challenges of modern innovation, and explains why people in Rainforests behave the way they do.

---

13 Matt Ridley, *The Rational Optimist: How Prosperity Evolves* (New York: Harper, 2010), 6-7, http://issuu.com/hcpressbooks/docs/rational_optimist.

The Invisible Currency of Innovation

Let us return to a hypothetical model we used previously in this book: a scientist who has discovered a possible cure for kidney cancer meets a businessman who has the expertise to turn that cure into a potential drug for real patients. In order for either person to realize the potential of their relationship, they must make an exchange. Essentially, each must give the other a piece of his brain and time. The scientist gives a portion of his discovery to the businessman, and the businessman gives the scientist a portion of his experience navigating the complex commercialization processes for drug therapies. A simplified way to demonstrate this might look like this:

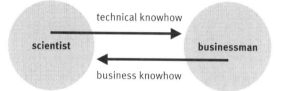

This exchange would be, in effect, not that different from a simple barter system on the Silk Road. It is an ancient ritual, and not that dissimilar from you and me exchanging an apple for an orange.

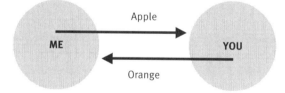

The problem with this diagram, however, is that it is too simple a model to really describe the way complex, modern economies act in reality. On one hand, there is often a time delay. One party provides something of value—a fruit, an idea, a personal introduction—but the other party may take weeks, months, or years before they give something else of equal value back in return.

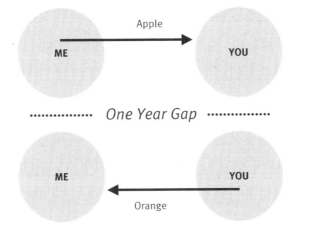

When we exchange basic goods and services, this problem is easy enough to solve. We create currency, which enables us to overcome the time delay. I can give you an apple, and you can give me an orange one year later. If you give me a dollar for that apple today, however, I do not need to worry about trusting you to give me an orange later because I have received the value of that orange in the form of a monetary currency. As historian Niall Ferguson says, "Money is not metal. It is trust inscribed."[14]

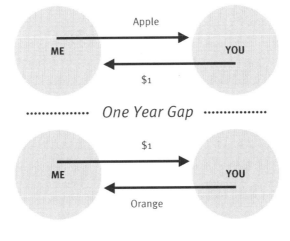

---

14 Niall Ferguson, *The Ascent of Money: A Financial History of the World* (Penguin: 2009), 30.

Or, you might decide to take your orange elsewhere, which is perfectly fine with me since I now have money I can use to purchase a different orange somewhere else. Currency dramatically increases our ability to trade in many ways, by bridging gaps in time, compensating for the differences in value between objects (e.g., if my apple is worth $1.05, and your orange is worth $1), or allowing a complex network of multiple transactions among a number of parties (e.g., a three-way exchange of an apple, an orange, and a pear). Money greases the gears of trade.

In the world of innovation, however, we are not just exchanging apples and oranges, or even silicon and plastics. A greater challenge arises when we are exchanging things that have no readily determined price, or are perceived by opposing parties to have widely different values.

If a scientist has spent an entire lifetime researching a possible cure for cancer, how can he or she really put a price tag on their ultimate discovery? In the scientist's eyes, it is priceless. It would have been difficult to accurately estimate the original value of the computer search algorithm that powered Google before there was a Google, especially when you consider that there were thousands of other technologists and entrepreneurs claiming at that time to have invented the next great search engine technology. Only in retrospect does its value appear to be billions of dollars. The technology could just as easily have been worth nothing. In fact, that is exactly what hundreds of venture capitalists thought when they rejected the opportunity to invest in Google at its founding.

At the start, there was no definitive way to know which was worth more— the technology used by Google or the system employed by the Anti-Google described earlier in this book. The value of an innovation—whether it is a cure for cancer or an Internet search technology—can be anywhere from zero to a trillion dollars depending on the perception of the parties involved. Almost invariably, as we have seen in our work, each party tends to value its own contributions far more highly than does the other party in an exchange.

To launch a new startup company with great potential, one must assemble a whole range of objects with values that are virtually impossible to price accurately. An entrepreneur will typically start with nothing except his ability to talk. From there, he must then be able to assemble a wide network of valuable people and resources to make his company successful—ideas, expertise, market insights, investment capital, legal services, intellectual property, accounting services, banking, manufacturing capabilities, sales and marketing skills, relationships with distributors, regulatory expertise, and so on. Each of these elements is critical to the company's success.

How do you organize hundreds of essential people and resources that are impossible to price accurately? You might conclude from this line of reasoning that the exchanges required to turn an innovation into a thriving venture are beyond the ability of the traditional transaction methods described above, and you would be largely right.

To solve this problem, people have created new tools, including the structure known as a company. If we insert a company in the middle of the basic exchange, it becomes a potential way for all parties to transact equitably. Each party gets a piece of the new company in exchange for their contributions to it.

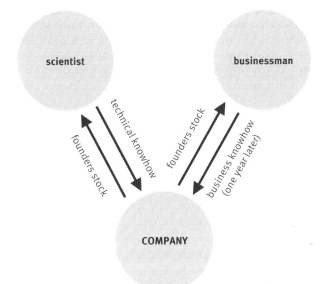

The idea of the company structure, therefore, is a critical artifice in the entrepreneurial innovation process because it replicates the role of currency in the world of goods and services, but it does so for the world of ideas and innovations. Equity (or stock) in an emerging company is the "trust inscribed" of the Rainforest. It is the currency of innovation, whether in the form of common stock, options, warrants, or preferred stock.

The company structure, however, is still not sufficient to explain the entire life cycle of innovation. A company, after all, is just a superficial form. What happens in the beginning, before a company is created to serve in the role of currency? We need to dig even further back in time.

At the start of every episode of entrepreneurial innovation, there is no outward form. Every company in the beginning is just a group of disparate people with an informally arranged set of ideas. There is no corporate entity in the beginning—there is only a vision of what is possible. As Stanford's

Ade Mabogunje would say, "A company is not a thing. It is an event."[15] Although we often treat companies as tangible entities, in Rainforests we think of companies as nothing more than transitory moments of human organization. If we view enterprise creation as a human relationship process—an event—then we gain a profound insight into the "big bang" of innovation.

Let us examine that moment of creation. The origin of every innovative endeavor in the history of human society has required an implied exchange based on good faith. That exchange might look something like this, if we continue to use our hypothetical example. The scientist must share what he knows with the businessman long before the businessman can reciprocate to provide the bulk of his contribution.

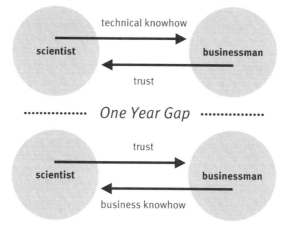

If there is no company yet formed, we are left only with a form of barter based on the *currency of trust*. Virtually every exchange in the Rainforest must start with some variation of this transaction. One thousand years later, we are still traversing the Silk Road, adapted to a modern-day context.

Trust, however, is hard. When it involves a lifetime of passionate work or expertise, and possibly represents billions of dollars at stake, it gets much, much harder. Human beings have human foibles, and tend to perceive value differently. People are not perfect economic organisms. They are not always "rational actors." Pride, dignity, and other emotions color their actions, and can even cause them to make decisions that are not in their own best interests. In reality, the basic barter transaction above does not happen naturally, as the differences in perceived value between parties is often vast. Far more typically, the transaction looks like this less inspiring version:

---

15 Mabogunje, interview (see chap. 2, n. 12).

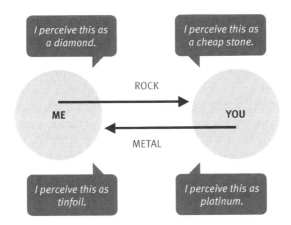

As a consequence, innovation often falters or dies. Where the accurate pricing of intangible elements like knowledge and expertise are impossible to ascertain, or where people have invested entire careers into developing specialized ideas or skills, the economic exchange often never happens. And that is what stops much innovation dead in its tracks.

We have seen this scenario play out thousands of times in real life. It is the story of the inventor who is never able to hire a great executive to grow their company. Or the startup that fails to license a critical technology because it is unable to negotiate conclusively with a university. Or the founder who is never able to raise capital because he is unwilling to share enough ownership of his company.

Transactions often do not occur because the parties place wildly differing values on their contributions. They each view what they are giving to be vastly greater than the value they are receiving. To be perfectly honest, it actually is impossible to put a price on, say, a potential cure for cancer. And therein lies a huge problem. The difficulty of consummating the series of transactions needed for innovation to occur is compounded by the fact that the elements required are so highly specialized—say, a lifetime of experience—that it is nearly impossible to determine or agree upon their actual value.

Where each person's participation is 100% necessary for the success of an endeavor—or at least is perceived to be by each person involved—how do the parties calculate the relative value of each person's contribution? This is not a theoretical exercise. It is a real, substantial, and perplexing issue faced by startup companies every day all over the world, in countless invisible transactions in cafes, conference rooms, and phone calls. We frequently see new entrepreneurs get stubbornly fixated on the paper value of their startup equity, often to their detriment. How do you convert the value of a lifetime of specialized knowledge—which is priceless to the person who has accumulated it—into the hard currency of startup equity?

If we want more innovation to occur—if we wish to foster more Rainforests—then we need to consummate more exchanges between people who possess highly differentiated and specialized ideas and skills. It is the Silk Road taken to the *n*th degree. The more that people possessing widely varied skills, insights, connections, and perspectives bump into each other, the better. The Silk Road helped realize great economic value in its time by connecting human skills and resources found in one place with highly differentiated human skills and resources in another. We present a corollary to David Ricardo's observations on specialization and exchange...

....

Rainforest Axiom #10: *The greater the diversity in human specialization, the greater the potential value of exchanges in a system.*

....

In a Rainforest, hyper-diversity tends to create interactions among people with hyper-specialization, which opens the door to a universe of possible hyper-exchanges. It is no accident that places like Silicon Valley have an exceptional amount of diversity among its people, whether by race, ethnicity, birthplace, training, experience, skills, personality, or otherwise. The melting pot offers inherent, but often latent, value.

By their nature, however, such ideas and skills are nearly impossible to value accurately. One key solution to this conundrum would seem to be the creation of trust. Trust, after all, is how people since the dawn of human history have bridged gaps when monetary currency was not enough to consummate a transaction. As a practical solution, however, trust is not so trustworthy.

If we examine the nature of trust in the Rainforest, we can start to uncover why the types of exchanges required to make innovation happen are the exception rather than the rule. The lack of trust helps explain why Rainforests are so rare. The micro mechanics of human relationships can throw a wrench into the transactional process, causing macro breakdowns and failures.

The Corporate Caveman

Trust is hard because our brains were designed for basic survival, not for building startup companies. In a fundamental way, we are cavemen dressed in corporate attire. If we wish to understand how to create Rainforests, we need to understand how we are wired. How that wiring works may be surprising.

Despite the huge leaps of achievement of human society over the past several hundred years, we are not that far from our ancestral heritage on the savanna grasslands of Africa.[16] In that environment, rich with grass and vegetation, blessed with a moderate climate, and with few trees to hide predators, human beings lived in a relative paradise. Given this nurturing ecosystem, archaeologists believe that early humans actually had a significant amount of leisure time. Our ancestors had the luxury of spending time on activities other than hunting and gathering. They developed social skills to help them better hunt and gather, but they also had time to evolve more complex social skills that facilitated the exchange of goods and services. Human beings are arguably the most social animal on earth, and it is that ability to exchange—whether food, clothing, information, or even scientific discoveries that might cure cancer—that has led to such tremendous prosperity in our civilization.

Clearly, there were still threats on the African savanna—from predatory animals, for example. Human beings had to develop the ability to quickly judge the presence of danger. Our ancestors had to assess in an instant whether the possible dangers arising from a particular situation were greater or less than the benefits derived from it. Human beings even today are born with a propensity to fear snakes.[17] Many parents have witnessed the fear that a toddler experiences when seeing a snake. Scientists have confirmed the same effect in chimpanzees and other primates. Fear is a primitive instinct that helped keep our ancestors alive.

16 Merlin Donald, *Origins of the Modern Mind: Three Stages in the Evolution of Culture and Cognition* (Cambridge: Harvard University Press, 1991), 2-3. "...the modern mind is a mosaic structure of cognitive vestiges from earlier stages of human emergence. Cognitive vestiges invoke the evolutionary principle of conservation of previous gains..."

17 Vanessa LoBue, David H. Rakison, and Judy S. DeLoache, "Threat Perception Across the Life Span Evidence for Multiple Converging Pathways," Abstract, *Current Directions in Psychological Science* 19 (2010): 375-379, doi: 10.1177/0963721410388801.

There were also threats from other human beings. If we survived by developing beneficial social skills, we could just as easily die from not developing them, or from developing the *wrong* social skills. Some of these fears had to be taught and handed down from one generation to the next. For example, parents have to teach children that someone brandishing a knife might harm them. But a chef brandishing a knife at a Benihana steak restaurant probably means them no harm. Such a distinction requires a fairly complex thought process and is learned through repeated social interactions with other members of society.

Social behavior, however, is not just learned. Human beings are also hard-wired to respond to other human beings in certain ways. Sometimes we do not need to be taught to be afraid. We can all point to personal experiences that demonstrate the power of our unconscious to trigger changes in our social behavior. We all understand at a deep level the meaning of such comments as, "Looking at that person makes me feel uneasy." Almost everyone has walked alone on a city street at night and experienced the sensation that someone dangerous is lurking around the next dark corner, although you consciously cannot point to any evidence that such a person is even there.

Our brains are practical biological tools, not precise computers. They are programmed to calculate value and risk and then roughly weigh the respective rewards and punishments of possible actions. The wiring of our brains, however, affects the way we process that information, and includes biases and imperfections. The brain makes decisions and rewards correct actions through the use of: the dopamine system, which is activated by pleasurable sensations; the orbitofrontal cortex, which helps govern decision-making; the amygdala, which controls emotional responses; and the striatum, which is involved in the reward process. The brain's punishment mechanisms are processed similarly, but do not include the dopamine system. As we learn more about these mechanisms, some economists see the dawn of *neuroeconomics*, a field studying how the brain's wiring affects the functioning of economies.[18]

---

18 Robert J. Shiller, "The Neuroeconomics Revolution," *Project Syndicate* (November 21, 2011), http://www.project-syndicate.org/commentary/shiller80/English.

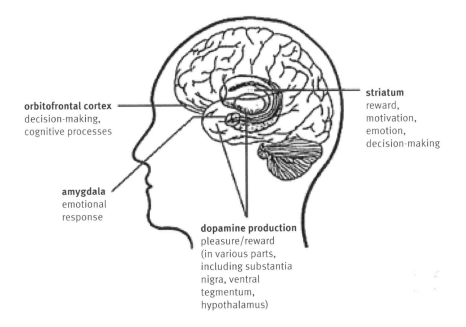

orbitofrontal cortex
decision-making,
cognitive processes

striatum
reward,
motivation,
emotion,
decision-making

amygdala
emotional
response

dopamine production
pleasure/reward
(in various parts,
including substantia
nigra, ventral
tegmentum,
hypothalamus)

The observations of philosopher David Hume—who famously wrote that reason is "the slave of the passions"[19]—are in fact being proven true by science. We are not wired to control our emotions. We now know that the amygdala can send signals to the prefrontal region of the brain, where the orbitofrontal cortex is located, but the prefrontal region cannot send signals directly to the amygdala. That is, the emotional part of our brain is wired to send signals to the thinking part of our brain, but not the other way around.

Furthermore, as people like Stanford Professor Robert Sapolsky have observed, an emotion like human fear is different from fear in other animals because we can be afraid of things that are not there but which might happen.[20] Our imagination plays a critical role in our ability to perceive danger, even when there is none.

19 Rachel Cohon, "Hume's Moral Philosophy," *The Stanford Encyclopedia of Philosophy (Fall 2010 Edition)*, http://plato.stanford.edu/archives/fall2010/entries/hume-moral/.

20 Robert Sapolsky, *Why Zebras Don't Get Ulcers: An Updated Guide to Stress, Stress Related Diseases, and Coping* (New York: W. H. Freeman, 1994); Robert Sapolsky and Marcia Reynolds, "Zebras and Lions in the Workplace: An Interview with Dr. Robert Sapolsky," *The International Journal of Coaching in Organizations* 4 (2006): 8, http://pcpionline.com/~files/Authors/IJCO200642715Sapolskyfinau.pdf. "So the damage comes when people are marinating in anticipation [of] the threat menace, which can last for months or years. It's the anxiety over the future that has the worst effect. You don't just turn on your stress response when you've been slashed by a predator, or when you've lost your job."

One reason that we fear so much is because we are so easily fooled. Being fooled by the wrong person—whether for our ancestors on the African savanna or for people living today in modern civilization—can sometimes mean death. Experimental work by researchers has shown that people identify false verbal claims at rates less than pure random chance.[21] As a result, it is not surprising that humans developed complex instincts for trust and fear. We more easily trust familiar people and environments, and are less trusting of new people and unfamiliar situations.

Ultimately, our ability to build social networks based on trust helped keep our ancestors alive, and we still rely on those innate social skills to survive in modern societies. Our social relationships are not just a source of pleasure and pain; our brains treat them as a matter of life and death. Indeed, neuroscientists have discovered that the pain we experience from social rejection has the same effect in our brains as the pain we experience from physical injury.[22]

Science is proving that we make decisions based on instincts and emotions that our conscious minds cannot control, nor even be aware of much of the time. Scientists have observed that even something as simple as lifting a finger can happen as much as ten seconds before the conscious mind is aware of the action.[23] As Professor Wolf Singer at the Max Planck Institute for Brain Research writes:

> The evidence...contradicts our intuition that we can always freely decide what we are going to do next and which factors we are going to consider when we plan future acts...We say 'we have decided in this way because...' and then we give the reasons that we are consciously aware of. However, much of the activity that actually prepared and determined the decision process escapes conscious recollection.[24]

Similarly, the process of building a startup company is one in which people must often rely on gut-level decision-making. Entrepreneurial innovation, by its nature, is virtually a never-ending series of educated guesses. Almost every decision made is based on substantially incomplete information.

21 Timothy R. Levine, Hee Sun Park and Steven A. McCornack, "Accuracy in Detecting Truth and Lies: Documenting the 'Veracity Effect,'" *Communication Monographs* 66 (1999): 125, https://www.msu.edu/~levinet/veracity.pdf.

22 Naomi I. Eisenberger, "Why Rejection Hurts: What Social Neuroscience Has Revealed About the Brain's Response to Social Rejection," to appear in: J. Decety & J. Cacioppo (Eds.), *The Handbook of Social Neuroscience* (2011): 590,595, http://web.mac.com/naomieisenberger/san/Naomi_Eisenberger_SAN_Papers_files/39-Decety-39.pdf.

23 Chun Siong Soon et al., "Unconscious Determinants of Free Decisions in the Human Brain," *Nature Neuroscience* 11, (2008): 543-545, doi:10.1038/nn.2112).

24 Wolf Singer, "A Determinist View of Brain, Mind and Consciousness," in *Brain Waves Module 1: Neuroscience, Society and Policy,* The Royal Society, Frankfurt, January 2011, 43, http://royalsociety.org/policy/reports/brainwaves1/.

There is usually not enough information or time to make precise mathematical calculations for even a single key decision, much less an entire month's worth. The innovation process cannot be divorced from the fragile dynamics of human emotions and instincts.

Our brains are imperfect tools for making decisions, so the decisions we make are not always the right ones. Professor Wolfram Schultz of Cambridge observes:

> We assume that brains evolved to assure the survival of genes and their carriers in *most* situations. Assuring survival in *all* possible, however unlikely, situations would require extra brain matter and function that would make brains less efficient and their carriers less competitive.[25]

Thus, our minds are imperfect by design. Their biological goal is efficient decision-making, not perfect decision-making.

For instance, we know that our brains can cause us to make prejudiced decisions based on tribal affiliations.[26] At an anecdotal level, we know that people tend to congregate with others who are similar to themselves, whether united by their race, ethnicity, culture, religion, or language. One of the interesting reasons we do so is because it simply takes more effort to do otherwise. Recent experiments by social neuroscientists have confirmed that the human brain actually has to "work harder" to trust people who have a different ethnicity, language, etc.[27] It is like the difference between reading a complicated textbook and a simple picture book—our brain has to use more energy to process the information it is receiving.

A number of scientists have found evidence for this using functional magnetic resonance imaging (fMRI) techniques to watch the brain in action. Researchers at Northwestern University, in one experiment, observed that the brain demonstrated more cognitive conflict when it was engaged in economic trust games with people of a different religion than it did when dealing with people of the same religion.[28] That is, our brains have to "work harder" to engage in win-win economic transactions with people who are

---

25 Wolfram Schultz, "Reward, Decision-Making and Neuroeconomics," in *Brain Waves Module 1: Neuroscience, Society and Policy,* The Royal Society, Frankfurt, January 2011, 53, http://royalsociety.org/policy/reports/brainwaves1/.

26 See for example Rhitu Chatterjee, "Xenophobia's Evolutionary Roots," *PRI's The World,* August 10, 2011, http://www.theworld.org/2011/08/xenophobias-evolutionary-roots/. Michael Wilson, a primatologist at the University of Minnesota: primates generally have "a very deep-rooted fear and suspicion of outsiders," Primatologist Frans de Waal of Emory University: "Sort of bred into the primate line is that you belong to a group and you don't necessarily like outsiders."

27 Katie Rotella et al., "Neural Bases of Trust for Ingroup and Outgroup Members," Poster presented at the 2010 Social and Affective Neuroscience Conference, Chicago, IL, October 29-31, 2010, http://www.socialaffectiveneuro.org/docs/SANS_program_2010.pdf.

28 Ibid.

perceived to be outsiders, regardless of the actual value of the economic transaction itself.

The evidence shows that these tribal biases are not just about race. For example, one can point to numerous conflicts around the world that erupt among groups of people—Serbs and Croats, for example—who look almost indistinguishable from each other. Social boundaries that are invisible to most people can be powerful divisions in other people's minds, rooted in deeply-held prejudices based on professional backgrounds, socio-economic status, cultural habits, religious affiliations, political beliefs, and even language accents. Our perceptions of tribal allegiances—your team, my team—transcend race or other physical characteristics.

This ingrained bias against people from different tribes impedes innovation. As we saw on the Silk Road, there is much greater potential for economic value to be created by exchange and specialization between people who bring highly different skills and ideas. Anything that reduces our ability to engage in win-win economic transactions across social boundaries will hamper the ability of a network to maximize its economic output.

This instinct towards tribalism also affects the way in which our brains perceive value. We do not all evaluate the same information in the same way. The economic problem we described before—in which one party perceives a diamond and the other party perceives a cheap rock—is accentuated when we are engaged in economic transactions across social boundaries. This might include, for instance, a scientific inventor and a businessperson trying to start a company together. Experiments in social psychology reveal that we value the ideas of people who are viewed as similar to us more than we value those contributed by people who are viewed as different.[29] Our brains use social identity as a filter for determining the value of information.

Indeed, it appears that we do not even hear the same information being communicated to us from different types of people. When people feel like they are not members of a group, their brains process less information communicated by members of the group.[30] Social psychologists call this phenomenon *emotional numbing*. Social exclusion "numbs" our ability to hear others.

---

29 Mirre Stallen et al., "The Influence of Group Membership on Advice Taking." Poster presented at the 2010 Social and Affective Neuroscience Conference, Chicago, IL, October 29-31, 2010, http://www.socialaffectiveneuro.org/docs/SANS_program_2010.pdf.

30 Asuka Murata et al., "The Effect of Social Exclusion on the Sensitivity to Vocal Tone: an ERP study." Poster presented at the 2010 Social and Affective Neuroscience Conference, Chicago, IL, October 29-31, 2010, http://www.socialaffectiveneuro.org/docs/SANS_program_2010.pdf.

Cavemen Doing Innovation

We see these unconscious behaviors at work with innovators everywhere in the world. Scientists versus entrepreneurs. Startups versus large corporations. Investors versus investees. These tribal conflicts can be obstacles to the development of Rainforests. The emerging body of research from social neuroscience and social psychology strongly suggests that our primitive negative instincts towards certain "other" people are more powerful than we realized. Furthermore, the evidence indicates that our unconscious wiring affects our economic behavior. As Stanford's Ade Mabogunje states, "Our cognitive machinery is exactly the same in Silicon Valley and in rural India. We can change the software but not the hardware."[31]

Conflicts in startup companies—as in Company X at the beginning of this chapter—are to be expected. We now know that these conflicts are exacerbated by our basic wiring, and are often not just about the actual issues at hand.

Rainforest Axiom #11: *The instincts that once helped our ancestors survive are hurting our ability to maximize innovation today.*

On top of the group bias problem, we have increasing evidence that demonstrates just how bad humans are as economic computers. We tend to overestimate the value of things in the present and underestimate the value of things in the future.

Neuroeconomics is starting to uncover the neurobiological basis for the properties of economic valuations and decisions. In some cases, these valuations lead to daily choices that could be disadvantageous to individuals and society…We know that certain reward values are coded 'inaccurately' in the brain. For example, we know that the reward processes in the striatum tend to discount the values of future rewards (temporal value discounting). This may be a factor that leads us to invest less in provisions for the future (such as education, healthcare or pensions) than we 'should' do.[32]

Let us go back to the hypothetical story of the cancer scientist. As the researcher and the businessman are trying to find ways to work together and build a business to commercialize their discovery, we see an intimidating obstacle course of unconscious challenges they need to

31 Mabogunje, interview; see also Merlin Donald, *Origins*.
32 Schultz, "Reward," 56.

overcome: a human neural bias against trusting people from different social groups, cognitive wiring that requires us to work harder to find win-win economic transactions across social boundaries, difficulty processing communication that comes from people outside their tribes, a tendency to value ideas and contributions from people in their own group more than those from people in other groups, and an inclination to undervalue the future rewards of economic activity, among other possible biases that we are still learning about.

And we are still talking about only the first pairing of two people in what will inevitably require a cast of thousands if it is ultimately to be successful. In addition, the pair must contend with the fact that scientists and businessmen tend to speak different languages—with their own specialized acronyms, slang, body language, and value systems—and they almost certainly have different circles of friends and acquaintances. At a profoundly deep level, human beings are not wired to innovate well together. From this perspective, it is perhaps amazing that such partnerships happen at all.

Behavioral expert Janet Crawford puts it succinctly: "Attention has a negative bias. It is much more useful to notice the tiger lurking in a tree than the tasty fruit on its branches."[33] As a consequence, we are wired generally to avoid loss more than to seek gain. Distrust is easier than trust.

Perhaps surprisingly, human behavior in the new social networks on the Web has reinforced our tendency to remain in our social ghettos, rather than empower us to move beyond them. Researcher Danah Boyd has demonstrated that young people in social networking communities like Facebook and Myspace tend to recreate online the groups they belong to offline—with the same homogenous race and class characteristics—despite their easy access to hundreds of millions of other types of people.[34]

Stanford researcher Mark Nelson has created a project in collaboration with Facebook that shows how human interactions across "friendship boundaries" in the virtual world actually reflect what is happening in the real world. For example, when tensions in the real world rise between Israelis and Palestinians, social activities (such as "friending" and messaging) between Israelis and Palestinians on Facebook decrease almost immediately. Our friendships are not immune from the larger forces affecting the tribes to which we belong. Even when the whole world is so close, we are still programmed to be members of our own groups. The world may be one click away, but people are still miles apart.

---

33 Crawford, interview.

34 Danah Michele Boyd, "Taken Out of Context: American Teen Sociality in Networked Publics" (PhD dissertation, Graduate Division of the University of California, Berkeley, Fall 2008), 293-294.

In this chapter, we have argued how our natural biology can be the nemesis of innovation. Humans are social creatures, and we tend to create tribes of social affinity. Tribalism, however, can separate us from people in other groups, even when we might create the greatest economic value together. The hardest relationships to build are quite frequently the ones that have the greatest potential value. The emotional part of our brains can control the logical part, but not vice versa. Thus, we will never completely eliminate the instinctual tendencies that push people apart. It takes great effort to behave in the ways most likely to create the greatest amount of innovation.

If distrust is easier than trust, then what makes people in Rainforests come together at all? People have found "shortcuts" to overcome these forces that impede innovation. Rainforests like Silicon Valley have developed ways to foster communication, trust, and collaboration among very different kinds of people. Determining exactly how that happens—by examining the ways human behavior can overcome psychological impediments—is critical to understanding and replicating the process of innovation. We turn to that question in the next section.

Chapter Four: Life in the Rainforest

Part II: The Roller Coaster

Animals have a body and soul too.
Without mind and feelings
what joy is there in life,
without yearning for the depths?

– Kazakh poet Abai (1845-1904), *Book of Words*[1]

---

1   Abai, *Book of Words* (Abai International Club, 2005), 59.

Atomic Power

Imagine the people in the Rainforest as a pool of atoms floating freely. On one hand, the atoms seem to be repelling each other in a disorderly fashion. They are wary of one another, as they have been trained to keep their distance for fear of a terrible cataclysmic collision.

On the other hand, the atoms also need to band together to survive. They seem to be pulling toward each other and pushing away from each other at the same time, in a back and forth dance, as if each pair of atoms was connected by some sort of invisible rubber band.

Over an extended period of time, the atoms appear to be arranging themselves into a kind of pattern, a complicated matrix in which they can be as close to each other as possible without getting any closer than they really need to be. There is an inherent tension that remains in each of the rubber bands that connect the atoms, as they find a comfortable distance from each other that reduces their otherwise chaotic collisions to a minimum.

We have seen how human beings are wired to repel each other, so now we turn our attention to what keeps us together, and makes possible the type of economic exchanges that are necessary for innovation to occur. What keeps the atoms from flying away as far as possible from each other? Given that we have such strong instinctual tendencies that hinder us from working together, why does systemic innovation happen at all? Why attract, when repelling is easier?

In essence, it is no different than the questions posed by economist Ronald Coase: Why have a company in the first place, when you could just hire independent contractors? Why do the benefits of coming together outweigh all the transaction costs that push us apart?

Throughout most of human history, repelling each other is what we have done best. Governments and corporations by the thousands have crammed smart people into incubators, innovation centers, or other similar structures, only to find that little of value has emerged and that vast amounts of capital have been wasted. People can be sitting in the same office and still have a vast gulf between them. In virtually all attempts to create artificial Rainforests, the invisible bonds tend to break, the rubber bands snap, and the atoms are left floating on their own.

In the second part of Chapter 4, we move from examining the Rainforest as brain scientists to a new vantage point as sociologists. We look at how social structures emerge, what incentives drive human behavior, and how entrepreneurs leverage human nature. With that understanding, we will have a fuller picture of life in the Rainforest.

Running Away From Tribes

What happens when you tear people out of their traditional social networks? What happens when people have no tribes?

The world's great experiment to answer these questions is America. The story of America is the building of a society not burdened by historical tribes. Generally speaking, Americans are less likely to be identified by family history. They are less chained to the past. Instead, Americans tend to be identified by self-reliance and their ability to contribute to the task at hand. As Professor Gary Weaver, an expert on cultural history, observed about America:

> These new beliefs and values of individual achievement and class mobility were rewarded and reinforced. Americans then began to identify themselves in terms of what they do. If you encounter an American at a party, he or she will often greet you with: "Hello, my name is Gary Weaver. I'm a professor at American University. What do you do?"
>
> People from many other cultures, however, identify themselves in terms of who they are. A West African might greet you by saying, "Hello. I'm Pap Seka, the son of Tamsier Seka from up river in Basse." The primary source of his identity is who he is — his father and his birthplace. His status is based upon family and heritage, not what he does as an individual or what he may do in the future.[2]

Moreover, what is true about America is even more true about California. Whereas America was the place to which people ran in order to escape the rest of the world, California was where people ran in order to escape the rest of America. Perhaps more than any other place on Earth, California is where the atoms were undocked from their moorings and left to float on their own.

People still run to California today. It is commonly regarded as the land of pioneers, nonconformists, artists, and rebels. It is the land of the free-spirit surfer and the iconoclastic biker. It is identified with both Ronald Reagan, who became a symbol for personal freedom and responsibility, and James Dean, who in movies like *Rebel Without a Cause* represented rebellion for the sake of rebellion. It is where Steve Jobs urged us to "think different." It is where iconoclastic sports like skateboarding were born. The Chinese proverb *"tian gao huangdi yuan"* is an apt description of the spirit of California: "Heaven is high, and the emperor is far away." In other words, authority may be powerful, but it is also distant, so you are responsible for your own fate.

---

2 Gary Weaver, "The American Cultural Tapestry", eJournal USA (June 1, 2006), 18-19, http://guangzhou. usembassy-china.org.cn/uploads/images/r4YPWf8G8Npaa6zJQxaKHQ/ijse0606.pdf.

The culture of America, and particularly that of California, is a product of freedom from tribes. But if the old tribal social fabric has been shredded, what new fabric takes its place? How do people interact when traditional social structures are absent? People still need to exchange with each other for mutual survival and benefit.

The Peruvian economist Hernando de Soto wrote about this question in his groundbreaking book *The Mystery of Capital.* De Soto argues that where the formal law is inadequate for serving the needs of society, people tend to develop informal laws to govern their economic behavior. Because the formal rules governing real estate transactions in many emerging countries are so complicated and costly, the vast majority of people in these places have simply developed their own "unwritten rules" to govern such transactions.

De Soto describes how the discovery of gold in 1848 along the American River in California caused a massive migration of people to search for gold. Within one year, there were 100,000 miners in the state. Two years later, there were almost 300,000.

> Faced with a legal vacuum in federal mining law, the miners, with some legal acumen, created a kind of acting mining law. Negotiating among themselves, they worked to protect their rights and increase the value of their property until the government could step in to validate their claims. Creating property rights through extralegal means was hardly a rarity. Extralegality was—as it is today in the Third World—rife...Most politicians came to support the miners' claims, and the courts proceeded to sanction their extralegal arrangements...This fusion of informal and existing legal models filled the vacuum of formal law on America's vast mineral lands.[3]

Today and throughout human history—whether in the Gold Rush, the Dutch guilds, the diamond business, or the cotton industry—we see a similar process. People tend to create informal rules when formal laws are insufficient to govern the practicalities of real-world interactions.[4] Similarly, entrepreneurial innovation, as it has developed in places like Silicon Valley, is built on its own set of unwritten laws. A successful Rainforest benefits from lower transaction costs because of unwritten behavioral norms that fill the gaps when traditional social structures don't exist.

---

3   Hernando de Soto, *The Mystery of Capital* (New York: Basic Books, 2000), 143-145.

4   See, e.g., Lisa Bernstein, "Opting Out of the Legal System: Extralegal Contractual Relations in the Diamond Industry," 21 *Journal of Legal Studies* 115 (1992); and Lisa Bernstein, "Private Commercial Law in the Cotton Industry: Creating Cooperation Through Rules, Norms, and Institutions," 99 *Mich. L. Rev.* 1724 (2001).

....

Rainforest Axiom #12: *Rainforests have replaced tribalism with a culture of informal rules that allow strangers to work together efficiently on temporary projects.*

....

It is no coincidence that the two industries most identified with California— Hollywood and Silicon Valley—are both industries that are by definition impermanent. They both require an environment that enables people to band together quickly for a specific purpose—whether a movie, a television show, or a startup company—and then disband until they reunite for the next project. Or perhaps they never meet again. A major Hollywood film, for example, can require thousands of people entering into a temporary partnership, as evidenced by the end credits of most movies, when a seemingly endless list of people scrolls in front of the audience.

Those people were assembled—like atoms organized out of the fast-moving chaos—to achieve a specific purpose. When that purpose is accomplished, the atoms are allowed to disperse back into the apparent chaos from which they came, enabling them to recombine later into something else. What Ade Mabogunje once observed—that "a company is an event"—is essentially the dominant underlying framework of the California economy. Creative reassembly—the ability to gather atoms together quickly and then let them recirculate again in the most efficient way possible—is what drives economic value in the Rainforest.

Changing Teams

Fortunately, there is no inherent reason that the Rainforest should happen only in California. The past does not necessarily determine the future. Neuroscience research is revealing that the way the human brain thinks of social groups is highly malleable, and is based on context.[5] We can create new tribes and social structures if we want.

Think of modern sporting matches. The typical American college football crowd is full of diverse students from across the spectrum of human society, but the diversity of that student body does not diminish the united enthusiasm of its cheering when the home team scores. Imagine a neighborhood pick-up basketball game, in which people who show up

---

5 Jay J. Van Bavel and William A. Cunningham, "Social Identity Modulates Automatic Face Perception: Group Membership Overrides the Effects of Race on Early Event-Related Potentials," Poster presented at the 2010 Social and Affective Neuroscience Conference, Chicago, IL, October 29-31, 2010, http://www.socialaffectiveneuro.org/docs/SANS_program_2010.pdf.

are randomly assigned to opposing teams—individuals are able to identify quickly with their own group members and fight hard for their side's victory.

Science shows how tribes can change. In one recent research experiment, scientists measured facial recognition bias—our brain's tendency to remember faces of our own race better than the faces of another race—and discovered that people easily overcame this bias when they were simply told that the faces they were seeing were members of their own group. As the scientists observed:

> The current study suggests that very early effects of race are *not* inevitable, but are sensitive to current motivational states and perceptual goals. While social categories clearly affect the earliest phases of social perception, the particular social categorization is sensitive to changes in the social context—top-down influences like social identity can influence automatic face perception in a dynamic fashion.[6]

Social scientists have long observed the effects of this neurological process in real-world situations. Perhaps one of the best known studies was conducted by Muzafer Sherif and his colleagues, who observed the effects of dividing boys into separate cabins during summer camp.[7] By splitting the boys into two groups, named the Rattlers and the Eagles, and introducing competitive games, the researchers were able to create intense rivalries between the teams, complete with name-calling, stealing of banners, threats, and even fights. However, when the researchers put the boys into a series of situations in which cooperation was required for mutual benefit, such as fixing a broken water system, they found that the boys soon learned to cooperate and even built significant friendships regardless of their team affiliations.

Common goals cause people to rise above tribe. The Rainforest functions best when old tribal definitions based on family and history are broken down, and new tribes based on personal interests and professional affiliations are allowed to take their place.[8]

---

6 Ibid.

7 Muzafer Sherif et al., "Intergroup Conflict and Cooperation: The Robbers Cave Experiment," Classics in the History of Psychology, http://psychclassics.yorku.ca/Sherif/chap4.htm.

8 Saxenian, *Regional Advantage,* 36 (see chap. 2, n. 24). Observes that: "continual shuffling and reshuffling tended to reinforce the value of personal relationships and networks…. Silicon Valley's engineers developed stronger commitments to one another and to the cause of advancing technology than to individual companies or industries."

Where Cooperation Comes From

With the old tribes gone, the Rainforest also creates the opportunity—and the need—for a new behavioral culture to fill the vacuum. How does new culture emerge?

Neoclassical economists have tended to disregard the concept of culture, believing that macro forces explain the world sufficiently, so they do not need to incorporate the micro behavior of human beings into their theories. Such a viewpoint looks at culture in the wrong way. True, culture may not have a noticeable effect on the allocation of resources at the macro-scale. It does, however, have a powerful impact on the seemingly spontaneous generation of economic value at the micro-scale, through the vast human web of invisible transactions that govern the exchange of ideas, insights, connections, information, and time.

How does culture affect the underlying mechanisms of the Rainforest? Culture is critical to the way economic systems function because it provides the rules of engagement between people that hopefully can maximize their collective well-being. The development of cultural norms of behavior comes from repeated interactions among individuals. The norms are maintained by the threat of punishment for defections. As Professors Singer and Steinbeis at the University of Zurich write:

> Human cooperation between nonkin has been an evolutionary puzzle, particularly when interactions are not repeated and the ability to form a reputation is limited (i.e., why help a stranger in a large city?). The use of game theory has been able to shed light on how such instances of cooperation may arise, and, by means of simulations and experimental tests, it has become apparent that *the use and threat of punishment* is a key variable in bringing this about.[9]

Scientists have been able to come to these conclusions by testing groups of people using two types of experimental games: Public Goods (in which all members contribute to a public good and can share its benefits), and Prisoner's Dilemma (in which two people can either cooperate or defect from one another).[10] The results of these experimental games have shown that Prisoner's Dilemma games inevitably lead to a lack of cooperation over time and therefore fail to provide sustainable mutual benefit.

---

9   Tania Singer and Nikolaus Steinbeis, "Differential Roles of Fairness- and Compassion-Based Motivations for Cooperation, Defection, and Punishment," *Annals of the New York Academy of Sciences* 1167 (2009): 43, (italics added), doi: 10.1111/j.1749-6632.2009.04733.x.

10 For additional information, see Wikipedia contributors, "Prisoner's dilemma" and "Public goods game," *Wikipedia, The Free Encyclopedia,* http://en.wikipedia.org/wiki/Prisoner's_dilemma and http://en.wikipedia.org/wiki/Public_goods_game (accessed August 2, 2011).

However, Prisoner's Dilemma games do succeed under one major condition: if there is a community that punishes violations. In those cases, a Prisoner's Dilemma game actually turns into a Public Goods game. In short, when the community has an interest in enforcing the rules of human interaction, and there is the threat of punishment for defectors, the norms that regulate interactions can become sustainable.

> Thus, it seems that to maintain stable cooperation in a society, the possibility for punishment has to be available constantly, which in turn means that the permanent threat of such punishment as a result of even accidental transgressions against social norms is highly prevalent. Polemically, one could argue that stable cooperation resulting from fairness norms comes at the cost of persistent anger over others' violation of fairness norms and the fear of being punished for one's own violations.[11]

For Rainforests to be sustainable, therefore, greed must be restrained. Innovators in a system eventually learn to tax themselves—that is, they give up some short-term gain—in order to participate in the system for the long-term.

As economist Adam Smith observed, a man who wants to achieve something "must flatten... his natural tone, in order to reduce it to harmony and concord with the emotions of those who are about him."[12] Self-restraint is essential for human systems to function. If you do not tax yourself, the system will punish you and possibly kick you out. If you tax yourself too much, you run the risk of not getting the full rewards of what you have contributed. What happens over time, therefore, is that a culture develops a set of "Goldilocks" standards of behavior that keep people at just the right distance from each other.

One way to demonstrate this in the Rainforest is to think about the way venture capitalists invest in startup companies. A venture capitalist is caught between trying to own as much of a company as possible and trying to leave enough equity in the hands of the entrepreneurial team to keep them fully incentivized to work for the company's success. Furthermore, a venture capitalist wants to preserve a reputation for treating entrepreneurs and other investors fairly in order to make sure that future promising companies will seek his capital. Any potential damage to a venture capitalist's reputation does not affect his fortunes immediately, but over time, the punishment can be severe, as the most promising companies avoid taking his capital, other investors no longer want to co-invest with him, and he eventually fails in the investment business.

---

11 Singer and Steinbeis, "Differential Roles," 43.

12 Adam Smith, *The Theory of Moral Sentiments* (orig. pub. 1759), Sec. 1, Ch. 4, Kindle edition.

Reputation, good or bad, matters greatly in the venture capital industry. The social feedback system in the Rainforest, with its inherent forms of punishment, is the equivalent of life or death for many of its inhabitants. The new social network sites that allow entrepreneurs to rate venture capital investors and post comments for the world to see—such as TheFunded.com—only reinforce these norms.[13]

The underlying social norms in any industry are not always obvious, even to people in the system. Clearly, not all venture capitalists treat all entrepreneurs fairly. However, the system reinforces the norms over time, so that most people who do not play by the rules are eventually pushed out. As Nick Binkley, a former venture capitalist and Vice Chairman of Bank of America, once said to us, "Predatory venture capitalists might win a few in the short run, but they do not last long in the business and are unable to build lasting firms."[14]

What venture capitalists do today is not different from what human beings have done for millennia. Human societies, through repeat interactions over time, have a tendency to find the right tension in those invisible rubber bands that connect people to one another. Anthropologists have looked at an extreme example of repeated human interaction spanning tens of thousands of years: the San tribes of the Kalahari Desert. Essentially "undiscovered" by the rest of the world until the 1950s, genetic analysis has proven that the San people are some of the oldest, most genetically unadulterated remnants of humankind's ancient ancestors.[15]

On the surface, the San people appear to have developed a socialist utopia—a highly altruistic society in which virtually everything is treated as a community good, and gift-giving is a constant. The underlying truth, however, is more complicated than it at first appears. As author and Harvard academic Steven Pinker has observed, the culture of sharing is not driven wholly by angelic altruism, but instead is "driven by cost-benefit analyses and a careful mental ledger for reciprocation. People share when it would be suicidal not to."[16]

Where one family might have an abundance of meat one month and another family an abundance of vegetables the next, it makes sense for the families to share the food resources together, lest they all die of malnutrition. The social

---

13 See http://www.thefunded.com.

14 Nick Binkley, personal conversation with author, January 27, 2011.

15 Spencer Wells, *The Journey of Man: A Genetic Odyssey* (Princeton: Princeton University Press, 2002), "These groups [including the San] are found today in Ethiopia, Sudan and parts of eastern and southern Africa, and the genetic signal they contain is very good evidence that they are the remnants of one of the oldest human populations. The signals have been lost in other groups, but today these eastern and southern African groups still show a direct link back to the coalescence point—Adam."

16 Steven Pinker, *How the Mind Works* (Norton: 1997), 505.

norms of sharing in the Kalahari evolved as a way to assure mutual survival. Violations of those social norms are severely punished, through gossip and the withholding of valuable resources. Human beings tend to develop behaviors that are an optimal balance of interests between individual and group.

We find the same set of behaviors in the Rainforest. Venture capitalists are constantly tempted to "defect" from social norms and grab more for themselves when the opportunity arises. When they succumb to that temptation, they can develop a reputation for being what are commonly known as "vulture capitalists." Over time, such damage to a venture capitalist's reputation can be far greater than the money he might lose by not maximizing his return on any particular deal. The most enduring venture firms tend to be those that have learned to "play by the rules".

....

Rainforest Axiom #13: *The informal rules that govern Rainforests cause people to restrain their short-term self-interest for long-term mutual gain.*

....

We use venture capital as only one example. Individuals throughout the Rainforest learn to restrain their own self-interest in the short run in order to benefit their self-interest in the long run. This applies to scientists making deals with businessmen, lawyers assisting entrepreneurs, companies partnering with other companies, and countless other interactions.

The Chicken or the Egg?

How does this process of cooperative behavior start in the first place? One of the biggest reasons that so few Rainforests exist is because they face a chicken-and-egg problem.

This problem was made clear to us in one of our Extreme Venture Capital projects, helping to establish an incubation program in an emerging market. We invested months of work building a program staff and selecting about twenty promising startup companies from the region. We spent a great deal of time working with these companies and identifying potential partnerships for them, both domestically and internationally. For an entire week, we held a torrent of meetings with them from early morning to late evening, providing valuable advice on these partnerships that could help grow their businesses. We were physically exhausted, but we also felt a great deal of pride and accomplishment.

On the last day of our trip there, our balloon was burst. Our project manager came to us just before we were about to depart and said, "So all these partnerships we have identified are great." He paused. "But how do we actually get these people to do it?"

The question hit us like a rock. But of course, it was valid. He was addressing a fundamental difference between the business culture of Silicon Valley and that in other parts of the world. The obvious value of partnering is one of the basic assumptions of the Valley. However, in most of the world, one of the biggest obstacles to overcome is the lack of a shared culture that values long-term, cooperative partnerships, and that "punishes" self-serving behavior that seeks only short-term gains.

People in many markets tend to treat transactions as zero-sum games. There is always a winner and a loser. The idea that one can engage in a transaction by voluntarily taxing oneself—by not trying to squeeze every last drop out of a deal—is simply outside the normal mental framework for conducting business. People find the idea of partnering in a positive-sum game with strangers where there can be two winners naïve. Trust can be scarce, and you do not want to be the fool that is left getting the short end of the deal.

In contrast, the culture of Rainforests tends to regard relationships as having the potential to be "win-win." Such a community recipe is like an updated version of the San tribes of the Kalahari. But instead of ingredients like meat and vegetables, we are dealing with the ingredients of innovation.

In the following chapter, we will address how to overcome the chicken-and-egg problem in emerging markets and how to build new Rainforests. Before we get there, however, we need to examine the nature of motivation. What motivates people to do what they do in Rainforests?

The Joy of Not Being Rational

If you think about it, there is nothing at all rational about riding a roller coaster. You pay money, often a lot, for the privilege of ending up in exactly the same place you started. You experience stomach-turning dizziness, and possibly a hoarse voice from screaming. Some get physically sick, and on rare occasions, people even die. Signs repeatedly warn you of the health risks before you even take your seat. Riding a roller coaster is actually a pretty irrational act. Yet, ride roller coasters we do.

The process of launching a startup company has many similarities to riding a roller coaster. It is a highly irrational act. You will invest blood, sweat, tears, and probably a lot of money for the privilege, and you will probably end up in exactly the same place you started, since the majority of such efforts fail. You will be sleep-deprived and stressed-out, and you will spend a great deal of time away from your loved ones.

If you wanted to avoid this agony, you could probably just find a regular job. You'd have paid vacations, more time with your loved ones, more sleep, and more opportunities to relax. Seen this way, launching a startup company is not all that rational. Yet, launch startup companies people do.

This leads us to another big mystery in our story so far. It is perhaps the most fundamental question: "Why bother at all?" Given all the things that one can do in life—spend time with family, sit on a beach, watch a good movie—why do people take on the huge challenge of starting a company in the first place?

Let us begin by examining a single person. An individual has a choice as to whether or not to start a company or engage in other innovative behavior. Some people choose to do so, but most do not. The conventional story about entrepreneurship is usually similar to the one attributed to the American author Horatio Alger, Jr.—that every honest and competent individual has the ability to attain financial success if they just persist through hard work, courage, and honesty.[17] It is a story that is consistent with the thinking of neoclassical economists, who believe that financial reward is proportionate to the amount of effort and risk that an individual is willing to invest. The idea—a distinctly American one—is that you can go from "rags to riches," and that it is solely up to you.

There must be a reason, however, why the Horatio Alger success story is rarely realized, even in places where the bureaucratic barriers are low, the rule of law is good, and the markets are open. If the Horatio Alger premise applied everywhere, the world would be brimming with such success stories. The reality is that the decision-making calculation of a real, live human is not so simple or clear-cut. It is far more than just a monetary calculation.

17 See Horatio Alger, Jr., *Ragged Dick, or, Street Life in New York with the Boot-Blacks* (New York: Modern Library, 2005). For more information, see http://www.thehoratioalgersociety.org/.

In the chart below, we weigh the pros and cons that a hypothetical individual might consider in a traditional, non-Rainforest calculation when deciding whether or not to do something innovative, like launch a startup:

Traditional Incentives of an Individual for Engaging in Innovative Behavior

Benefits	Costs
• Some possibility of making more money	• Sacrifice a stable income and career, perhaps forever • Risk social disapproval from family, friends, potential spouses • Difficulty and fear of working with strangers outside conventional circles of trust, culture, ethnicity, language • Difficulty and extra effort in communicating effectively • Huge investment of time, effort, stress • Possibility of losing everything (depending on laws regarding bankruptcy, partnerships, etc.)

When we examine the incentives and disincentives such an individual faces, it is clear that the personal risks of being innovative are not all that appealing. Winning at innovation requires a tremendous investment of effort compared to the reward, and a great deal of luck. It is likely that the effort invested will not pay off for most participants.

The basic calculation for the vast majority of the billions of people in the world is that innovative behavior is simply not worth it. Some people may talk about the appeal of innovation in a broad sense, but the actual moment-to-moment behavior of individuals is what counts. It is one thing to talk about innovation; it is another for someone to make the huge personal sacrifices actually required to be successful at it.

Innovative behavior is not driven by rational maximization, as neoclassical economists would argue. There are in fact other forces that motivate people in Rainforests to engage in innovative behavior: what we call *extra-rational motivations.* The research of neuroscience professors Chris Frith and Tania Singer has led to some rather counter-intuitive conclusions about human motivation:

> ... [there is] a need to revise the idea that emotion/intuition is the enemy of reason. It is not in dispute that these two systems may often be in conflict. Rather, the data suggest that decisions dictated by reason are not always good, while decisions dictated by emotion are not always bad.[18]

Extra-rational motivations—those that transcend the classical divide between rational and irrational—are not normally considered critical drivers of economic value-creation. These are the motivations that cause the New ROI—return on involvement— that we highlighted in Chapter 3. These motivations include the thrill of competition, human altruism, a thirst for adventure, a joy of discovery and creativity, a concern for future generations, and a desire for meaning in one's life, among many others. Our work over the years has led us to conclude that these types of motivations are not just "nice to have." They are, in fact, "must have" building blocks of the Rainforest.[19]

They are essential because money alone is not a sufficient motivator for the type of behavior that is necessary for causing innovation on a systemic scale. Writer Dan Pink has pointed out that, beyond a basic level of survival, human beings actually are less creative when they are incentivized by more financial reward.[20] Economic research is also generating increasing evidence that is counter-intuitive:

> As long as the task involved only mechanical skill, bonuses worked as they would be expected: the higher the pay, the better the performance. But once the task called for 'even rudimentary cognitive skill,' a larger reward 'led to poorer performance.'[21]

---

18 Chris D. Frith and Tania Singer, "The Role of Social Cognition in Decision Making," *Philosophical Transactions of the Royal Society* 363 (2008): 3875–3886, doi: 10.1098/rstb.2008.0156.

19 See Chester Barnard, *Organization and Management: Selected Papers* (Cambridge: Harvard University Press, 1948), 15: "...a long catalogue of non-economic motives actually condition the management of business, and nothing but the balance sheet keeps these non-economic motives from running wild. Yet without all these incentives, I think most business would be a lifeless failure."

20 Daniel Pink, *Drive* (see chap. 1, n. 13).

21 Ibid. Pink cites findings of D. Ariely, U. Gneezy, G. Lowenstein, & N. Mazar, *Federal Reserve Bank of Boston Working Paper No. 05-11; NY Times, 20 Nov. 08.*

Once someone has enough income to live, additional financial incentives can cause that person to turn off their creative brains in favor of repetitive actions that do not require creativity—like laboratory rats taught to push a lever to get more food.

What happens in a Rainforest, then, is that the fundamental risk-reward calculus must be altered. Individuals must employ a different accounting system. In the chart below, we present a different checklist of human incentives—one that reflects what we have observed in working Rainforests today:

Rainforest Incentives of an Individual for Engaging in Innovative Behavior

Benefits	Costs
• Perceived and possibly real opportunity of making more money (following role models that have validated the path already) • Joy of discovery, novelty, adventure, creativity, passion • Social approval (as a peer member of a community of innovators) • Joy of friendship, sharing, love, working on a team, building new trust, common values and goals • Fulfillment from the possibility of making a difference in society, leaving a legacy for future generations • Thrill of competition • Freedom and independence	• Little social punishment, often encouragement, from family and friends for taking a worthwhile risk • Some anxiety from meeting new people, but offset by the joy of making new friendships • Huge investment of time, effort, and stress, but viewed in a neutral or even positive light because pursuing a personal passion • Little risk of losing everything because new opportunities emerge in the process of experimentation • Much lower probability of failure because of support from a broad community of fellow innovators

For a Rainforest to thrive, extra-rational motivations must transform the decision-making calculus of individuals. These motivations are critical to tipping the balance of individual behavior in favor of innovation.

Corrected Vision

Governments and corporations often try to incentivize innovation by focusing on financial mechanisms, such as tax breaks, subsidies, grants, and loans. But the overall results of this strategy have been poor. No doubt, the financial incentives for innovation must be meaningful, lest people feel like fools for pursuing it. However, such incentives cannot be the only ends in themselves.

Extra-rational motivations are what give people joy and satisfaction during the journey. As a result, the journey becomes the end, not just the means. Recent science supports this idea, as fMRI imaging shows that human brains are wired to enjoy the pursuit of a vision more than the actual achievement of that vision.[22]

Although Gordon Gekko in the movie *Wall Street* said that "greed is good," greed unchecked is *not good* when it comes to innovation. Greed that is restrained so that a community of people can mutually pursue highly beneficial economic activity, however, can be powerful indeed.

If we diagram the actual cost-benefit analysis that a real person might make when considering a potentially innovative transaction, it might look something like this:

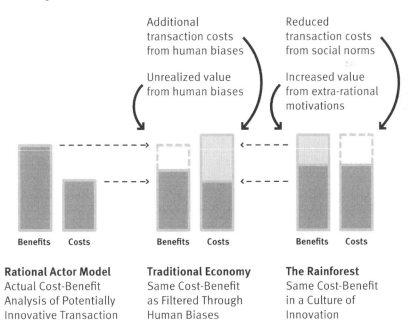

Additional transaction costs from human biases

Reduced transaction costs from social norms

Unrealized value from human biases

Increased value from extra-rational motivations

| Benefits | Costs | | Benefits | Costs | | Benefits | Costs |

Rational Actor Model
Actual Cost-Benefit
Analysis of Potentially
Innovative Transaction

Traditional Economy
Same Cost-Benefit
as Filtered Through
Human Biases

The Rainforest
Same Cost-Benefit
in a Culture of
Innovation

---

22 Sarah E. Henderson and Catherine J. Norris, "An fMRI Study of Anticipation: Is the Journey More Important than the Destination?" Poster presented at the 2010 Social and Affective Neuroscience Conference, Chicago, IL, October 29-31, 2010, http://www.socialaffectiveneuro.org/docs/SANS_program_2010.pdf.

On the left side of this diagram is a neoclassical economist's paradise, in which humans are like computers and all potentially valuable transactions that ought to happen actually do happen. In the middle is most of the real world, where the imperfect human brain unconsciously creates a perceived value of a transaction that is less favorable than the actual value of a transaction. On the right is the Rainforest.

As we move from left to right, we see how the actual cost-benefit valuation of a transaction (on the left) is warped through the imperfect filters of the human brain (in the middle), but then is balanced (on the right) with the additional value of extra-rational motivations and the reduced transaction costs derived from unwritten social rules.

The Rainforest depends on extra-rational motivations and social norms to push the cost-benefit analysis closer to, or even beyond, its original shape. The process is not dissimilar to wearing a pair of eyeglasses to correct faulty vision. It may be "natural" to see things poorly, but that does not mean we shouldn't correct our vision. In the Rainforest, *this form of "corrected vision" actually helps people see the full potential value of economic transactions, which they would otherwise have been blind to.*

....

Rainforest Axiom #14: *Rainforests function when the combined value of social norms and extra-rational motivations outweigh the human instincts to fear.*

....

Recent science is validating the power of this extra-rational reward system. Building trust-based teams that can transform the world in positive ways affects the brain in the same addictive way that a narcotic can. As Ade Mabogunje says, "Trust is like cocaine."[23] Human beings derive sustenance from social connections beyond the money they earn from these relationships. We derive pleasure from giving as well as receiving.[24] Neuroscience is proving that our brain's reward system is activated by a variety of incentives—including ones the "rational actor" economic model never envisioned.

> Many socially and emotionally positive situations activate the brain's reward system, including *fairness* in the ultimatum game; *cooperation* in prisoner's dilemma; *reciprocation and intention to trust* in the trust game; and *altruistic punishment* of players who were uncooperative in the trust or prisoner's

---

23 Mabogunje, interview.

24 Tristen K. Inagaki, and Naomi I. Eisenberger, "Neural Underpinnings of the Provision of Social Support," Poster presented at the 2010 Social and Affective Neuroscience Conference, Chicago, IL, October 29-31, 2010, http://www.socialaffectiveneuro.org/docs/SANS_program_2010.pdf.

> dilemma game. *Donations to charities* activate the striatum, despite one's own money loss.[25]

Additionally, scientists have observed that the process of discovering new and interesting things with others can strengthen relationships, through activating the reward-based dopamine and norpepinephrine systems. Arthur Aron, a professor of social psychology at the State University of New York at Stony Brook, has observed this phenomenon in married couples and found evidence that marriages become stronger when couples engage in novel activities together.[26]

We are finding scientific validation for many "soft" human aspirations: the desire to treat people fairly and to be treated fairly, the pleasure of being a member of a community and pursuing a shared goal, the thrill of adventure and discovery, the joy of giving to someone in need, and the addictive quality of trusting and being trusted. These drivers are in many ways the things that make our lives worth living. We are wired to feel that way.

Cold-Blooded Love

When we emphasize the importance of extra-rational motivations, it is not as naïve idealists. It is actually a cold-blooded observation to say that these motivations are necessary to incentivize a system of individuals to engage in Rainforest behavior.

Whether we are conscious of these motivations or not is a separate issue. Our brains have been hardwired to derive pleasure from altruism and love, but they are in fact selfish behaviors. Yes, we enjoy helping people in need. Yes, we take joy in offering a hand to a friend or a family member. But, as Steven Pinker observes:

> People love their children not because they want to spread their genes (consciously or unconsciously) but because they can't help it...Genes "try" to spread themselves by wiring animals' brains so that the animals love their kind and try to keep them warm, fed, and safe.[27]

Love shapes our actions because we are unconsciously driven to want the dopamine reward that comes from loving another person, even if it prevents us from earning an extra dollar in the short run.

---

25 Schultz, "Reward, Decision-Making," 55-56 (italics added).

26 Arthur Aron et al."Couples' Shared Participation in Novel and Arousing Activities and Experienced Relationship Quality," *Journal of Personality and Social Psychology* 78 (2000): 273-284, doi: 10.1037//0022-3514.78.2.273; Tara Parker-Pope, "Reinventing Date Night for Long-Married Couples," *The New York Times*, February 12, 2008, http://www.nytimes.com/2008/02/12/health/12well.html.

27 Pinker, *How the Mind Works*, 400-401.

This phenomenon extends beyond our family members, to our larger social communities. Altruism is a beneficial quality that can help groups thrive and defeat competitors. E.O. Wilson argues that altruism is a genetic trait that can be manifested in a group whether or not individuals are genetically related to one another.[28] He states, "Within groups, the selfish are more likely to succeed. ... But in competition between groups, groups of altruists are more likely to succeed."[29] The ability to create alliances is an evolutionary human trait that allows certain groups to win. As a result, human beings have evolved the instinct to sacrifice ourselves for the benefit of groups to which we belong, what biologists call *eusociality:*

> The genes that favor this type of group cohesion would also favor an innate sense of morality and group loyalty. It would explain how so often group or tribe loyalty overrides even family loyalty. It would help to explain why, for example, it is the squad or the platoon that men fight and die for, more even than country or religion.[30]

We are programmed to take pleasure in serving the greater good of our tribe, whether that tribe happens to be a local sports team, a startup, or the human race.

A scientist or an entrepreneur aspiring to bring a cure for cancer to the market—with all the obstacles that such an endeavor involves—is almost certainly not driven by pure financial gain. As veteran Silicon Valley venture capitalist Kevin Fong says, "At a certain point, it's not about the money anymore. Every engineer wants their product to make a difference. You want your work to be recognized for what it does for people."[31] We are all beneficiaries of the "love" that has motivated countless scientists, engineers, and entrepreneurs over the years.

There are different degrees of love, of course. These varying degrees of love manifest themselves in the elasticity of the invisible rubber band that connects two people. One's children, for example, can usually get away with a lot more than one's friends, as every weary parent knows. As Steven Pinker notes, "People feel a spontaneous pleasure in helping a friend or a spouse,

---

28 Martin A. Nowak, Corina E. Tarnita and Edward O. Wilson, "The Evolution of Eusociality," *Nature* 466 (2010): 1057, doi:10.1038/nature09205.

29 Howard W. French, "E.O. Wilson's Theory of Everything," *The Atlantic* (November 2011).

30 Richard Conniff, "Discover Interview: E.O. Wilson," *Discover* (June 2006, published online June 25, 2006).

31 Kevin Fong, personal interview with author, August 17, 2011. See also Saxenian, *Regional Advantage*, 113. Saxenian quotes venture capitalist Don Valentine: "[T]hat's why ventures are started: from lack of responsiveness in big companies... The only reason good people leave is because they become frustrated. They want to do something they can't in their present environment." Quoted in David Sheff, "Don Valentine, Part Two", *Upside*, June 1990, 52.

without anticipating repayment or regretting the favor if repayment never comes...[T]he line of credit is long and the terms of repayment forgiving."[32]

It is not as if the wellsprings of such relationships are infinite, of course. The invisible rubber band can indeed snap if a friend or a family member keeps asking for favors without ever returning anything of value. However, the nature of love is such that the ledger is not precise. When two people have to calculate the exact value of every single transaction between them, it is not only impossible to make those calculations accurately, but the act of negotiating every transaction is so costly that the relationship can be destroyed in the process. The Rainforest can only thrive if people are motivated by reasons that elevate them above the *quid pro quo* exchanges that one might find in a retail transaction between strangers at Wal-Mart.

We can see the power of extra-rational motivations throughout the world of innovation. Entrepreneurship is frequently called an addictive disease, with only a little bit of humor.[33] Most entrepreneurs would agree that entrepreneurs generally stop being fully rational when pursuing their dreams. As Susan Gauch once remarked sarcastically, "The great thing about being an entrepreneur is the flexibility of choosing which ninety hours a week you want to work."[34] This work of art by Hugh MacLeod[35] seems to state it succinctly:

---

32 Pinker, *How the Mind Works*, 507.

33 See for example Jeff Stibel, "Entrepreneurship as Disease," HBR Blog Network, *Harvard Business Review*, September 14, 2010, http://blogs.hbr.org/cs/2010/09/entrepreneurship_as_disease.html.

34 Susan Gauch, telephone conversation with author, circa 2006.

35 Hugh MacLeod, "I'm not delusional. I'm an entrepreneur" (2010). Reprinted courtesy of gapingvoid ltd.

One example of the impact of extra-rational motivations is evident when governments, corporations, or foundations issue prizes or challenge grants to achieve technical milestones. Teams that compete for those prizes frequently spend more than the amount of the prize itself. Shaifali Puri, the Executive Director of Scientists Without Borders, recently held a challenge in which the participants invested a total of *sixteen times* the value of the actual prize money.[36] Her organization regularly employs such challenge prizes to drive innovation.

In the same spirit, the Google Lunar X PRIZE advises contestants to prepare for a highly intense and expensive battle:

> Teams in competitions such as the Orteig Prize, the Ansari X PRIZE, and the DARPA Grand Challenges have spent as much as 5 times the prize purse value to fund their entries; and expenditures of 2.5 times the prize purse value by individual teams are relatively common. We expect that teams pursuing the Google Lunar X PRIZE will follow these historical trends.[37]

Viewed in this light, acts that are not rational—such as spending more money to win a prize than the amount of the prize itself—can lead to remarkably innovative outcomes.

Challenge grants turn the forces of human nature in the service of innovation, not against it. People are able to enjoy the process of creating new "tribes" of teammates, the thrill of competing against other tribes, the possible pride of winning, the feeling of satisfaction in accomplishing something that has great value to many people, and the sheer value of adventure and novelty for their own sake. These motivations are not just features of this type of contest; they are its essence. They make these contests what they are.

The Rainforest is in many ways a massively expanded version of a challenge grant. There is an implied understanding that its inhabitants are part of a voluntary, extended community participating in a great, never-ending human contest for building better things, changing lives, making friendships, contributing to something bigger than themselves, discovering the unexpected, experiencing both the thrill of victory and the agony of defeat, and perhaps even making a lot of money. If you actually ask most people in the startup communities in Silicon Valley or similar places why they do what they do, you almost always find extra-rational motivations driving their behavior.

---

36 Shaifali Puri, personal conversation with author, December 2010.

37 "Google Lunar Prize FAQ," Google, 2011, accessed August 30, 2010,
    http://www.googlelunarxprize.org/prize-details/faq.

Pied Pipers

Entrepreneurship in the Rainforest leverages the natural aspects of human motivation. This is in contrast to conventional wisdom, which says that entrepreneurship is primarily about one person's determination and courage, à la Horatio Alger. Although these are essential traits, they are not entirely sufficient. There are lots of people in business with determination and courage. Few of them are successful entrepreneurs.

An entrepreneur leads people into acts that are not always economically calculable. As Ade Mabogunje says, "To lead, you have to move people. An entrepreneur is the storyteller who helps people take that leap of faith."[38] This is a dramatically different view from the traditional concept of a businessperson as a manager (an allocator of finite resources) or as an exploiter (one who takes advantage of others). Richard Branson, the founder of the Virgin Group, once wrote:

> For me, building a business is all about doing something to be proud of, bringing talented people together and creating something that's going to make a real difference to other people's lives. A businesswoman or a businessman is not unlike an artist. What you have when you start a company is a blank canvas; you have to fill it. Just as a good artist has to get every single detail right on that canvas, a businessman or businesswoman has to get every single little thing right when first setting up in business in order to succeed. However, unlike a work of art, the business is never finished. It constantly evolves.[39]

Ade provides another unusual simile: "An entrepreneur is like a pied piper. We actually enjoy their music. Through the means of a story, he or she creates a social movement."[40]

38 Mabogunje, interview.

39 Richard Branson, "Richard Branson: Five Secrets to Business Success," *Bnet.com*, September 10, 2010, http://www.bnet.com/blog/smb/richard-branson-five-secrets-to-business-success/2155.

40 Mabogunje, interview.

What makes an entrepreneur an entrepreneur is the ability to organize otherwise independent atoms, to lead people to collaborate on products or services that, in the beginning, are nothing more than mere ideas. When there are only ideas, he or she must convince people to join the effort by describing a desirable future, a story about what might be. An entrepreneur envisions how to make a new business—like a new work of art—appear from fragmented components. There is joy in the alchemy that happens when organizing these pieces.

This conception of entrepreneurship also runs counter to a recurring myth: that of the lone hero fighting against the rest of the world. That myth is hard to dispel. When we imagine an entrepreneur at work, we often have an iconic image of an individual working late at night in their basement or pounding on a hundred doors to get a first sale, which of course is often true. Successful entrepreneurship, however, is critically dependent on human interactions.

Entrepreneurship is not a monologue. Paul Graham, the founder of the Y Combinator incubator, advises entrepreneurs to "get a co-founder" as one of their first critical steps.[41] There is simply too much for one person to do. As we will show in Chapter 5, science is validating the notion that two heads are better than one, and that many heads can be even better than two. Behind every successful story of entrepreneurship, if one digs below the surface, are the contributions of countless people who provided critical help, who were driven by more than base economic self-interest, and without whom success would never have been achieved.

Perhaps there is no simpler story demonstrating the power of extra-rational motivation than the one provided by our late friend Clint Kopp, a veteran inventor and entrepreneur. At one time, he tried to convince a long-time friend of his to join a new startup company with him. He provided his friend with hard facts about the breakthrough technologies involved, the vast size of the markets to be captured, and the possibility of building great commercial value—all the usual reasons that economists claim motivate

---

41 Paul Graham, "Why to Not Not Start a Startup," (blog), March, 2007, http://www.paulgraham.com/ notnot.html. "If you don't have a cofounder, what should you do? Get one. It's more important than anything else. If there's no one where you live who wants to start a startup with you, move where there are people who do. If no one wants to work with you on your current idea, switch to an idea people want to work on."

people. None of it worked. In the end, Clint was able to get his friend on board by urging him in a simple way. He put his hand on his friend's shoulder, and said, "Come on, my friend. This will be fun."[42]

It is indeed possible for people to be shoulder-to-shoulder and not to be miles apart. In fact, the Rainforest depends on such connections.

The Tapestry of Life in the Rainforest

Let us weave together these disparate ideas into a bigger tapestry. The implications from the atomic view of innovation—how two individuals combine into a pair—are profound. Societies and companies can attempt to build top-down institutions that might have the outward forms of innovation, but unless the individuals in that structure have learned how to create effective relationships, the structure is almost certain to crumble. The macro system cannot sustain itself unless the micro latticework at its foundation is stable.

You can perhaps see why so many promising innovation projects fail. A government that builds an expensive technology park, as many have done, is just constructing a hollow shell if the individuals who populate it do not have the personal characteristics that facilitate collaboration. A large corporation that creates a venture division to invest in exciting new technologies is just shuffling names on an organizational chart unless its employees have a shared culture that encourages people to pursue goals for reasons that go beyond their paychecks. Such hollow initiatives are like building expensive computer hardware without the software to run it—like an iPhone without its operating system. Human software matters in Rainforests because successful innovation derives from the ability of two people to join together.

---

42 Clint Kopp, personal conversation with multiple parties, circa 2008.

The Rainforest Axioms show how different disciplines of study—biology, neuroscience, psychology, sociology, economics, law, and others—are necessary to explain the mechanisms of innovation ecosystems:

Axiom #1: *While plants are harvested most efficiently on farms, weeds sprout best in Rainforests.*

Axiom #2: *Rainforests are built from the bottom up, where irrational behavior reigns.*

Axiom #3: *What we typically think of as free markets are actually not that free.*

Axiom #4: *Social barriers—caused by geography, networks, culture, language, and distrust—create transaction costs that stifle valuable relationships before they can be born.*

Axiom #5: *The vibrancy of a Rainforest correlates to the number of people in a network and their ability to connect with one another.*

Axiom #6: *High social barriers outside of close circles of family and friends are the norm in the world.*

Axiom #7: *Rainforests depend on people who actively bridge social distances and connect disparate parties together.*

Axiom #8: *People in Rainforests are motivated for reasons that defy traditional economic notions of "rational" behavior.*

Axiom #9: *Innovation and human emotion are intertwined.*

Axiom #10: *The greater the diversity in human specialization, the greater the potential value of exchanges in a system.*

Axiom #11: *The instincts that once helped our ancestors survive are hurting our ability to maximize innovation today.*

Axiom #12: *Rainforests have replaced tribalism with a culture of informal rules that allow strangers to work together efficiently on temporary projects.*

Axiom #13: *The informal rules that govern Rainforests cause people to restrain their short-term self-interest for long-term mutual gain.*

Axiom #14: *Rainforests function when the combined value of social norms and extra-rational motivations outweigh the human instincts to fear.*

Real-world social interactions that generate high economic value often create *social friction,* and that friction creates heat. That heat is a powerful trigger that alters the laws of economics at the micro level. If we wish to encourage more successful interactions among diverse individuals in building a Rainforest, there must be low-cost ways to reduce the heat generated—to cause the *dissipation of social friction.*

When we consider the seismic effects of modern innovation—routine transactions that now occur between people on opposite ends of the Earth, multi-billion dollar companies seemingly born overnight, or online tools that topple iron-fisted authoritarian governments in mere days—it is perhaps surprising that such powerful effects could be founded upon motivations that sound as simple as love and altruism. Neoclassical economists assume human beings are somewhat one-dimensional, and that we all define our happiness by the same basic, rigid material values of food, security, or wealth. The quote, however, from *The Matrix* at the beginning of this chapter underscores a critical point: human beings are not motivated by the mundane. Boredom is, in fact, a powerful behavioral driver in the opposite direction. Innovation only thrives when people desire to ride the roller coaster of life.

The real-life story of Company X at the beginning of this chapter—the argument between a startup CEO and an inventor—is a useful case in point. Eventually, the two gentlemen were able to forge a productive relationship based primarily on their common desire to build something big, transform their industry, and maybe even transform the world. They were excited by the prospect of making money, but neither was in it just to make a salary. If that were the case, the company would have easily splintered, because each person had many ways to earn a living. Based on their shared vision, they developed a mutual respect for each other that elevated their relationship above day-to-day concerns, and kept the company moving forward.

Now, we confront another layer of mystery: what is the code of behavior in Rainforests that enables such activity? Rainforests can only thrive if such a code is adopted throughout a broader community, not just among a few individuals. We turn to the invisible, unwritten rules that enable people to combine and recombine efficiently in innovation ecosystems—what we call the Rules of the Rainforest.

Chapter Five: The Rules of the Rainforest

The Missing Third Tablet

Cats like me and you
Have got laws
That they adhere to,
Laws outside the laws
As laid down
By those we don't subscribe to.

—Chrissie Hynde and the Pretenders, "Revolution" [1]

---

1 Lyrics reprinted courtesy of Hal Leonard Corporation.

Zero-Sum Boundaries

It can be surprisingly easy to cross the Qalandia checkpoint going into the Palestinian West Bank. We have experienced this fact firsthand in our work there, where we have helped mentor entrepreneurs and design a startup venture fund. The border guard might give you a wave of the hand, a hint of a nod, or a simple tilt of their semiautomatic weapon. They acknowledge you, but they do not stop you. After all the terrible things you have heard about the decades-old conflict between Israelis and Palestinians—and when you think of all the blood and treasure that the world has lost in the Middle East in the name of this feud—it can be surprising. They just let you in.

Of course, if you think about it, there isn't a big reason to stop people going there. After all, most people are struggling to go in the opposite direction. It is a simple enough process to walk or drive into the Palestinian Territories.

When you cross from Jerusalem to Ramallah, you see some differences. The first thing you notice is that things look a little rundown. You expect this to be the case. Palestinians have limited access to trade with the rest of the world, so economic activity is literally constrained by barriers. You also notice the construction. There is noisy building activity all around due to the influx of foreign aid over the years.

But what is the same on both sides of the border is something intangible— the trading culture. You cannot help but notice it. You see it in your daily interactions throughout the region. Taxi drivers haggle with you over miniscule amounts. A shopkeeper in the Mehane Yehuda market might push you until you agree to buy a larger bag of dried fruits. Every transaction has a winner and a loser. One person has overpaid, and another has underpaid. Daily life is a series of zero-sum games outside of close family and friends.

Speaking at the biggest annual technology conference in the West Bank, in front of an audience of hundreds of entrepreneurs, investors, and global development officials, we pointed this out. We stated words to the effect of: "A zero-sum game mentality is a major obstacle to an innovation economy. When people do not approach relationships with the possibility of creating positive-sum games, then the system as a whole will reflect a zero-sum output."[2] Years later, numerous Palestinians still tell us that we described their situation precisely.

This zero-sum mindset goes beyond contemporary politics in the Middle East. It is deep in the history and culture of the region. This small area of land, located at the geographical crossroads of three continents, was one of

2 Victor W. Hwang, speech at Expotech conference (paraphrased from memory), November 2009.

the first places that humans settled outside of Africa. According to National Geographic's project to trace genetic evidence from the M89 Y-chromosome marker, this migration happened about 50,000 years ago.[3] Today, about 90% of the world's population carries that marker, which means that almost all of us are descended from people in the Middle East. The entire world has genetic tribal stakes in that region. Living on limited real estate, people have been constantly bumping into each other, hustling, bustling, haggling, and trading for millenia.

Win-win behavior only becomes part of a culture if it actually pays off. In much of the Middle East, and in most of the world, win-win has not paid off historically. As a result, people treat day-to-day interactions as win-lose propositions. If I pay you one more penny for this bag of nuts, then that is one penny you have stolen from me. If I build on this piece of land, then you cannot. To think otherwise would be foolish.

Zero-sum games are innovation killers. The zero-sum attitude explains much of the difficulty in growing new companies throughout most of the world. Innovation is, after all, a team sport. When we compare traditional zero-sum culture to the positive-sum culture of Rainforests, we see a stark contrast.

What is fascinating is how—in the middle of what is quite possibly the most intense zero-sum environment in the world—Israel has been able to succeed at growing so many technology startup companies. The answer to that mystery is telling, and we shall explore it in this chapter.

Successful innovation requires self-sacrifice. It is a form of self-taxation to give up something of value in the short-term for a larger benefit in the long-term. It is also a risky exercise, so it is not easy to do. Trusting the wrong person today could mean injury tomorrow. In our work over the years, we have discovered different rules of behavior among people who live in thriving innovation systems compared to those who do not. The rules of behavior that favor innovation include basic human concepts like trust, fair dealing, and willingness to dream.

What are the social rules that support innovation, how do they work, and where did they come from? To answer these questions, we begin with a journey that starts at the dawn of human civilization and takes us all the way to the Silicon Valley of the present. On that journey, we will meet Moses, a bunch of cowboys, and the denizens of a café in Northern Italy.

---

3   "The Genographic Project," NationalGeographic.com, accessed August 30, 2011, http://www. nationalgeographic.com/xpeditions/lessons/09/g912/haplogroupO.pdf. Other sources argue that the origins of the M89 marker were somewhere in the region stretching from the Middle East to South Asia.

The Missing Commandments

EXTERIOR MOUNTAIN TOP—DAYTIME

Lightning strikes, thunder booms. The prophet Moses, with long white beard and flowing robe, appears holding three stone tablets engraved with ancient characters.

MOSES
(proclaiming confidently)

>Hear ye, hear ye!
>The Lord has given unto you
>these Fifteen...

Moses drops one of the three tablets, which smashes into innumerable little stone pieces.

>*(with only a slight pause)*

>... Ten! Ten Commandments,
>for his people to obey.

This classic scene from the comedy movie *History of the World, Part I* is funny in part because it suggests that there is a whole tablet of missing commandments, and that no one seemed to notice their absence all these millennia. The history of innovation is similar in this way to the world that director Mel Brooks envisioned, but arguably, it has lacked the same comedy.

We can also think about innovation in terms of tablets of commandments. The "commandments" the world has been given for creating economic value have proven to be incomplete. The world was provided two of the tablets, and we were told by the experts that those were the only two tablets we would ever need. The absence of the mysterious third tablet— the commandments of innovation—has caused enormous frustration for executives and policymakers who have tried to foster innovation.

True, the first two tablets of commandments have proven extraordinarily useful. The first tablet instructs us to invest in the building blocks of economic production, such as human capacity and infrastructure. This tablet includes "thou shalt" commandments like:

....

Thou shalt educate people

....

Thou shalt build necessary public goods (roads, bridges, police, courts, military, etc.)

....

Thou shalt invest in science to generate more knowledge and discoveries

....

The second tablet, on the other hand, has commandments that instruct us to reduce the artificial barriers between people, freeing them to do as they desire. This tablet includes "thou shalt not" commandments that let people move about and transact as they wish:

....

Thou shalt not create burdensome regulations

....

Thou shalt not allow corruption

....

Thou shalt not unduly interfere in freedom of contract

....

Thou shalt not let inflation grow out of control

....

Most economists generally agree with these two tablets: one to enhance the basic factors of economic production, the other to allow the invisible hand of the free market to do its thing. Together, they make up the Washington Consensus, the idea that free markets combined with basic investments in things like education and infrastructure are all that are needed to unleash economic growth. We can see the powerful effects of these two tablets in the growth of newly liberalized economies—in Eastern Europe, China, India, most of Latin America, and many other places. There is an explosion of activity that happens when the shackles are removed from people and they can transact as they wish.

The commandments in the first two tablets work, but only to a point. We know something big has been missing from these commandments because the marginal economic benefits they provide seem to diminish over time. Countries and corporations invest in people and infrastructure, they give them freedom, but then what? The results often fall short of expectations. We see this in corporations that fail to deliver on exciting, heralded new initiatives. We see this in economies that try to stimulate innovation through startup incubators, technoparks, public venture funds, entrepreneurial education, business assistance, scientific research, and numerous other methods without much success.

Just as in the Mel Brooks movie, what is contained in the third tablet has been a big mystery. The missing instructions in the third tablet are what we call the Rules of the Rainforest. These Rules consist of a set of unwritten norms of behavior that promote rapid collaboration and experimentation in a network of people.

Written Laws vs. Unwritten Rules

If you were a modern-day "Moses" and could help God build a society from scratch, how would you do it? You might first create a basic set of formal written laws to govern who owns what and what happens when people hurt each other or buy things from one another. If someone accidentally injures someone else, you could make them pay for the hospitalization. If one person defrauds another, you could make them pay the money back or put them in prison.

But those laws could not possibly fit every circumstance. They would not solve every case in which people are hurt or defrauded. You would therefore also let people make their own contracts with each other, so they could devise rules to govern the customized details of their distinct transactions. Let them take responsibility for their own law-making, so to speak.

However, even this does not work perfectly; people still get hurt and cheated. In Jerusalem, many a taxi driver has no problem squeezing an extra shekel from passengers. Yet in Japan, taxi drivers rarely behave that way. Why the difference? The answer lies in the unwritten rules—the cultural norms that govern the majority of our behavior. The norms fill in the gaps that the written laws and written contracts don't cover.

There are two ways for people to agree to do something together. One way is through a legal contract. Such a contract can be dreadfully detailed, spelling out every possible contingency in case something goes wrong. Think of the vast legal documentation—often thousands of pages—necessary for a billion dollar company to acquire another billion dollar company.

The other way is for parties to share a mutual set of unwritten rules that provides guidance for the countless little details that a formal contract cannot possibly cover. The commercial law in the U.S. even acknowledges this fact, as it expressly leans on "customary commercial terms" to help fill in the gaps of contracts between parties.[4] In daily routine, these "customary" terms take on even greater importance. A taxi driver in Japan simply "knows" that one does not cheat passengers, even though no one signs a physical contract when they enter the back of a cab. A mother in America who asks another mother to drive her child to school does not need to draft a full contract to govern that transaction—there is an implicit understanding that the favor is meant to be returned at some point, that the accepting mother will take care of that child as if it were her own, and that honoring and maintaining these types of exchanges is good for the community as a whole because everyone benefits over time from such a system.

Written contracts and informal norms are two sides of the same coin.[5] Contracts are time-consuming and costly to negotiate. Norms cost little, and provide a way to bypass a lengthy contracting process, like a form of social shorthand. As legendary Silicon Valley attorney John Goodrich once remarked to a surprised associate, "Good businessmen don't need to hire lawyers!"[6] He was making the point that people who can do business on a handshake—based on unwritten norms—would not need to engage extensive legal services to protect themselves against each other.

---

4   Richard A. Epstein, "Confusion About Custom: Disentangling Informal Customs from Standard Contractual Provisions," 66 *University of Chicago Law Review* 3, 821-835 (Summer 1999), 821-823.

5   Cass R. Sunstein, "Social Norms and Social Rules," (John M. Olin Law & Economics Working Paper No. 36, 2D Series, The Law School, The University of Chicago, Chicago, 1995), 4, http://www.law.uchicago.edu/files/files/36.Sunstein.Social_0.pdf. Cass states in his essay, "I urge that behavior is pervasively a function of norms; that human norms interact with human goods in surprising ways; that changes in norms might be the best way to improve social well-being; and that government deserves to have, and in any case inevitably does have, a large role in "norm management." Far too little attention has been played to the place of norms in human behavior and to the control of norms as an instrument of legal policy."

6   Anonymous source, said casually to an associate at Wilson Sonsini Goodrich & Rosati, circa 2000.

However, norms require trust, and creating a sufficient level of trust for norms to develop and remain in place is not easy. Norms usually come from shared values or lengthy relationships, not from top-down, authoritarian mandates. Humans create norms from the bottom up to streamline economic activity by reducing its transaction costs. It is self-interested behavior over the long term. Social scientists have found significant evidence that communities, over time, naturally develop norms through repeated interactions of people in a social network. As Francis Fukuyama notes:

> Market interactions in a commercial society lead, as Adam Smith observed, to the development of bourgeois social virtues like honesty, industriousness, and prudence. A society composed entirely of Kant's 'rational devils' will develop social capital over time, simply as a matter of the devils' long-term self-interest.[7]

The same thing happens in the Rainforest. People in places like Silicon Valley have developed an unwritten set of behavioral norms that lowers the cost of repeated transactions among them. They usually are not even conscious of it. These norms can feel like second nature to insiders, but they aren't so obvious to outsiders. The norms have the aggregate effect of bridging differences, communicating transparently, building trust, and creating new opportunities for collaborative experimentation where none would have existed otherwise.

The Rainforest requires these norms to thrive. Entrepreneurial innovation can only flourish when it moves away from the expensive tool of the legal contract and towards the inexpensive means of the social norm. Innovation is hard enough, risky enough, and expensive enough without having to negotiate a million little contract terms to do it.

---

7   Francis Fukuyama, "Social Capital, Civil Society and Development," *Third World Quarterly* 22 (2001): 16, http://intranet.catie.ac.cr/intranet/posgrado/Met%20Cual%20Inv%20accion/Semana%206/ Fukuyama. Notes that social capital is spontaneously generated all the time through the playing of iterated prisoners-dilemma games. Cites Robert Ellickson and Elinor Ostrom who have catalogued many empirical cases of cooperative norms arising as a result of repeated community interaction. These are particularly interesting because these communities involve many people and should theoretically be much harder to solve through iteration than a two-player game.

The Three Derivatives

In Israel, one sees a curious dichotomy. In this land of intense zero-sum games, the technology startup industry behaves differently. It is a community within a community, with its own internal rules of behavior and its own sense of trust. In an ocean of zero-sum games, it is a cultural island that thrives on positive-sum transactions.

In the book *Start-Up Nation*, authors Dan Senor and Saul Singer describe this normative culture: deep trust forged within startup teams due to their shared experience of service in the Israeli military; teams with a diversity of talents due to the military's mixing of people from all walks of life; and the unifying social connections of a tight community and global diaspora:

> In Israel, the seemingly contradictory attributes of being both driven and "flat," both ambitious and collectivist, make sense when you throw in the experience that so many Israelis go through in the military. There they learn that you must complete your mission, but that the only way to do that is as a team. The battle cry is "After me": there is no leadership without personal example and without inspiring your team to charge together and with you. There is no leaving anyone behind...And when you complete your military service, everything you need to launch a start-up will be a phone call away, if you have the right idea. Everyone knows someone in his or her family, university, or army orbit who is an entrepreneur or understands how to help. Everyone is reachable by cell phone or e-mail...As [entrepreneur] Yossi Vardi told us, "Everybody knows everybody."[8]

The evidence points to the notion that trust, social norms, and connectivity are critical to innovation. This observation is true not just in Israel—it is in the DNA of Rainforests everywhere.

Now, in your role as a modern-day "Moses" helping to design a new society, you would face a vexing problem. History shows that these norms develop naturally, not intentionally. *So how does one intentionally create an organic system?* In our daily human experience, direct action causes results. An engineer can "do" this or that series of tests and, over time, stands a good chance of ending up with a better product. A venture capitalist might advise his team to follow this or that path, and then watch as the company shifts direction. However, direct actions do not create sustainable innovation: building Rainforests requires systemic change. The table below attempts to outline why systemic change requires an entirely different approach:

---

8   Dan Senor and Saul Singer, *Start-Up Nation: The Story of Israel's Economic Miracle* (New York: Twelve, 2009), 231-232.

The Three Derivatives of Innovation

	What	Method	Effort	Examples	Parallels
Basic Equation	Innovator	Creates direct value	"Massive"	Inventor, entrepreneur	Hand-crafted artworks **(home gardens)**
First Derivative (advisors of innovators)	Mentoring innovators **(one-to-one)**	Advise innovators in value creation	"Heavy lifting"	Coaches, advisors, consultants, investors, board directors, university technology transfer, lawyers, accountants	Manufacturing assembly line **(agricultural plantation)**
Second Derivative (groups of advisors and innovators)	Creating networks of mentors **(many-to-one)**	Organize networks to support innovators in value creation	"Light lifting"	Larta Institute, CONNECT, Endeavor, incubators	Supply chain management **(nature preserve)**
Third Derivative (systems of groups, advisors, and innovators)	Causing entire communities to collaborate for mutual gain **(many-to-many)**	Cause Rainforest culture and normative behavior to emerge in a broad network	Self-sustaining	**?**	eBay, stock exchanges, Hollywood **(tropical rainforest)**

The First Derivative is based on helping one innovator at a time in a linear process. Like a manufacturing assembly line, it is based on one-to-one relationships that do not scale easily.

The Second Derivative is based on organizing groups of people to help one innovator at a time. It is based on a many-to-one relationship model, so it is more scalable. Programs like Larta Institute, CONNECT, and Endeavor are good examples. Their method is to construct a localized Rainforest of mentors and advisors around each startup. This method of assistance is still labor-intensive, but it is much more efficient than the heavy lifting of the First Derivative. Furthermore, the team approach means that a wider array of skills is accessible to each startup, and the building of small networks aids the creation of trust within those networks. However, it still takes significant effort to organize the right people, mobilize the right resources, and maintain the right funding that supports such initiatives every year. When the subsidies stop, the programs usually stop. Constructing lots of miniature "nature preserves" by hand is still hard work.

The Third Derivative is the transformation of human culture. If people in a community are able to learn behavioral patterns that reduce the cost of transactions between them, the system can become self-sustaining. By transforming human culture, we can transform a set of people into a many-to-many system. The Third Derivative, however, requires the missing commandments. What are these missing commandments, and where can we find them?

Let us put on a different hat. So far, we have acted like biologists, neuroscientists, psychologists, and sociologists in the Rainforest. Now, let us become anthropologists. To discover the "real" history of Silicon Valley and identify the DNA of that culture, we need to go back in time and discover where it came from.

Back to the Frontier

In 1893, the World's Fair in Chicago captured the public's imagination. The Fair was full of things most Americans had never seen, tasted, or heard of before: the Ferris Wheel, neon lights, hamburgers, iced tea, breakfast cereals, and ragtime music, to name a few. People flocked to see the latest scientific inventions and discoveries. Buffalo Bill even set up his Wild West Show right next door.

The World's Fair was one of the most exciting events ever staged in America. About one in five of all Americans attended, traveling from far and wide, including celebrities such as Thomas Edison, Mark Twain, Helen Keller, Harry Houdini, and Scott Joplin.

Few of them particularly wanted to hear an academic speech on the hot evening of July 12. A young, unknown professor from the University of Wisconsin named Frederick Jackson Turner was delivering a talk on history to a small, bored audience. He had only become a professor four years earlier, and few people had ever heard of him. There were many more interesting things to do and see at the World's Fair.

Turner's presentation was called "The Significance of the Frontier in American History." Although it created little fanfare at the time, in the following years, the ideas in his work would become increasingly prominent. That presentation—in the middle of one of the most exciting events ever—would launch Turner on a trajectory that eventually made him one of the leading historians in America.

Turner believed that the westward movement of the frontier boundary was the major defining feature of American culture. His "Frontier Thesis" argued that the American identity was forged at the juncture between the civilization of settlement and the savagery of wilderness.[9] The moving "frontier line" meant that American culture had evolved away from traditional European-style institutions on the East Coast—such as established churches, aristocracies, strong governments, and landed gentry. These institutions were essentially useless in frontier life, since one had to tame the undeveloped land. The further one moved away from the East Coast, the greater the sense of individualism and self-reliance.

---

9 Wikipedia contributors, "Frontier thesis," *Wikipedia, The Free Encyclopedia,*
   http://en.wikipedia.org/wiki/Frontier_thesis (accessed August 15, 2011).

Turner was the first to define the uniquely American ideal of the rugged and egalitarian individualist. It is an idea which still resonates today in national politics, media, and culture. This "cowboy culture," as it might be called, did not exist prior to the frontier. The culture developed as a matter of necessity.[10]

A visitor to Silicon Valley today still feels the legacy of the frontier culture. It is palpable. You can see the physical evidence in the rustic wooden architecture found even in modern buildings. You sense the love of open space in the rolling hills and among the trails in the redwood forests. You notice the large number of ranches and horses dotting the hills. You hear the fierce individualism in the roar of motorcycles—like modern-day horses—racing along the ridges of the mountains. You observe the variety of eclectic, individualistic hobbies that people pursue.

The modern high technology industry of Silicon Valley would never have existed without the culture that developed on the American frontier, but not just because of its emphasis on individualism, as most would assume. Silicon Valley is also the heir of the frontier spirit because of its unique collectivism. As Frederick Jackson Turner observed over a century ago, it is the tension between the individual and the collective that matters. *The frontier was conquered not just by individualists, but by a culture that enabled individuals to work together pragmatically on mutually beneficial projects.*

As we discussed in Chapter 4, the American experience was a giant social laboratory—probably the grandest experiment of its kind in human history—to discover what happens when people are cut free from their ancient ties to land and tribe, and are forced to survive as individualized atoms.[11] It was an atomistic society, so there was basically a blank slate for social behavior. One had only to survive. Still, the atoms had to work together and form temporary alliances. The American frontier was like a reality survival show, only writ large across a continent and played over a span of centuries.

---

10 David Dary, *Cowboy Culture: A Saga of Five Centuries* (Kansas: University Press of Kansas, 1989), xi-xii. "It was a culture based on mobility, custom, and the survival of the fittest. It was influenced and shaped by many things. It was a culture with little permanence."

11 Robert V. Hine, *Community on the American Frontier: Separate, But Not Alone* (Norman, OK: University of Oklahoma Press, 1980), 201.

People usually think of Silicon Valley as an anomaly in the otherwise "normal" history of the world, but what if we reversed that proposition? What if we envisioned Silicon Valley as the natural endpoint of a 50,000-year story? Perhaps it could be the latest stage in the evolution of human society, *from a culture based on tribes to a culture based on pragmatic individuals.*

The story began on the African savanna. Vast numbers of people then moved to the Middle East. From there, the genetic record shows that they migrated to Europe, Asia, and finally the Americas.[12] The California coast is arguably the furthest point one can travel from the roots of human civilization, from the ties that bound people to the past, and from the rules of behavior imposed by our ancestors' experiences.[13] Silicon Valley happened exactly when and where it should have happened—at the end of the story so far. California today consists largely of people, or their descendants, who are such individualists that they could not even fit into an entire nation of rebels. It is the world's ultimate non-tribe.

But people still have to learn to "get along." Even today, people who move to Silicon Valley are surprised at the ease of starting conversations with new people, the lack of hierarchy, the openness to sharing information and ideas, the willingness to collaborate, the tolerance for mistakes, and the rapid style in which new ideas are embraced and attempted. The cultural legacy of the frontier—balanced between individualism and pragmatic cooperation—has created a new economic paradigm.

The great irony is that this distinctly American culture—often criticized for its lack of permanent community or traditions—has actually created a new form of community unto itself. When new people move to Silicon Valley, many of them actually feel like they are joining a tribe. There is a sense of pride, a sensibility, and a willingness to participate and play by the new tribe's internal rules. Ironically, this new type of community—birthed from the idea of running away from older communities—has led to consistently greater economic output over time than traditional tribes have ever achieved.

What are the norms that created the balance between individual and community ideals, which has led to such powerful economic results? In the historical evidence of the American frontier, we discover the Rules of the Rainforest hidden throughout.

---

12 "The Genographic Project," NationalGeographic.com, accessed August 30, 2011, https://genographic.nationalgeographic.com/genographic/lan/en/atlas.html.

13 For similar perspectives, see Robert M. MacIver, *Community* (Chicago: University of Chicago Press, 1970), 252-253. MacIver sees history as a continuous widening of community beyond our primitive origins. "Our life is realized within not one but many communities, circling us round, grade beyond grade."

Cooperation Born of Necessity

Imagine crossing a different boundary: from a civilized society into a place where there was absolutely no society at all. If you were a newcomer to Independence, Missouri in the early or mid-1800s, you would probably be preparing to make just such a journey. You might have spent many days and perhaps your life savings to get to Independence. Perhaps you rode a horse, or took a steamboat or a train. In any case, you were now on the western edge of civilization as most people knew it. Beyond that point was essentially a lawless, frontier wilderness. Less than ten miles to the west of you was what people called the "Great American Desert."

You came to Independence to seek a better life for yourself and maybe your family. This city was the starting point for three of the major trails heading west—the Santa Fe, California, and Oregon Trails. If you were heading to California, you still had about six months and 2,000 miles to go. This was not a journey for the weak-willed.

But you were not alone. Independence was bustling with many others just like you. People interested in making the journey across the frontier would meet in Independence and form larger groups to help ensure their mutual survival. Once on the trail, you never knew when you might have to deter attacks by Native Americans, kill predators to keep your livestock safe, help pull wagons from the mud, or provide medical care to injured group members.[14] You had no choice but to band together with complete strangers for the purpose of pooling your skills and resources to increase your chances of living through the journey. It was a matter of pure pragmatism.

On the American frontier, the spirit of rugged individualism was balanced by the practical necessity of working with others. Frederick Jackson Turner wrote: "In the spirit of the pioneer's 'house-raising' lies the salvation of the Republic." That is, the ability to create community out of self-interested individuals would be the defining hope of America. Many historians have validated this idea of the frontier as an "incubator-of-cooperation."[15]

---

14 Boorstin, *The Americans*, 54 (see chap. 3, n. 11).

15 Lacy K. Ford, Jr., "Frontier Democracy: The Turner Thesis Revisited," *Journal of the Early Republic* 13 (1993):149, http://works.bepress.com/lacy_fordjr/31/. He writes: "This frontier-as-incubator-of-cooperation argument was pioneered by Stanley Elkins and Eric McKitrick, 'A Meaning For Turner's Frontier, Part I: Democracy in the Old Northwest,' *Political Science Quarterly*, 69 (Sept. 1954), 321-353; and Daniel Boorstin, *The Americans: The National Experience* (New York 1965), esp. 113-168. 17 Don Harrison Doyle, 'Social Theory and New Communities in Nineteenth-Century America,' *Western Historical Quarterly*, 8 (Apr. 1977), 151-165 (quotation at 157). Earlier works that emphasize conflict on the frontier include Allen G. Bogue, 'Social Theory and the Pioneer,' *Agricultural History*, 34 (Jan. 1960), 21-34; and Robert R. Dykstra, *The Cattle Towns* (New York, 1968)."

Individualism is a fine idea in theory, until one has to face the realities of finding food, water, clothing, shelter, information, protection, and human companionship. Despite common stereotypes, evidence shows that the frontier was not full of Lone Ranger types. Rather, it consisted largely of individuals and families who had to build social networks, traveling groups, small communities, and frontier posts to help them clear land, plant crops, sell goods, and exchange with one another. Just as in the startup world, individualists had to "get along" to survive, and new types of communities were formed. As author Daniel Boorstin writes:

> ...of all American myths, none is stronger than that of the loner moving west across the land...The courage to move to new places and try new things is supposed to be the same as the courage to go it alone, to focus exclusively and intensively and enterprisingly on oneself...But groups—especially the casual, informal, readily formed and readily dissolved groups in which travelers move—keep no diaries, write no letters, compose no autobiographies...To cross the wild continent safely, one had to travel with a group. Between the American Revolution and the Civil War, those who pushed far west of the established settlements... *seldom traveled alone.*[16]

In the frontier areas, the mixing of people from different cultures was not easy by any means. Diversity tends to create social friction. Towns on the frontier were cultural crucibles in which people from different groups collided with one another. Significant conflicts and even violence between members of these groups often occurred, such as "southerners caning Yankees, vigilante mobs chasing abolitionists, Christians squabbling over the doctrine of infant baptism, police raids on Irish grog shops." [17]

People had to get along to survive, however, and so they did. Over time, frontier townspeople learned to start "containing these conflicts within acceptable boundaries as the key to social stability and economic growth." Those boundaries were created by civic, religious, and political institutions that diminished conflict so that "like-minded members of frontier communities pursued common goals." [18] People learned to channel their tribal and competitive instincts into practical means of collaboration. Without a formal legal system in the frontier territories, pioneer communities often had a simple, spontaneous "group conscience" that served as an unwritten code of laws.[19] Each group making the westward trek had to create its own set of rules for internal self-governance. These rules

---

16 Boorstin, *The Americans*, 51-52 (italics added).

17 Ford, "Frontier Democracy," 149. Ford cites Don Harrison Doyle, "Social Theory and New Communities in Nineteenth-Century America," *Western Historical Quarterly*, 8 (Apr. 1977), 151-165 (quotation at 157).

18 Ibid., 150.

19 Boorstin, *The Americans*, 82.

were usually quite simple because they were highly informal and needed to be easily understood.[20]

From the cultural norms that facilitated cooperation among pioneers, we have identified seven simple Rules of the Rainforest. Silicon Valley is an extension of the American frontier culture: marked by social networks where individualism is always tempered by the need to participate within a community.[21] The Rules are the unwritten "laws outside the laws" that continue to govern social behavior today.

The Rules

Two people are sitting in the balcony of the Café Venetia on University Avenue in Palo Alto. One hundred and fifty years ago, this location was a cattle ranch. Today, it is a pleasant and bright coffee shop in the middle of Silicon Valley. No doubt countless startups made their early forays into the world here.

One person is an entrepreneur with an idea for starting a new company. He cannot succeed on his own. He needs help from an array of engineers, salespeople, marketers, investors, advisors, and other professionals. Sitting across from him is a marketing expert who knows the target industry well. Her expertise in this sector is vast, and her relationships are broad and deep. They are meeting for the first time, introduced by a distant mutual acquaintance. It sounds so simple, but it is not.

He would clearly benefit if he had access to her experience, knowledge, and networks. However, he is also concerned that she could take his idea and give it to his competitor. Or she could even start her own company to compete with his. This is a real and common situation that occurs at the beginning of almost every person-to-person relationship in the Rainforest. It happens many thousands of times every day. It is, in many ways, a modern version of the same friend-or-foe challenge our ancestors faced when meeting someone unfamiliar on the African savanna.

Which way will the conversation go? Will it be the zero-sum game played by taxi drivers in Jerusalem? Or will it be the positive-sum game that Larry Bock created when he started Athena Neurosciences? It could go either way.

---

20 Ibid., 66.

21 Saxenian, *Regional Advantage*, 31-32 (see chap. 2, n. 24). Saxenian cites Don Hoefler, "Silicon Valley—U.S.A.," *Electronic News* (Jan. 11, 18, and 25, 1971), in which the term "Silicon Valley" was coined: "The wives all know each other and remain on the friendliest terms. The men eat at the same restaurants; drink at the same bars, and go to the same parties. Despite their fierce competition during business hours, away from the office they remain the greatest friends."

As they sit face-to-face in the coffee shop, what enables our entrepreneur to lower his defenses and work with this new person? The answer is the Rules of the Rainforest, our missing third tablet of commandments.

Rule #1: *Thou shalt break rules and dream.*

Rule #2: *Thou shalt open doors and listen.*

Rule #3: *Thou shalt trust and be trusted.*

Rule #4: *Thou shalt experiment and iterate together.*

Rule #5: *Thou shalt seek fairness, not advantage.*

Rule #6: *Thou shalt err, fail, and persist.*

Rule #7: *Thou shalt pay it forward.*

The Rules are simple, like the frontier's unwritten laws, because they are informal and must be understood—and practiced—by people in situations just like this one. The Rules make this conversation work to both parties' benefit. Let us walk through this story and show what the Rules mean in practice.

Rule #1: *Break rules and dream.*

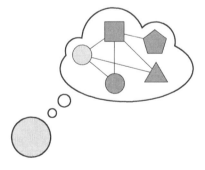

In the Café Venetia, our entrepreneur and our marketer are facing each other over lattes. Before they even speak, they must harbor a desire to break old conventions and dream of new possibilities.

Our entrepreneur wants to convey his genuine excitement about transforming an industry. He talks of the long-term future, not the short-term. He discusses the great scale of the market opportunity. But his payoff is not just about money. He also talks about his broader motivations—the great challenge, the adventure, the novelty, even a chance to make the world a better place. His defiance of the old ways almost seems "naughty," like a child might be.[22] For a Rainforest to thrive, people must accept that rule-breaking and believing in grand aspirations are acceptable forms of social behavior. They enable someone to believe that what has previously been considered impossible is in fact possible.

In most places, people with big dreams are considered naïve. In our work, we have observed how *fatalism* often permeates daily life and impedes innovation. From the Middle East to East Asia to Scandinavia to Latin America, many people often feel that what they get is what they deserve. There is a Swedish saying—*The tallest blade of grass gets cut first*—implying that dreaming, aspiring, striving, or just acting different are foolish behaviors. In the Palestinian Territories, an entrepreneur once remarked sheepishly, after hearing our grand suggestions for his startup's strategy, "How could we possibly do that? We are just a little startup in Palestine."

Fatalism is like a disease that eats away at people's willingness to aspire to greater things. Without aspiration, without the willingness to believe, nothing can be born. Every great company in the world at its beginning was little more than two people sitting in a coffee shop. Breaking through this mindset can be a dramatic process. We witnessed this phenomenon in Saudi Arabia at a Startup Weekend, an event where entrepreneurs build brand new companies in the span of a weekend. By the end of the event, many of the Saudi men and women we worked with were openly crying from the shock of the newfound liberation they experienced. One man was still in disbelief and said to us through his tears, "I came here with nothing. I'm leaving here with new friends, a new company, and a new job." [23]

The idea that quixotic quests are not to be laughed at, but are to be embraced, is a fundamental building block of Rainforests. According to Shannon Callahan, the head of talent at Silicon Valley venture firm Andreessen-Horowitz, startups cannot compete effectively for talent against big companies based on salary alone. Startups don't have enough cash to pay full "market rates" to justify the risk for new hires. "They have to take the conversation to the vision of what they are building, the contribution a person can make at that [size of a] company. They have to feed a person's

---

22 Tomio Geron, "What Y Combinator's Paul Graham Looks For In Founders," *Forbes*, May 24, 2011, http://www.forbes.com/sites/tomiogeron/2011/05/24/what-y-combinators-paul-graham-looks-for-in-founders/.

23 Participant, Startup Weekend in Riyadh, Saudi Arabia (paraphrased from memory), November 2011.

desire to build the next coolest company, rather than be a part of the current coolest company."[24]

The history of the frontier shows that dreaming was actually justified. Indeed, it was essential. Lacy Ford observes, "from the microeconomic vantage point of individual households, whether North or South, a decision to move to the frontier in search of a better life stood a good chance of proving correct." The opportunities on the frontier were economically worthwhile.[25] A young pioneering family would, on average, do better than the family that had not taken that risk. However, it was more than economic. The organizer of each wagon caravan had to inspire and encourage people to join the difficult journey, and then work to maintain their spirits.[26] Historian Robert V. Hine describes the thrill of participation and sense of community that people felt when crossing the frontier in a long wagon train:

> The dirt and the hail and the desert bound them all together in the way hardship so often unites people. In busy seasons panoramas would suddenly open, eastward or westward, and the sight of hundreds of wagons like lines of emphasis under the hills would inspire a feeling of involvement in a larger enterprise.[27]

It is not enough for the entrepreneur in the Café Venetia to dream. The marketer must reciprocate and dream too. If she does not, then she might treat this conversation like a short-term, zero-sum game, with a temptation to defect and pocket immediate gain for herself. Rainforests thrive because people honor the dreams of others as well as their own.

24 Nicole Perlroth, "Forbes Q and A With Andreessen-Horowitz's Secret Agent," *Forbes,* February 4, 2011, http://www.forbes.com/sites/nicoleperlroth/2011/02/04/forbes-q-and-a-with-andreessen-horowitzs-secret-agent/.

25 Ford, "Frontier Democracy," 153. In his work, he cites James A. Henretta, "The Study of Social Mobility: Ideological Assumptions and Conceptual Bias," *Labor History,* 18 (Spring 1977), 165-178, and other studies to point out that "the data provides almost incontrovertible proof that there was enough genuine upward mobility to sustain the popular perception of America, and its frontier, as a land of unique opportunity."

26 Boorstin, *The Americans,* 59.

27 Hine, *Community,* 64.

Rule #2: *Open doors and listen.*

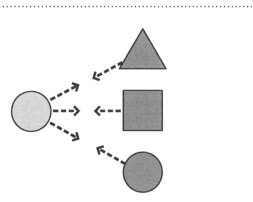

Our entrepreneur and our marketer have started drinking their lattes and are talking. What happens next? Opening doors to meet new people and then listening to them are essential rules of the Rainforest. The entrepreneur and marketer have already taken the first step by showing up at the café to meet. Now, they need to hear each other.

Remember the recipe of Larry Bock. To build his team, he would meet lots of people, and then simply listen to them talk. A thriving Rainforest requires that people treat every conversation like an open invitation, and be willing to learn by listening to the other party.

This is harder than it sounds. Most people are naturally suspicious. They might be closed-minded. They may simply be shy. It can take a tremendous effort to get them to openly and honestly engage in even simple conversations with strangers. Contrast that with a typical chance meeting that could happen in Silicon Valley. One day, two people could be strangers, and the next day, they could be in business together. This seemingly innocuous occurrence in a Rainforest would be considered a stunning result in many other regions of the world.

Social scientist Fukuyama calls it "spontaneous sociability."[28] Think of the conversations that happen around the water cooler in a corporate office. This kind of behavior creates opportunities for people with complementary skills, experiences, insights, or ideas to bump into each other. Clint Kopp used to attribute the success of life science company Baxter in the 1970s in

---

28 Francis Fukuyama, *Trust: The Social Virtues and the Creation of Prosperity* (New York: Simon & Schuster, 1996), 47. Fukuyama states: "Spontaneous sociability is critical to economic life because virtually all economic activity is carried out by groups rather than individuals."

part to the company's cafeteria, which encouraged conversations among diverse people.[29] He remembered how many great products were first sketched on the backs of napkins there.

Regions that became hubs for prominent numbers of "refugees" from other parts of the world—such as Israel, Taiwan, Singapore, or the United States—often thrive economically. It is probably not a coincidence. The refugees in such regions may have the same ethnicities or share similar value systems, but have been mixed and mingled to generate new, unexpected relationships and novel ways of thinking. This recipe leads to numerous types of economic transactions that otherwise would never happen.

Opening doors becomes even more powerful when there is a greater diversity of doors to open. Silicon Valley is a product of the collision of the frontier culture with the hyper-diversity of modern California. Silicon Valley's emergence coincided with a sharp increase in the diversity of people in California. As one proxy for measuring diversity, we can examine the percentage of foreign-born people. In 1900, the western and mountain states had about the same foreign-born percentage as the northeastern states.[30] By 1980, California had won that title outright with 15.1%.[31] In the past three decades, that percentage has skyrocketed. By 2008, 26.8% of California's population was born outside of the United States, the highest such rate in the country.[32] Many of those immigrants are involved in the Silicon Valley startup community. Berkeley researcher Vivek Wadhwa discovered that 52.4% of startups in Silicon Valley were founded by at least one immigrant entrepreneur.[33] This level of diversity sets California apart from the other western frontier states.

Economic research is validating the importance of diversity in Rainforests. In a model of complex systems, for instance, researchers demonstrated

---

29 For additional information about how the "Baxter Boys" built the global biotech industry, see Monica C. Higgins, *Career Imprints: Creating Leaders Across an Industry* (New York: John Wiley & Sons, 2005).

30 Campbell Gibson and Emily Lennon, "Foreign-Born Population by Historical Section and Subsection of the United States: 1850 to 1990," U.S. Bureau of the Census, Population Division, March 9, 1999, http://www.census.gov/population/www/documentation/twps0029/tab14.html.

31 Campbell Gibson and Emily Lennon, "Nativity of the Population, for Regions, Divisions, and States: 1850 to 1990," U.S. Bureau of the Census, Population Division, March 9, 1999, http://www.census.gov/population/www/documentation/twps0029/tab13.html.

32 Campbell Gibson and Emily Lennon, "Place of Birth by Citizenship Status" and C05005, "Year of Entry by Citizenship Status," U.S. Census Bureau, 2008 American Community Survey, CO5002, http://factfinder.census.gov/, accessed October 2009 http://www.census.gov/compendia/statab/2011/tables/11s0038.pdf

33 Vivek Wadhwa, "Foreign-Born Entrepreneurs: An Underestimated American Resource," Ewing Marion Kauffman Foundation, 2009, http://www.kauffman.org/entrepreneurship/foreign-born-entrepreneurs.aspx.

that diversity trumps raw ability for problem-solving in groups.[34] A team of randomly selected people will outperform a team comprised of selected experts because experts can be too similar to one another and possess less diversity of ideas. The process of opening new doors and listening is the real way that entrepreneurs "learn." Businesses are not built by constructing abstract theories while sitting at a desk. They are built in a non-linear, unpredictable manner based on constant iteration and testing in the real world. Details such as the price that a customer pays, the cost of making a product, the time it takes to close a sale—these all require real dialogue to determine. Therefore, entrepreneurs not only *should* open doors; they *must* open doors.

Rainforests facilitate this process because conventional walls and hierarchies have been broken down. These walls might include something as basic and obvious as the divisions between, say, scientists and business-people. But they might also include the divisions between wireless engineers and biomedical product designers, small startup entrepreneurs and Fortune 500 executives, and angel investors and large financial institutions. Rule #2 increases the knowledge transfer that happens between people who otherwise might be confined to their groups. Without the willingness to open doors, intermingling happens slowly. Without the willingness to listen, knowledge remains latent. Thus, opening doors and listening leverages the most value out of a community's inherent resources.[35] Any contribution is potentially valuable, so everyone is worth listening to.

Similarly, on the frontier, extremely diverse people had to work together out of pragmatic necessity. Cattle drives, for instance, required at least six to eight cowboys to work together in extremely harsh conditions. Robert Hine writes that "the cohesive energy could even unite such heterogeneous elements as Anglo derelicts, derided Mexicans, and black former slaves."[36] When the transcontinental railroads were built, people of different social classes were often crammed into the same train coaches. Cooperating with people from highly different backgrounds was a practical necessity in the difficult and sparsely populated landscape of the American frontier. We see

---

34 Lu Hong and Scott E. Page, "Groups of Diverse Problem Solvers Can Outperform Groups of High-Ability Problem Solvers," PNAS 101 (2004): 16385, doi:10.1073/pnas.0403723101. Hong and Page also note these other sources. "Overall, diverse societies may be more robust, as they have the potential to adapt to new and changing circumstances (Bednar J (2009) The *Robust Federation: Principles of Design.* Cambridge: Cambridge University Press). In contrast, societies that lack intra-cultural diversity may be prone to collapse (Diamond J (2005). *Collapse: How Societies Choose to Fail or Succeed.* New York: Viking)."

35 Two and a half centuries ago, Adam Smith highlighted the importance of the human dynamic when people interact, communicate, and connect. In describing a hypothetical interaction, he wrote, "These two sentiments... may, it is evident, have such a correspondence with one another, as is sufficient for the harmony of society. Though they will never be unisons, they may be concords, and this is all that is wanted or required." Smith, *Moral Sentiments*, Sec. 1, Ch. 4.

36 Hine, *Community*, 58-59.

this legacy today in Rainforests, where the norm is to open doors to diverse people and hear what they have to offer.

....

Rule #3: *Trust and be trusted.*

....

In the Café Venetia, the lattes are half empty. The entrepreneur has described his idea. It is a big and daring dream. The marketer has reciprocated and is excited by the prospect. They have been listening closely to each other. Now the entrepreneur is wondering whether to share his private strategy with the marketer. What does he do? The entrepreneur is concerned that his idea will be stolen, but if he is not willing to trust the marketer, the conversation will be a nonstarter. One person must take the first risk to trust the other.

Rainforests cannot thrive without trust among strangers. The hard part is having the courage to take the first step. It means being willing to suffer the occasional knife in the back as part of the cost of doing business. This type of thinking would be considered radical in many places. Giving trust first is what fools do, it might be said. In business, there is constant temptation to violate trust for short-term economic gain. The common saying "business is business" implies that taking advantage of the other side is an acceptable action. This behavior, however, would kill a Rainforest. Business is not just business in the Rainforest; business must be suffused with trust.

Likewise, people on the frontier had to learn to create trust quickly, or risk death. Pioneer families joining a wagon caravan in Independence would have to learn to trust complete strangers literally overnight to protect themselves against hostile Native Americans or bandits on the trail. The same lesson applies to startup companies in the Rainforest: trust fast or die. Michie Slaughter, the former head of organizational development at Marion Laboratories, recalls: "Our founder Ewing Kauffman used to say, 'Trust everybody that you work with. You'll get screwed every once in a while, but… people will want to do business with you."[37] Similarly, venture capitalist Kevin Fong has observed the role of trust in deal-making in Silicon Valley over the past decades:

> The friction of getting deals done here is faster. You don't lawyer everything to the nth degree. If you negotiate with a New York law firm, they want to negotiate every detail. They are probably right on the legalities, but you can spend hours and days to get everything right. But here, basically, you get it mostly right and then move on. *Everything is done with a handshake in the Valley.* If it's a failure, no one cares. If it succeeds, then everyone is happy.[38]

The underlying importance of trust applies in all human systems. Fukuyama describes how conducting business in systems that are low on trust tends to be expensive and inefficient.

> The economic function of social capital [read: trust] is to reduce the transaction costs associated with formal coordination mechanisms like contracts, hierarchies, bureaucratic rules, and the like…. No contract can possibly specify every contingency that may arise between the parties; most presuppose a certain amount of goodwill that prevents the parties from taking advantage of unforeseen loopholes. Contracts that do seek to try to specify all contingencies—like the job-control labour pacts negotiated in the auto industry that were as thick as telephone books—end up being very inflexible and costly to enforce.[39]

Although trust has a cost, the absence of trust in Rainforests would have an even higher cost. As practicing venture capitalists, we sometimes hear from entrepreneurs who are eager to get our capital but are unwilling to share even basic information that lets us make an informed decision about their companies. Not only does the lack of information prevent us from assessing the opportunity—the lack of trust preempts any relationship we might develop. No transaction ultimately happens. The Rainforest dies a small death.

---

37 Michie Slaughter, telephone interview with author, June 3, 2011.

38 Kevin Fong, interview (see chap. 4, part II, n. 31) (italics added); Saxenian, *Regional Advantage*, 149. Saxenian also observed this behavior. She quotes an Apple purchasing manager: "We have found you don't always need a formal contract… If you develop trust with your suppliers, you don't need armies of attorneys."

39 Fukuyama, "Social Capital," 10 (see chap. 2, n. 33).

Entrepreneur Mark Pydynowski, the co-founder of our portfolio company Somark Innovations, has witnessed how trust differs between Rainforest and non-Rainforest communities:

> There is a big difference when I talk with entrepreneurs in California and those in the Midwest. In California, people are generally willing to share a lot about their ideas. In the Midwest, entrepreneurs who seek me out for advice are often not willing to tell me anything about what they are doing. They are so afraid of sharing that they end up hurting themselves.[40]

A single conversation stifled by a lack of trust does not seem significant, but multiply such a conversation thousands or millions of times, and the macro effects can be profound. On the other hand, if people in a Rainforest understand that sharing information comes with an implied code of honor, the positive macro-effects can be considerable. People are more willing to share, more potential collaborations are explored, more transactions are consummated, and innovation is accelerated.

This is not to say that ideas are not stolen in Rainforests. Of course they are. However, there is a penalty for violations of trust. When a venture capitalist forwards a business plan to another venture capitalist, there is the social expectation by all parties that the entrepreneur who wrote that plan has previously approved that transfer. The expectation is maintained in part because one might be on the other side of the table tomorrow—today's venture capitalist could be tomorrow's entrepreneur. It is a notion of right and wrong that echoes what the philosopher John Rawls called the "veil of ignorance"—you never know which side you will be on.[41]

The human disposition to distrust makes it is relatively easy for a startup company to splinter apart. In the life of a startup, there are numerous opportunities for stakeholders to screw one another—an employee can steal an idea to launch a new company, an investor can squeeze an entrepreneur by waiting until a company is at a financial dead end before investing, or an entrepreneur can simply take venture capital and run away with it. As startup guru Paul Graham says, "Startups do to the relationship between the founders what a dog does to a sock: if it can be pulled apart, it will be."[42]

40 Mark Pydynowski, telephone interview with author, June 3, 2011.

41 For additional information, see Wikipedia contributors, "A Theory of Justice," *Wikipedia, The Free Encyclopedia,* http://en.wikipedia.org/wiki/A_theory_of_justice (accessed August 26, 2011). Rawls offers a model of a fair choice situation (the "original position" with its "veil of ignorance") within which parties would hypothetically choose mutually acceptable principles of justice. Specifically, Rawls develops what he claims are principles of justice through the use of an entirely and deliberately artificial device he calls the *Original position* in which everyone decides principles of justice from behind a veil of ignorance. This "veil" is one that essentially blinds people to all facts about themselves that might cloud what notion of justice is.

42 Paul Graham, "What It Takes," *Forbes.com,* November 8, 2010, http://www.forbes.com/forbes/2010/1108/best-small-companies-10-y-combinator-paul-graham-ask-an-expert.html.

Given the strain of the startup experience, Rainforests cannot function without trust. People in Rainforests often develop instincts to "sniff out" trust, the way animals in a real rainforest use their sense of smell to identify potential threats.

Trust in Rainforests requires a style of transparent communication which is not common in many parts of the world. Our work in places with strong family cultures, such as East Asia, Latin America, or the Middle East, has revealed a cultural tendency for people to keep their "real" opinions to themselves out of courtesy or conflict-avoidance. Passive-aggressive behavior—which causes miscommunication and misinterpretation—can easily turn into resentment in a fast-paced environment. In places like the post-Soviet countries, people often struggle to have a genuine debate without causing a nasty argument. Trust depends on social patterns that encourage openness without defensiveness, honesty without argument, and opinions without grievances.

Rule #4: *Experiment and iterate together.*

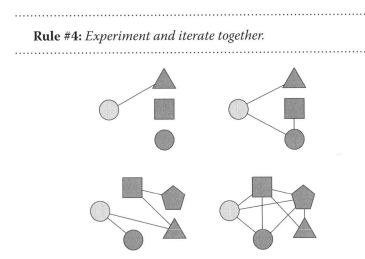

Back at the Café Venetia, our protagonists have finished their lattes. They have built enough trust that they are sharing important information with each other. The entrepreneur has shared some aspects of his proprietary technology; the marketer has shared some valuable insights about customers. What happens next?

The entrepreneur and the marketer know they want to work together, but they have no idea how exactly they will do that, or if their collaboration will yield anything of value. It could be huge, but it could also be a bust. Will customers respond to the idea?

The Rainforest requires that people be willing to experiment together. Innovation is a continuous process of trial and error, failure and improvement. It does not rely on a perfect initial design, but on experimentation and perseverance. Thus, people learn not to *build for perfection*, but to *build for iteration*.

Most people are not comfortable with the uncertainty that comes with experimentation—in some places even more so. In one country, for instance, after we had helped a government on several technology projects, one official asked us pointedly, "So can you guarantee that all of these new projects will be successful?" Naturally, we explained that innovation was unpredictable and that many, if not most, of the projects would fail. Suddenly, in the eyes of the official, we could see a clear flash of fear. We realized that uncertainty for him was a huge source of anxiety. The idea that success could be measured by looking at invisible processes—iterative experimentation and lessons learned, for example—was a completely alien concept. Another official once said to us that his goal was to "control, monitor, and exploit" innovation. For him, the process of innovation was like the controlled output of a plantation, not an unpredictable Rainforest, so uncertainty would be the equivalent of failure. This type of mindset, however, stifles the growth of Rainforests.

On the frontier, impermanence and uncertainty was the norm. There was no choice but to "give things a try". Families in Independence might join wagon trains of 100 to 150 people when it made sense to do so, but they had no problem leaving the groups either. A person traveling in the frontier might belong to a number of parties before deciding where they ultimately wanted to go.[43]

This willingness to "try it out" creates a form of *rapid cycle iteration* in the Rainforest. There is no substitute for experimentation and iteration when it comes to prototyping new products and testing them out in the real world with real customers. Natural selection works the same way in a real rainforest. The more genetic variations and mutations that are created, the more likely it is that a plant or animal that is better adapted to its environment will be produced. Innovation in Rainforests is akin to the process of evolution.

---

43 Boorstin, *The Americans*, 71, 95.

Experimentation is driven by action, not theory. Jeff Hammerbacher, the former leader of the data team at Facebook, once described the early days of Facebook: "It wasn't the kind of culture where it was a good idea to say, 'Hi, I have an idea.' It was the kind of culture where it was a good idea to build a prototype of your idea, and then to show people."[44] This culture was demonstrated in the data team's hack-a-thon sessions (computer programming marathons), where products like Facebook chat and Facebook video were developed in a single night and then showcased in internal "prototype forums" for feedback. This type of prototyping and real-world testing is widespread in Rainforests.

Back at the Café Venetia, as the entrepreneur and the marketer shake hands, they must share the notion that a journey together is worth a try. In a traditional economy, there would be many reasons not to bother trying (and risking failure) at all. A Rainforest only works when people believe in the value of experimentation and iteration together.

....

Rule #5: *Seek fairness, not advantage.*

....

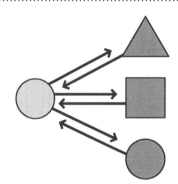

Several weeks have passed since that first conversation at Café Venetia. The entrepreneur and the marketer have been doing valuable work together. They feel that they are both benefiting from the collaboration, and they are enjoying the project. Clearly, 1+1 is greater than 2. The entrepreneur is now thinking of formally engaging the marketer for the long term. They have returned to the Café Venetia to discuss this matter. What now? How do they decide the terms of that relationship?

The Rainforest requires that individuals strive to create fair transactions with each other, not advantageous transactions. This is not easy in most of the world, where business is about "winning" against the other person.

---

44 Lester Holt, "The Facebook Obsession," CNBC video, 2:19, December 23, 2010, http://video.cnbc.com/gallery/?video=1707620781.

The entrepreneur wants to offer the marketer some stock options in his startup company. At first blush, the granting of stock options looks like a one-time transaction, but this is an illusion. A single grant of stock options is actually a series of invisible, repeat transactions. Let us say that the entrepreneur gives X value in options in exchange for the expected value of the marketer's contributions to the company.

Day One

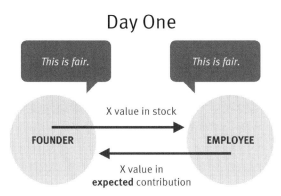

Despite outward appearances, this transaction is not over. The transfer of equity in a startup is a transaction that is silently repeated every single day. Both parties are constantly re-evaluating the transaction to determine whether or not they got a fair deal. And since startup companies are highly unpredictable, what is a fair deal one day may not feel like one the next.

Day Two

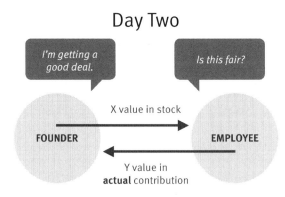

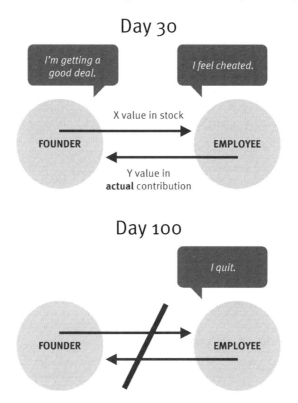

Remember that equity is just a proxy currency for trust. It is stress-tested continuously. If someone feels he is not being treated fairly, the relationship can fracture, a company can splinter, and innovation can be lost. There is no magic formula for the right amount of equity for the entrepreneur to give to the marketer. The answer is what both parties will consider fair over the course of their long-term relationship. They just need to keep in mind that they will have to work together every single day and cannot afford to have anyone feel slighted.

Inevitably, there are going to be times when one person feels they are doing too much, or the other person is contributing too little. Founders of a startup are expected to actively contribute to the success of the company every day, but sometimes that's not possible. A sense of unfairness among team members can lead to a rapid breakdown in trust and cause resentment among parties. Startup teams must constantly recalibrate to maintain fairness.

The same rule applies to venture capital investing. If investors feel they got a "great deal" in a startup company, they soon find that the startup team has a lot less motivation to work for the success of the enterprise. Veterans of the Rainforest know that successful companies need to be led by motivated entrepreneurs who feel they got a fair deal. Phil Wickham, a venture capitalist who now runs the Center for Venture Education, calls it the *Fairness Doctrine*: the unwritten expectation in Rainforests that everyone will do the right thing and treat the other person fairly in the end.

This ideal of fairness was found on the American frontier as well. Every individual in a wagon caravan was expected to do his or her fair share of duties, and people who refused were punished. Gene Autry, the famed cowboy, even had his own rule: "A cowboy never takes unfair advantage— even of an enemy." [45] A system in which people feel that they will be treated fairly lowers barriers to transactions, reduces fear, and keeps people incentivized to pursue aspirations together.

....

Rule #6: *Err, fail, and persist.*
....

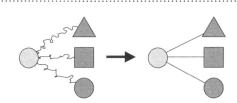

Another few months have passed since that first meeting at the Café Venetia. The entrepreneur and the marketer tried one strategy to procure an important first customer. It failed terribly. The customers wanted something entirely different. What now?

The expectation of people in the Rainforest is that there will be many ups and downs. There will be wrong turns and false starts. The key is to get up and try again. Remember how the failure of the Anti-Google led the Gauches to try again with another, more successful startup.

Failure is no fun. It can even be devastating. In many places we work, we hear would-be entrepreneurs tell us variations of this statement: "I would love to be an entrepreneur, but if I failed, my entire family would be ashamed, I would never find a good spouse, and my career prospects would be ruined for the rest of my life." An entrepreneur from Sweden once told us, "The problem in Sweden is that one can never win. If you fail as an entrepreneur, you will face shame, and people will stop talking to

---

45 Rudy A. D'Angelo, "The Cowboy Codes," accessed August 30, 2011,
   http://rudydangelo.tripod.com/cowboy_codes.htm .

you. However, if you succeed as an entrepreneur, people will assume that you must have done something improper, and people will stop talking to you, too." In such places, where the price of doing something wrong is so extraordinary, the personal calculus necessary to take the risks needed to succeed as an entrepreneur usually doesn't add up.

In the Rainforest, error and failure are still unpleasant, but they are not the end of the road. If people learn from the experience and improve the odds of success the next time, failure and error are actually positive indicators in a system. From a macro view, *there is no real failure in the Rainforest, only learning*. Failure is merely a hypothesis that has been tested and shown to be false. It is not the failure that matters; what matters is the knowledge you have gained through that failure, and the perseverance you have shown picking yourself up and trying again. Venture capitalist John Doerr once said at a conference we attended: "We only invest in people who have crashed an F-14 fighter plane."[46] Just as a scientist learns through failed experiments, an innovator learns through failed ventures.

This idea of serial persistence also permeated the frontier experience. Robert Hine observes that, "Among pioneers there was a common bond, so ingrained that conformity to it was assumed, and nonconformists were instinctively ostracized. The essence of the bond was *endurance*, the triumph over a hostile wilderness.[47] Like the frontier, the Rainforest does not only encourage people to endure; it depends on it. The process of building an innovative enterprise is so hard, so unpredictable, and so complex that before succeeding, entrepreneurs always make thousands of mistakes, and may even fail several times. When we consider the systemic effects in a Rainforest, the willingness to err and fail can be a good thing.

46 John Doerr, overheard by the author, circa 2004.
47 Hine, *Community*, 120 (italics added).

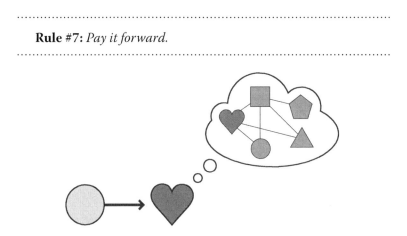

Rule #7: *Pay it forward.*

Our heroic duo is sitting at the Café Venetia again, one year later. They are celebrating over cappuccinos and tiramisu. They have just landed their major first customer through their mutual efforts. Revenue is coming into the company, and they are growing. At the end of the conversation, as they prepare to leave, a student at the next table interrupts them: "Excuse me, but I couldn't help overhearing your conversation." The student is thinking of entering the same industry upon graduation. He wants their advice.

One of the great surprises for newcomers to Silicon Valley is that, if you want, you can talk to almost anybody. In almost any other field of business, getting in front of the most influential individuals is impossibly difficult. In the Rainforest, it can be shockingly easy.

The reason for this is because it is in everyone's best interest for there to be little hierarchy. The organizational structure of the Rainforest is mostly horizontal, not vertical. One never knows where the next Facebook or Genentech will come from: an introverted college student wearing a hoodie, or a biochemist and a geneticist with an interesting discovery. Experience shows that it pays to be open-minded to new people, to be helpful, and to treat each person as if they might have "the next" valuable opportunity.[48]

One of the fundamental Rules of the Rainforest is the idea of "paying it forward"—doing a favor for someone without expecting to get paid back directly. The phrase was coined in the year 2000 in the book *Pay It Forward*,[49] but the concept existed in the Rainforest long before the phrase did. There is a cooperative spirit in the air of Silicon Valley. As John Doerr

---

48 Saxenian, *Regional Advantage*, 51. Saxenian describes how Hewlett-Packard had a "decentralized organizational structure that represented an important departure from traditional corporate organization." This meant that "good ideas could come from anywhere."

49 Catherine Ryan Hyde, *Pay It Forward* (New York: Simon & Schuster, 2000).

said, "I've never met a successful entrepreneur who wouldn't take time out of his or her day to help an aspiring entrepreneur think about a new business."[50]

Paying it forward is not done simply to be charitable. People believe it "comes back around" in the end, like the concept of karma in Buddhist, Hindu, Sikh, and Jain philosophies. You hear this sentiment often in Rainforests. When you help someone, you may not expect them to repay the favor directly, but you do expect that someone else will repay the favor in some other way. It is as if individuals are making a transaction with the Rainforest as a whole, based on faith that the system ultimately rewards people who are helpful to others.

We find evidence of this behavior on the frontier too. Robert Hine writes about the "long tradition of frontier cooperation," when tasks were too large for a single individual to perform. Sometimes this meant clearing land, house and barn raising, building roads, threshing crops, or finding stray cattle:[51]

> Diaries tell of women nursing the sick of neighboring wagons, then washing the clothes of the afflicted family; of men carrying the injured to shelter in spite of danger to themselves; of parts donated for the repair of one another's wagons; of posses swiftly organized to pursue thieves; of men walking because they had given their wagons to families in trouble; of whole trains traveling only a few hundred yards a day because of the combined group assisting each wagon over an obstacle; of blacksmiths, wheelwrights, and barbers offering their services. Personal as they were, these acts must have been infused with spirit of the group, like the salt of the loaf.[52]

Despite the individualism of the frontier, these types of acts could sometimes create what one farmer called "inner neighborhood."[53] This willingness to "pitch in" was critical for survival in such harsh conditions.[54] Similarly, in the early days of Silicon Valley, it was "not uncommon for production engineers to call their friends at nearby competing firms for assistance when quartz tubes broke or they ran out of chemicals." [55] As Berkeley's Annalee Saxenian notes, "Many of these cooperative practices were simply attempts to be neighborly."[56]

50 Michael S. Malone, "John Doerr's Startup Manual," *Fast Company,* February 28, 1997, http://www.fastcompany.com/magazine/07/082doerr.html.
51 Hine, *Community,* 104.
52 Hine, *Community,* 65.
53 Hine, *Community,* 105.
54 Hine, *Community,* 108.
55 Saxenian, *Regional Advantage,* 44.
56 Ibid.

"The system works because of all the free stuff," Ade Mabogunje of Stanford once said. That free stuff might be anything: an idea given over drinks, a valuable introduction, or mentoring of an entrepreneur in a fast-changing market.[57] Think of all the free market information, patent data, how-to videos, and online tips that are easily accessible for startup companies. Stanford's President Fred Terman, who was motivated more by patriotism than financial return, played a key role in the growth of Silicon Valley when he offered licensing of Stanford's intellectual property with minimal barriers.[58] Stanford's relaxed licensing policies have helped many researchers and students pursue their entrepreneurial dreams, and more than a few have succeeded. Cisco, Sun Microsystems, Yahoo!, and Google are just a few examples. Rainforests thrive on such "free" stuff.

Interpreting the Rules

A skeptical reader might say, "These Rules are too broad. How can they possibly work in practice?" We can say that people should treat each other fairly, but at a pragmatic level, does that mean that buying 40% of a company costs $5 million or $10 million? The concept of fairness seems useless when it is too abstract.

The answer, in this case, is that it depends on the specific circumstances. In this case, the factors might include the strength of the public stock market, the valuations of acquisitions in a particular sector, the potential market size, the novelty of the technology, customer adoption speed, the source of the capital, and the quality of the team, to name a few.

The Rules of the Rainforest are like a legal foundation, but they need to be applied and interpreted. They are not that different from, say, the Bill of Rights in this manner. We do not regularly think about our right to freedom of speech, but we manifest our inherent belief in that right through our daily actions. Our freedom of speech remains intact, but its interpretation varies depending on whether we are yelling "Fire!" in an Internet forum or in a crowded theater.

---

57 See also Fukuyama, "Social Capital," 10. He notes that the informal exchange of intellectual property—like the sharing of scientific data—is essential to the creation of technology communities because "formal exchange would entail excessive transaction costs and slow down the speed of interchange." He also cites Annalee Saxenian, *Regional Advantage,* which gives numerous examples of informal intellectual property exchange in Silicon Valley.

58 C. Stewart Gillmor, Fred Terman at Stanford: *Building a Discipline, a University, and Silicon Valley* (Stanford: Stanford University Press, 2004), 154. "Stanford's patent policy in [the 1950s] differed markedly from industry and even from many peer universities in that it placed the rights, when possible, in the hands of faculty, staff, and students." See also "Secret History of Silicon Valley - Berkeley Edition. mov," YouTube video, 1:06:10, lecture by Steve Blank, posted by "techistory," March 19, 2011, http://www.youtube.com/watch?v=eajSutMIRPY&feature=player_embedded.

Similarly, the Rules of the Rainforest are manifested in real-world situations. This is a dynamic process that leads to constantly shifting interpretations. It is like the common law, the basis of our legal system in America. The common law system allows the interpretation of laws to change over time, as judges build on precedents created by prior rulings and adapt to changes in the real world. Therefore, in certain situations, buying 40% of a startup does cost $5 million, while in other situations $10 million seems perfectly fair. The participants of the Rainforest are actively interpreting the Rules all the time.[59]

The "C Factor"

If you gave a puzzle to a group of three people to solve, what factor would have the biggest influence on their ability to solve that puzzle? Their intelligence? Their motivation? Their group cohesion? The answer to this question helps us understand why the Rules matter.

Researchers at Carnegie-Mellon and MIT's Center for Collective Intelligence set out to find the answer. They were seeking to measure "collective intelligence"—the ability of a group of people working together to perform cognitive tasks. They wanted to discover what they called the "C Factor"— the variable with the strongest correlation to collective intelligence. They recently gathered 699 people and divided them into teams of two to five people. They asked these groups to work on a variety of tasks, including solving visual puzzles, brainstorming, making collective moral judgments, and negotiating over limited resources.

Their answer might be surprising, as it runs counter to conventional wisdom. They discovered that a group's ability to solve tasks is "not strongly correlated with the average or maximum individual intelligence of group members." Instead, what they found was that a group's ability to solve tasks is correlated to "the average social sensitivity of group members, the equality in distribution of conversational turn-taking, and the proportion of females in the group."[60] In other words, the quality of a group's collective output appears to depend on how effectively a group can unlock its human-

59 Mabogunje, interview (see chap. 2, n. 12). Ade has speculated whether the common law heritage of America (as opposed to the civil law heritage of other countries) facilitates the growth of innovation, as people feel empowered to interpret rules to fit evolving circumstances. The concept of the "law" in America is much more dynamic than in most countries. There is significant legal literature analyzing correlations between economic output and civil law systems (which focus on policy-implementing by states) versus common law sytems (which focus on dispute-resolving among private contracting parties). See, e.g., Rafael La Porta, Florencio Lopez-de-Silanes, and Andrei Shleifer, "The Economic Consequences of Legal Origins," *Journal of Economic Literature* 2008, 46:2, 285–332, 286, http://www.aeaweb.org/articles.php?doi??10.1257/jel.46.2.285.

60 Anita Williams Woolley, Christopher F. Chabris, Alexander Pentland, Nada Hashmi, and Thomas W. Malone, "Evidence for a Collective Intelligence Factor in the Performance of Human Groups," *Science* 330 (2010):686, DOI:10.1126/science.1193147.

to-human dynamics. The key is in the linkages, not the nodes. The way a group's members communicate and relate to one another is more important for solving problems than the inherent abilities of individual people in the group.

In another study, scientists discovered that two people achieve better answers when each person is able to communicate his level of confidence in a particular answer—not just facts and figures—with the other person.[61] This result makes sense when we think about how innovation works. Since we are never certain about the *right* answer, the best we can do is to come up with the *probable* answer. Communication—how we transfer thoughts between one another—is the connective tissue between people.

The Rules of the Rainforest work because they govern the ways in which people interact to foster communication and enhance that "C Factor." They lower the invisible social barriers that prevent people from sharing ideas, listening to each other, working together, and forging bonds of trust. It is probably not a coincidence that the Rules correlate to many of the highest human ideals. People are wired to aspire toward ideals that can generate powerful collective benefits.

The Legacy of the Frontier

If you could sit down today not in Palo Alto, but at a café in Venice, Italy, what would you see? That traditional café in Italy would be a connecting point for the people in the neighborhood to gather and exchange information, refresh daily relationships, and enjoy the companionship of old friends. The social circles in that café would be incredibly tight—hard to penetrate, but highly beneficial for its members. Howard Schultz, the CEO of Starbucks, once stated: "Coffeehouses in Italy are a third place for people, after home and work. There's a relationship of trust and confidence in that environment." [62] Schultz saw how they were "the mainstay of every Italian neighborhood."[63]

---

61 Ryota Kanai and Michael Banissy, "Are Two Heads Better Than One? It Depends," *Scientific American*, August 31, 2010, http://www.scientificamerican.com/article.cfm?id=are-two-heads-better-than.

62 Alex Witchel, "Coffee Talk With: Howard Schultz; By Way of Canarsie, One Large Hot Cup of Business Strategy," *The New York Times*, December 14, 1994, http://www.nytimes.com/1994/12/14/garden/coffee-talk-with-howard-schultz-way-canarsie-one-large-hot-cup-business-strategy.html.

63 Matt Rothman, "Into the Black," *Inc.*, January 1, 1993, http://www.inc.com/magazine/19930101/3340.html.

In contrast, if you sat down at the Café Venetia in Palo Alto, the social circles you would find would be vastly wider. You would encounter people from near and far, strangers meeting for the first time, innovators sharing information with each other or people halfway around the world through their laptops and mobile phones. You would see recruiting, experimenting, criticizing, strategizing, reading, emailing, or any number of entrepreneurial activities. You might find someone getting feedback on a business model or testing a product idea. You might notice a scientist asking an entrepreneur how they could build a company together, or an investor being pitched by a startup. You could overhear a new college graduate getting advice from a successful entrepreneur, or people who have never met each other before discussing a potential partnership. Almost anything is possible.

And the interactions would not be confined to the walls of the café. Imagine that you could see streaks of light that represent the web of human connections—like invisible Silk Roads—emanating from the Palo Alto cafe. You would see rays of light as people emailed, commented, and Skyped each other around the world, perhaps about products to be sold, employees to be hired, capital to be raised, or ideas to be pursued. That web of light would reach out and probably encompass the whole planet. Just because both cafés serve up similar types of drinks does not mean that they are serving up similar types of human relationships.

The unique properties of the social network around the café in Palo Alto are a cultural legacy inherited from the American frontier. Frederick Jackson Turner feared that the demise of the American frontier would diminish the uniquely American spirit that helped conquer it. What we have discovered, however, is that the frontier spirit lives on. We see the same individualism today in Silicon Valley—an individualism that is unfettered by tribal obligations, but is also empowered by a distinct set of norms that enable strangers to collaborate and experiment together. The Rules of the Rainforest allow them to create positive-sum games for mutual gain.

However, we are still left with a big question: given all that we understand about the invisible mechanisms of the Rainforest, how do we actually build Rainforests? In the next chapter, we lay out the "secret" recipe.

Chapter Six: How to Build a Rainforest

Sex and the Valley

I have seen a medicine
That's able to breathe life into a stone,
Quicken a rock, and make you dance canary
With spritely fire and motion...

— **Shakespeare,** ***All's Well That Ends Well*** **(II.1.72-75)**

Banking on Innovation

It was June 27, 2011, and Al Watkins was feeling rather happy. After 24 years at the World Bank, he was being toasted upon his impending retirement at the early age of 62, a milestone that was mandated by the rules of the institution. Six years before, Al had been appointed by the former President of the Bank, James Wolfsensohn, to serve as the institution's leader on issues of science, technology, and innovation.

On that day in June, he had organized a luncheon for the Chief Scientist of Israel. Many of Al's colleagues surprised him by treating the event as his valedictory. They spoke warmly about his numerous contributions over the years. They honored his insights and wisdom. They talked about his key role defining the World Bank's agenda on innovation and serving as the World Bank's main window to the global scientific community. Then, as Al humorously describes, they "thanked me for my service and then announced that they are happily continuing without me."[1]

When Al first joined the World Bank in 1987, the institution was notably different than it was on that day in 2011. The original aim of the World Bank—started in the aftermath of World War II to reconstruct devastated countries—was to finance the building of the hard assets of economic growth. These hard assets included things like roads, bridges, buildings, electrical systems, railroads, oil pipelines, and the like. For a global development *bank* to structure the financing for such arrangements was not a difficult conceptual leap. There was a sovereign guarantee for the debt, and the risk to the bank as a preferred creditor could be measured and controlled to a reasonable degree in a broad portfolio.[2]

Over time, the countries that were seeking World Bank assistance started to ask for new types of help. They were not just seeking hard infrastructure assistance; they were now seeking technical assistance to help build new types of "soft infrastructure," including connections between universities and businesses, research institutes, training engineers, and technology commercialization programs.[3] The Bank helped foster many of these efforts around the world in the 1970s and 1980s, including programs in Spain and South Korea.[4]

1 Al Watkins, e-mail to author, June 27, 2011.

2 Al Watkins, telephone interview with author, July 21, 2011.

3 Alfred Watkins and Joshua Mandell, "Global Forum Action Plan: Science, Technology and Innovation Building Partnerships for Sustainable Development," Science, Technology, and Innovation (STI) Group, World Bank, Washington, DC., September 1, 2010.

4 World Bank, Report No. 12138, "Bank Lending for Industrial Technology Development Vols I and II," June 30, 1993.

The models for these programs were a function of their time. They were designed to help large companies find technologies from elsewhere in the world and adapt them for local implementation. These companies were massive, vertically-integrated enterprises—many state-owned or state-supported—that had the ability to transfer new technologies all the way from concept to marketplace, like a virtual assembly line.

Al describes, "The system was designed to help these guys catch up. The notion of innovation was to help them learn technologies that already existed."[5] For instance, the World Bank supported these efforts by sending thousands of engineers to study proven technologies at schools in the United States.[6] The automotive and electronics industries in Japan are good examples of the success of these models.

Today, however, the situation is vastly different. As Al notes, "The world has changed, so the strategies that worked in the 1970s are not so relevant anymore."[7] Emerging economies can no longer depend on large, vertically-integrated companies to commercialize new technologies. State-owned businesses have largely been privatized. Nations still train engineers, but they no longer feel it is sufficient for technology development. Governments are increasingly seeking to spur entrepreneurial activity across the entire system, not just for large companies. Today, countries are ambitiously seeking to create entire innovation economies.

In this chapter, we shift our perspective again. We take off our anthropologist hat, and we put on our business administrator hat. We look at how to manage complex human systems from the perspective of leaders charged with that responsibility. What are the practical tools to build Rainforests, why do these tools work, and how do we implement them?

The Price of Trust

Developmental institutions, governments, and corporations are looking for answers to these questions. Our own work at T2 Venture Capital has taken us from small town halls to national sovereign governments to multilateral global institutions, all of them dealing with the same frustrations and lack of effective tools. These challenges are certainly not of the same stripe as investing in physical infrastructure projects or working with vertically-integrated companies. "The vertical structure imposed its own logic on the system," observes Al. "Now, developing countries don't have those, so you have to operate in a different world."[8]

---

5 Al Watkins, interview.

6 Ibid.

7 Ibid.

8 Ibid.

Al wondered how an institution like the World Bank could enhance economic activity by utilizing the technical knowledge that was scattered across the globe.[9] He remembers, "I observed how Russian scientists were so isolated from the rest of the world, and I realized that the key was to help those scientists make links to the outside world to export that knowledge. And in developing markets, like in sub-Saharan Africa, I realized that the key was to help people make links to import knowledge to be applied to solve local problems. The answer in both cases, however, was the same: to help isolated people get connected."

One informative story stands out from Al Watkins' tenure at the World Bank. He was leading the Bank's effort to put together a deal between a sovereign government and a major multinational corporation. It was a way to connect innovative, high-technology products with customers who were willing to pay for them. As a result, many scientists and engineers would remain gainfully employed and would start to learn the art of customer service. The deal made a lot of sense. After years of effort and the commitment of many millions of dollars, the deal was about to close.

And then suddenly it was falling apart. The only solution Al could find was highly counter-intuitive and controversial—he got the World Bank to pay for the other side to hire a blue-chip law firm to negotiate directly against the World Bank. Al recalls:

> People said this had never been done before. Nobody had ever used World Bank money to hire a lawyer to negotiate against the World Bank. But, in the end, it gave the other side the confidence to go forward with the deal. They were afraid they were going to get screwed because there was an imbalance of power. They felt that the fact that they couldn't see the trap just meant it was well hidden, not that it wasn't there. Until people feel that their interests are going to be protected, it's very hard to do a deal.

In the end, the whole thing boiled down to trust. The World Bank had to pay a price to gain the trust of the other side. The biggest invisible bottleneck in innovation is not necessarily the economic desirability of a project, the quality of the technology, or the rational willingness of the customer. The real cost frequently boils down to the social distance between two vastly different parties. As Al Watkins learned in his tenure at the World Bank, if you can bridge that social distance, there is great economic value to be realized.

And if you can replicate those bridges across an entire system, the potential value can be astronomical. Al jokingly refers to this as "Sex and the Valley."

---

9 Watkins and Mandell, Global Forum Action Plan.

Promiscuity—in an economic sense—facilitates innovation and cultivates new ideas and new connections. As he observes, "Chance encounters often turn out to be the most fruitful connections, although they are not the neat and orderly connections that you would generate if you were planning to connect people in a more systematic, less promiscuous fashion."

The Power of Decentralization

The evolution in Al Watkins' thinking is validated by the mathematics of Rainforests. In the past, governments would try to spur innovation primarily through a traditional model of business assistance based on "First Derivative" thinking we described in the prior chapter. It is a "heavy lifting" model that makes the agency the primary "do-er."

You can see examples of this model in the way most American universities operate their technology transfer offices, the way many governments have supported technology commercialization, and the way some major corporations think of venture development. An example of such an approach might look like this:

Traditional "First Derivative" Approach

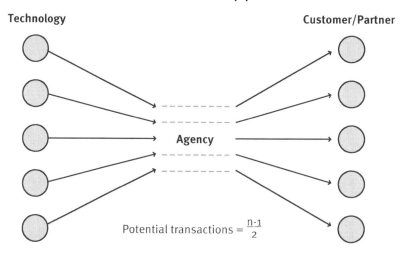

Technology   Customer/Partner

Agency

Potential transactions $= \frac{n\text{-}1}{2}$

A central agency serves to broker transactions between technologists, on the left side, and customers or partners, on the right side. But there are limits to this approach. Mathematically, an agency-led effort to boost innovation can never yield greater than (n-1) divided by 2 economic transactions, where n is the number of nodes in the social network. The system as a whole must pay for the costs of that agency, and many of those costs are highly variable.

They depend on the distance between parties, the amount of trust in the system, and the influence the agency wields.

Perhaps most importantly, the moment that the agency in the middle is no longer there, the entire process grinds to a halt. The system is, in effect, a form of centrally-planned economic activity that is not fundamentally different from a Soviet-style system. Without subsidies, it dies. The centralized, linear approach can be a useful first step—as it was in Japan or South Korea in the 1970s—but over time, this approach is rarely sustainable.

This path can become an endless cash drain for a government, university, or corporation. And when people stop and ask "Why is it still not working?" the most common traditional answer is "You need to keep doing more of it and for longer." We have participated in numerous conferences where intelligent people are told that the answer is to increase commitments and to never give up. As the saying goes, insanity is doing the same thing over and over again and expecting different results.

Innovation is chaotic, serendipitous, and uncontrollable, so processes that are linear and controlled are rarely self-sustaining. In contrast, what we strive for in a Rainforest is a system that yields immense impact, is low-cost, and generates internal sustainability. The only possible way to achieve these goals is to build a community of innovators where transaction costs have been reduced through the creation of trust, social norms, connectivity, and diversity. This model is based on what we call the "Third Derivative." In a perfect world, the total potential relationships in such a system might look like this, what mathematicians call a *complete graph*:

Rainforest "Third Derivative" Approach

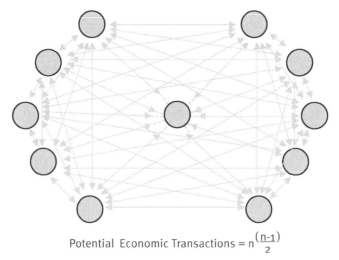

$$\text{Potential Economic Transactions} = n\frac{(n\text{-}1)}{2}$$

Every party can mix, mingle, and potentially transact with every other party. Such a perfectly efficient network would help people access the right expertise, customers, partners, and capital without the rigid and limited role of a central agency. It is a more decentralized "social network" model in which the agency serves as the experienced facilitator and connector, not the sole or primary "do-er," and helps to create social trust and social norms. Mathematically, the number of potential economic transactions skyrockets by *n times* greater than that of the centralized approach.

What is the difference in impact between these two approaches? If we consider that each community has a large number of latent potential 1+1>2 transactions, several potential 1+1=10 transactions, and a handful of potential 1+1=100 transactions, then the more such transactions we can foster, the greater the economic output of the entire system. We believe this model is a more accurate reflection of the underlying mechanisms of real-world communities like Silicon Valley, with keystones serving as the agents that catalyze such system-wide effects. In a perfect Rainforest, every relationship has the potential to become a transaction. While no network is perfectly efficient in real life, a Rainforest aspires to treat each potential relationship as a genuine possibility for mutual gain.

To build sustainable Rainforests, therefore, we need to create environments that foster as many self-generating economic transactions as possible, rather than going through the strenuous process of custom-creating every economic transaction one at a time. A linear development model will never yield more than a linear output from the system:

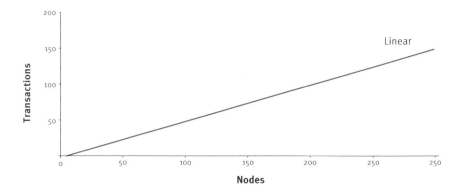

The Rainforest development model, on the other hand, attempts to catalyze a universe of possible transactions. Even if such a system is only able to realize a tiny percentage of its potential, it vastly outperforms the linear system. In the graph below, the flat line indicates the traditional linear development model, the steepest line represents the Rainforest model at

100% efficiency, another line shows the Rainforest model at 5% efficiency, and another line is the Rainforest model at 1% efficiency:

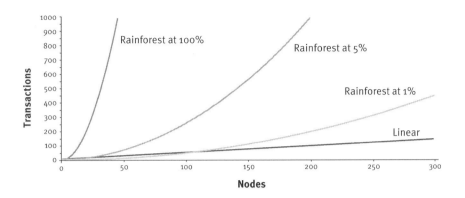

If we extend the x-axis even further, we see the powerful effects when the number of nodes starts to grow beyond a few hundred:

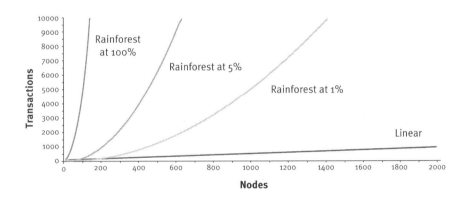

We do not need a Rainforest to be anywhere near perfect efficiency in order to realize its economic impact.

The question then becomes: can such systems be created where they do not exist today? This question is as relevant in America's heartland as it is a sub-Saharan village. Additionally, as Al Watkins might ask, how can we transition an economic system that is based on the linear model—whether in Japan, South Korea, Taiwan, Malaysia, or many other places—to a decentralized Rainforest model? To answer these questions, we need a recipe for the Rainforest.

Managing a Rainforest

W. Edwards Deming was not always a quintessential management icon. He was once just a nerdy statistics consultant and professor. As the Japanese economy recovered from World War II, Deming was invited by the U.S. Army in 1947 to advise the Japanese government in preparation for its 1951 census.[10] Deming accepted the opportunity. He had developed the sampling methods used in the 1940 U.S. census, and hoped his knowledge of statistical process control might be useful in post-war Japan. For a statistician, Deming was not a timid soul.

Eventually, Deming was invited by the Japanese Union of Scientists and Engineers to teach his methods and ideas to numerous Japanese managers and engineers. The knowledge that his students gained from those lectures, the first series of which ran from June through August 1950, were subsequently applied to Japanese industries and produced transformative results. For decades, Deming was almost entirely unnoticed in the U.S. even as he observed companies like Mitsubishi, Nissan, Toyota, and Sony become world leaders in quality and profitability. Then, an NBC television special in 1980 profiled his key role in Japan's development. Deming soon became a star.

What can Deming teach us about how to "manage" a Rainforest? The notion that corporate management concepts can be applied to an entire economic system seems odd at first blush. However, if great minds have spent decades studying how to better manage companies, then wouldn't it make sense to apply some of the best ideas from managerial science to the "management" of Rainforests? After all, aren't they both just networks of human beings? Indeed, a better question might be: why *can't* we manage Rainforests?

We believe that we can. Companies and Rainforests are made of the same atomic building blocks—people—and they both seek the same goal of increased economic output. Looking closely, we find both striking similarities and profound differences between managing a traditional business and building a Rainforest.

---

10 Various histories of Deming's life are available, and we have extracted bits and pieces of information from general sources. For more information see Mary Walton, *The Deming Management Method* (U.K.: Penguin, 1986), 3-21.

Deming developed a comprehensive philosophy for managing successful companies. His core ideas focused on the company as a system geared towards maximizing the quality of its output. To manage a Rainforest, we follow concepts that both resemble and differ from Deming:

Deming	Rainforest
Appreciate individuals as vital parts of a system, not just as "bits and pieces."[11]	Appreciate individuals as vital parts of the Rainforest, not just as "bits and pieces."
A "constancy of purpose" for the entire system, so that all individuals could work toward that common purpose through "continual improvement."[12]	Do not import a top-down purpose on the Rainforest, but set individuals free to pursue their own dreams based on extra-rational motivations.
Quality control should expect "common causes" of variation, but not "special causes" of variation.[13]	Innovation is discontinuous and should tolerate a large amount of error and failure.
Reduce corporate barriers—whether bureaucratic, misaligned incentives, or otherwise—that prevent individuals from striving for the overall output of the system.[14]	Reduce social barriers—whether physical, psychological, emotional, transactional, or otherwise—that prevent individuals or teams from connecting to pursue mutual gain. Social norms and trust are encouraged to reduce barriers.
Transform individuals who "get it" into role models for others in the system.[15]	Transform individuals who "get it" into role models for others in the Rainforest.

The Deming philosophy and the Rainforest philosophy are in fact two sides of the same coin. They both emphasize cultural transformation, not just tinkering with a few gears here and there. Deming says to "drive out fear"; the Rainforest says to "tolerate errors." Deming wants to reduce adversarial relationships; the Rainforest wants to build trust and fairness. Deming considers the most important things (with the greatest potential impact) to

---

11 W. Edwards Deming, *The New Economics: For Industry, Government, Education* (Cambridge: The MIT Press, 1994), 57. We have selected various key concepts from Deming to highlight the similarities and differences between the Deming approach and the Rainforest approach. Deming loyalists will accept our apologies for the need to simplify the nuance and complexity of Deming's work for our purposes here.

12 Ibid., 24, 41, 51.

13 Ibid., 174, 208-226.

14 Ibid., 64.

15 Ibid., 92-93.

be unknowable; the Rainforest wants its weeds to flourish—because their unplanned results can be more valuable than those of the farmed crops.

However, whereas Deming encourages normal variation and rates of defect, the Rainforest expects serendipity and frequent failure. Deming's ideal company strives to give people their "pride of workmanship"; the Rainforest works to encourage extra-rational motivations and allows people to pursue their dreams.

The two models are used at different points in the management life cycle. The Deming framework applies to existing companies trying to scale up manufacturing of defined products with ongoing revenue streams, like a plantation. In contrast, the Rainforest framework applies for the "soup" of human beings that exist in the beginning, usually before a product is defined, before revenue is realized, and perhaps even before a company or team is formed at all. We can visualize the complete management life cycle as the interplay between the systems of Deming and the Rainforest.[16]

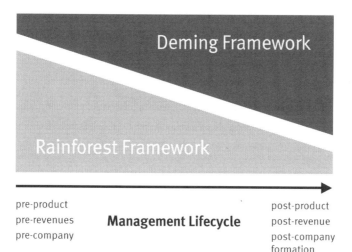

pre-product
pre-revenues   **Management Lifecycle**   post-product
pre-company   post-revenue
                                                 post-company
                                                 formation

As a company grows, it usually makes sense to tilt its management techniques from Rainforest to Deming. That said, even a mature company needs innovative new products, and even nascent companies need to think about improving quality and operational efficiency. A black-and-white approach to management does not work sustainably. For example, Berkeley researcher Annalee Saxenian has described how Silicon Valley semiconductor companies lost their innovative edge in the 1980s when

---

16 As Beinhocker notes in The *Origin of Wealth*, 355-356 (see introduction, n. 3.), the dichotomy between innovation and execution has been observed by various writers. Tom Peters and Bob Waterman, *In Search of Excellence* (New York: Harper & Row, 1982) (organizations must be "tight" in executing and "loose" in adapting); Dick Foster and Sarah Kaplan, *Creative Destruction* (New York: Broadway Business, 2001) (balance between "operating" and "innovating").

they shifted to "mass production as a natural and inevitable stage of their industry's maturation."[17]

Innovation by nature is generated at the "atomic level" where it is driven by serendipity, but it is harvested with "classical tools" where one strives for statistical exactitude. The classical tools of harvesting innovation consist of traditional "MBA topics" and include studies like operational management, financial accounting, and market analysis. The tools for generating innovation are "softer" ones, but they are no less important because they are invisible, intangible, and harder to quantify. As Henry Doss, a management expert and former senior bank executive, says, "One cannot create innovation efficiently using classical tools. Simultaneously, one cannot harvest innovation efficiently at an atomic level."

A simple way to demonstrate this is by comparing what Deming faced decades ago in Japan to the situation we encounter today when building a Rainforest. Deming introduced this flow diagram—"on the blackboard at every conference with top management in 1950 and onward"—as a tool to help Japanese managers turn their companies around:[18]

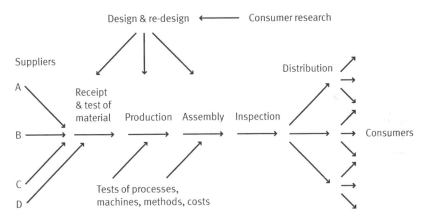

In contrast, when someone builds a new startup in a Rainforest, this diagram cannot even be drawn usefully. There are few or none of the right people identified, nor are there processes for connecting those people. There is merely a collection of individuals floating in a more or less random soup. If we take the Deming flow diagram and blow apart the individual atoms, we would end up with something like this, where the interconnecting processes do not even exist:

---

17 Saxenian, *Regional Advantage*, 81 (see chap. 2, n. 24).
18 Deming, *The New Economics*, 57-58.

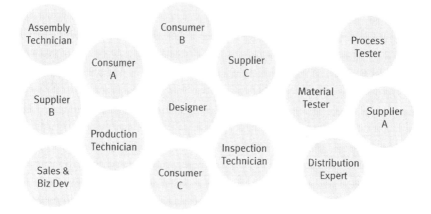

In a real startup situation, one could easily imagine even more atoms in this fragmented soup. Before there is a company to optimize (a la Deming), there are people who need to be brought together (a la Rainforest).

We surmise that one of the major reasons large corporations often fail at innovation—whether they create venture arms, new product divisions, or otherwise—is because they typically create new business divisions in a formal sense without the "cultural walls" separating the Deming and the Rainforest communities. A mature company that wishes to foster both the high quality encouraged by Deming and the disruptive innovation emerging from a Rainforest should enable both environments to exist simultaneously, while consciously and methodically maintaining their distinct cultures.

3DM, Part I: Third Derivative Management

The ideas of W. Edwards Deming make for interesting reading and lectures. However, it was not until those ideas were turned into a practical framework that things really took off. That framework—Total Quality Management—has become one of the most popular corporate management techniques in the world. Real-world companies can apply this framework to measure themselves and then make changes to improve productivity. In 1988, the U.S. government began to give the Malcolm Baldridge National Quality Award to companies that exemplified the TQM model, which was largely derived from what Deming had taught the Japanese many decades before.

As the Deming philosophy gave rise to TQM, we propose a parallel management system based on the Rainforest philosophy. We call it 3DM—Third Derivative Management—because its purpose is to transform an entire system by changing its culture. 3DM provides a tool to help diagnose, measure, and affect changes in human networks to transform them into Rainforests.

The elements of 3DM must include not only the "traditional Commandments" that focus on building human capacity and reducing artificial restraints, but also emphasize the removal of constraints that affect how people interrelate, collaborate, and transact with one another. The model has the effect of increasing social friction among diverse individuals while also providing mechanisms for the dissipation of that social friction. 3DM helps transform culture by encouraging the behaviors that accelerate creative reassembly.

The first step in 3DM is to map an innovation ecosystem in a region, community, company, or other human network. In our work, we have developed a Rainforest Canvas to ensure that we are asking the right questions. Here, we provide you a version that includes some of the questions we ask, plus one that is blank for you to use as a practical worksheet.

The Rainforest Canvas

T3 VENTURE CAPITAL

Leaders:
- Who has the reputation, resources and commitment to lead new initiatives?
- Who will champion new initiatives within their own organizations?
- How can leaders and champions be more inclusive?

Resources:
- What resources are available to aspiring entrepreneurs?
- What sources of capital are there in the marketplace?
- How does this capital flow and interact with growing businesses?
- What is the volume and quality of talent in the labor pool?
- What are the main sources of innovative ideas/discoveries/inventions?
- What resources are available to service and support organizations that interact with entrepreneurs?

Infrastructure, Capability & Community:
- What is the density and quality of service providers?
- What boundary spanning organizations exist?
- What is the local level of serial entrepreneurship?

Stakeholders:
- Who are the entrepreneurs?
- Who are the stakeholders?
- Who are the inventors?
- Who are the capital providers?
- Who are the support organizations?

Activities:
- What are people already doing to stimulate innovation?
- How are these people collaborating with each other?
- What activities drive participation in the community?
- What events create "buzz" and generate interest?

Infrastructure, Capability & Community:
- What is the density and quality of service of physical infrastructure?
- What are the core sectors of the local economy?
- What are the strongest regional comparative advantages?

Engagement:
- Where, when and how do stakeholders interact?
- How do ideas, talent and capital come together?
- What are the lines of communication between partners?
- How do members of the community collaborate with each other?
- How does the community engage external or global partners?
- How does the community encourage/recruit new constituents?
- How do young people get involved?
- What forums exist that allow the breakdown of social and professional hierarchies?

Culture:
- Where do people come from?
- What are their value systems?
- What are their motivations?
- What are the 'amenities of place'?
- How do we create and maintain a sense of urgency?

Frameworks:
- What is the regulatory environment for innovation?
- What legal/bureaucratic barriers stand in the way of entrepreneurship?
- What widespread social norms surround the innovation ecosystem?

Stakeholders:
- What is the role of government?
- Who are the other key participants in the innovation ecosystem?

Role Models:
- Who are the local entrepreneurs that have built successful companies?
- Who are the local entrepreneurs that haven't yet been successful and what can we learn from their failures?
- What regions have similar attributes and resources?
- What organizations have shared visions/values?
- Are there other regions with successful innovation ecosystems that we could learn from or emulate?

Culture:
- What kind of innovation social networks exist already?
- How do people deal with uncertainty, risk and randomness?
- How is failure perceived?
- Do people build for perfection or iteration?

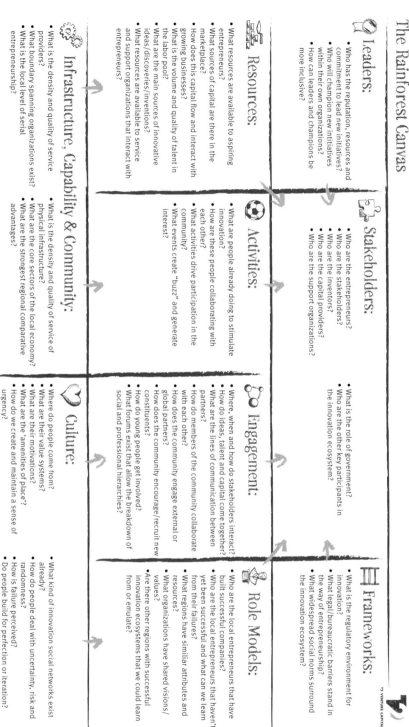

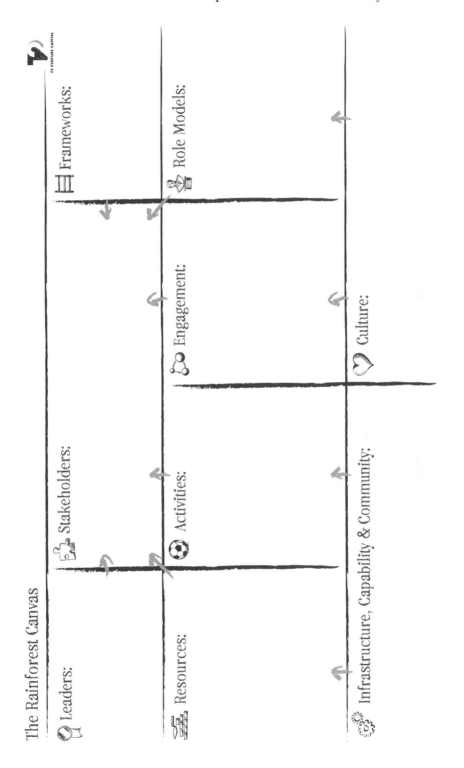

The Rainforest Canvas

T2 VENTURE CAPITAL

Leaders:

Stakeholders:

Frameworks:

Resources:

Activities:

Engagement:

Role Models:

Infrastructure, Capability & Community:

Culture:

Once we have mapped out what an ecosystem looks like, the next step in 3DM is to apply the Rainforest Recipe to devise solutions that can close gaps in the ecosystem. This recipe attempts to capture the various ideas discussed in the book so far:

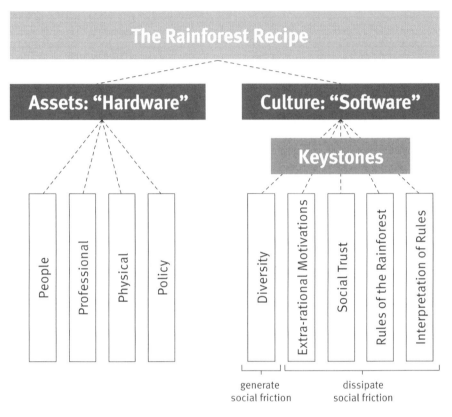

The left side of the Recipe is like the "hardware" of a Rainforest (its basic underlying framework), while the right side is like its "software" (what makes it come alive). The software, as Shakespeare might say, "breathes life into the stone" of the hardware.

3DM, Part II: The Hardware

The left side of the Rainforest Recipe is the equivalent of the traditional "Commandments" of innovation. They are necessary, but not sufficient for innovation to thrive. On this side, we can point to four key pillars—the 4 P's—that constitute the infrastructure required for innovators: people, professional, physical, and policy.[19] These pillars are basic preconditions for a Rainforest—like water, air, and soil. Our questions at this stage might include the following:

- **People.** What is the quality of the *educational systems* in place, including primary, secondary, and higher education, job training, and skills transfer mechanisms? What are the strengths of the *scientific research and development* base and the novelty of the technologies being produced? What technologies are accessible from elsewhere? How vibrant and talented is the base of *entrepreneurs and managers* in a community? Who are the *integrative leaders* who have influence and impact and can become keystones? How strong is the overall pipeline of *knowledge workers*, and how integrated is the workforce development strategy?

- **Professional**. What is the health and engagement of the broader *business service provider* industry surrounding the innovation process (including bankers, accountants, lawyers, real estate brokers and landlords, executive recruiters, consultants, and others)? How robust and engaged are the *trade organizations, professional groups, and civic associations* that touch the innovation process, particularly those groups that cross traditional social boundaries to create new forms of social affiliation? Who invests directly in innovative ventures, whether *individual angels, institutional venture capital, corporate/ strategic capital, or government-sponsored proof-of-concept funds*, and how well are individuals who manage such funds connected in a continuum of capital? Which institutions invest or might be willing to invest indirectly in innovation as *limited partners* in other funds? What *academic institutions and networks* exist to connect professors, researchers, and students so they can work collaboratively? What *media organizations and journalists* touch upon the innovation process and are able to disseminate information? How integrated are all these groups through collaborations, partnerships, alliances, and other mechanisms?

19 Various frameworks assess the "hardware" of innovation, perhaps the best of which is Soumitra Dutta, ed. "The Global Innovation Index 2011: Accelerating Growth and Development," INSEAD, Fontainebleau, France, 2011.

- **Physical.** Are the *communication and information networks* robust enough to support the efficient flow of knowledge and ideas? Are other infrastructure networks, such as *energy and transportation*, strong enough to support the effective movement of people and goods?

- **Policy.** How effectively do the *legal and regulatory systems* support the free flow of people, goods, ideas, and knowledge through legal protections that ensure freedom of movement, freedom of speech/press, reduced corruption and bureaucracy, and legal enforcement/due process? How strong is the *policy support of business* through laws governing freedom of contract/labor, protection of property rights, taxation, immigration, and reduction of government barriers? What *financial systems* are in place to support the availability of credit, flexibility in capital formation, and efficiency of capital flows? How reasonable are the barriers to convert privately-held securities into publicly-tradable securities via *initial public offerings*?

3DM, Part III: The Software

After we invested in one of our startup companies, Somark Innovations, its founders decided to move the company from its original home in St. Louis to a new home in California. This caused some discontent in St. Louis. The company had been a darling of the community, winning numerous prizes and the Federal SBA Young Entrepreneur of the Year award. Many people were saddened by its departure. The founding CEO, Mark Pydynowski, was asked by the St. Louis business community to explain why the company had moved.

Mark's answer touched a little bit on the asset infrastructure of St. Louis. But primarily, his concerns were about the culture. He explained that, in St. Louis, law firms were unwilling to share risks with young startups by deferring fees, venture investors were not open to coaching young entrepreneurs, technical talent was scared by the idea of accepting equity in lieu of some salary, and relationships with customers and partners were hard for a startup to develop, among other things. The culture of St. Louis, he felt, did not reward the type of behavior that was necessary for his startup to grow:

> When discussing failed startups with St. Louis investors, they seemed to label the founders with a Scarlet Letter. When I had the same discussion with similar investors on the coasts, they seemed to label founders with the Purple Heart. I am still perplexed by the stark contrast.[20]

---

20 Mark Pydynowski, personal interview with author, June 3, 2011.

Most of the world faces the same type of quandary as St. Louis: what can regions possibly do about culture? Conventional wisdom says we cannot do much. The "tyranny of the prevailing style of management" (as Deming would say) has little to offer. [21]

We should be able to do better. The right side of the Rainforest Recipe deals with the cultural "software" of building Rainforests. At the top of the diagram are keystones. Keystone individuals and keystone institutions are the agents that do the work of Rainforest culture. Below the keystones are five pillars. Although people are naturally separated by social barriers...

...these five pillars help lower those barriers. *Diversity* increases interactions between people, as they communicate across barriers. *Extra-Rational Motivations* give people positive reasons to talk. *Social Trust, the Rules,* and *Interpretation of the Rules* reach over the barriers, so that people can collaborate and transact with one another. Here are some questions we might examine in assessing these pillars:

- **Diversity**. How diverse are the people in a system, particularly when you assess the numbers of people who bring specialized insights, expertise, experience, relationships, and know-how? How frequently do significantly diverse people "bump into" each other? Are people collaborative or secretive? Are customers talking with inventors, engineers, entrepreneurs? Is the private sector engaged early—pre-transaction—to validate proof-of-customer relevance for new ideas? Diversity includes people with domain knowledge, as well as market, business, finance, management, and other skills that help startups grow. Diversity is not necessarily based on traditional characteristics like gender, race, ethnicity, and religion, but it doesn't exclude them either. Diversity can also include non-traditional measurements, such as the number of people with varying fields of scientific expertise or business experience (e.g., the value of crossing skills between wireless technology engineers and health care researchers).

- **Extra-Rational Motivations.** How many people are in the innovation business for reasons that go beyond the traditional motivations of the "economic rational actor?" These might include people seeking competition, challenge, novelty, adventure, legacy, or opportunities

---

21 Deming, *The New Economics,* Preface xv.

for altruism. Is there a critical mass of validation and encouragement from peer support networks for having extra-rational motivations as a legitimate reason to pursue a goal?

- **General Social Trust.** How well do people, particularly strangers, trust each other across social boundaries? The levels of trust among members of an innovation community are frequently a microcosm of their society as a whole. To what extent do unconstructive societal habits such as cynicism, zero-sum game mentality, and defections from Prisoner's Dilemma games infect the people who are involved in innovation?

- **Rules of the Rainforest.** How robust are the social norms in a community? How well do they build and maintain trust among innovators?

  » **Break Rules and Dream.** What is a community's willingness to violate and/or rewrite conventions (rebellion)? What is the willingness to accept dreams (vision) as legitimate ends? What is the willingness to accept dreamers (visionaries) as legitimate messengers? What is a group's propensity to accept the validity of extra-rational motivations and promote their legitimacy to others?

  » **Open Doors and Listen.** Does the community value how individuals intermingle with one another, particularly across social boundaries? How often is the participation of people in networking events organized around non-traditional social categories? What is the speed and the number of referrals and connections between strangers from disparate social groups? How open-minded to diversity is a community—which can range from basic tolerance, to political correctness, to overt welcoming of different people? Is there a willingness to accept social friction as a potential positive force? Does a community value listening over speaking (which promotes the "diffusion and absorption of knowledge")? Does a community demonstrate a willingness to listen to customers and solve their problems?

  » **Trust and Be Trusted.** Are people willing to take the initiative to trust others? Does a community create alternative proxies for trust (e.g., professional affiliations, referrals, respected brands, common motivations)? How does a community demonstrate the transparency of its motivations as part of its routine transactions? Does a community demonstrate the ability to speak transparently without creating conflict between parties?

» **Experiment and Iterate Together**. How active is networking activity? Are people willing to try innovative experiments together (e.g., test proof-of-concept, proof-of-market)? Are people willing to build for iteration, rather than build for perfection? What is the overall speed of iteration? Does a community value action over delay? Does leadership recognize that experimentation comes from the bottom up, not the top down?

» **Seek Fairness, Not Advantage**. When making collaborative transactions, are parties willing to sacrifice some of their immediate self-interest in order to enhance their long-term self-interest? To what extent have precedents for fairness become routine in a system (e.g., fair valuations for angel or venture capital investments)? Do participants demonstrate humility in realizing that they cannot "do it alone"? Do people recognize that respect must be earned through continuous action and that traditional hierarchies of seniority, wealth, power, tribe, etc. are not as relevant?

» **Err, Fail, and Persist**. Is there social tolerance for mistakes and failure as part of a normal course of doing business? Are participants tolerant of the routine ups and downs of entrepreneurial innovation? Are they comfortable with uncertainty and the idea that innovation is governed by probability, not perfectibility? Does a peer support network exist to help people through challenging times?

» **Pay It Forward**. Are people generally willing to help others without expecting to get paid back? Is there an abundance of people willing to mentor or coach others who are entering the game? To what extent are participants pro-actively making referrals to help others expand their networks?

• **Interpretation of the Rules.** Does a community demonstrate flexibility to adapt its interpretation of the Rules to changing circumstances? Does a community have the ability to punish violators of the social norms (e.g., social feedback mechanisms, whether through tight social networks that affect reputation, cutting off future deal flow, online reviews or active blogging, etc.)? Are there positive mechanisms to drive collective intelligence (e.g., open communication of opinions, horizontal hierarchies, willingness to listen to the opinions of many people in a group, etc.)?

3DM is a tool—in the humble footsteps of Deming and TQM—that allows us to diagnose the strengths and weaknesses of a system, leverage the strengths, and implement targeted efforts to overcome the weaknesses. 3DM incorporates the hard assets of innovation and the soft tissue that connects those assets into what we consider "culture." Taken as a whole, 3DM integrates a community's hardware and software to maximize the output of the whole system.

The Rainforest Tools

We have seen the best minds of a generation of economists, dragging themselves through arcane formulae looking for fixes to the world's ills. For instance, we recently listened to a detailed presentation by a former Minister of Finance talking about his nation's macroeconomy during the Great Recession. In the middle of his speech, we started to feel sorry for him. It was not because he wasn't smart—he was extraordinarily sharp. It was not because he was saying anything wrong—his analysis was absolutely correct.

It was because we realized that he and his peers in the field of macroeconomics have so little control over events. All they can do is watch their macroeconomic indicators happen in slow motion, like someone watching two cars about to collide and who is completely helpless to do anything about it. Macroeconomists have two levers they can pull to influence economic activity: fiscal policy (how much a country spends) and monetary policy (how much money a country prints). Other than that, their best tool is often just prayer.

3DM attempts to provide new levers that a leader—whether a Minister or a corporate CEO—can pull to increase innovation-based economic output. So, what is the therapy for building a Rainforest culture?[22] Rather than thinking like macroeconomists, to change behavior, we must think like psychiatrists. And instead of treating individuals, we must work with communities. We have already described how the Rainforest of Silicon Valley emerged from the beliefs and attitudes of the American frontier. The process was unintentional, organic. It might be described in this way:[23]

Beliefs > Attitudes > Behaviors

---

22 Sunstein, "Social Norms," 23 (see chap. 5, n. 5). Professor Cass Sunstein would call leaders seeking to build Rainforests *"norm entrepreneurs*—people interested in changing social norms". He says that successful normative change requires the use of *norm bandwagons* and *norm cascades.*

23 Thanks to Ade Mabogunje and Mark Nelson for this helpful way of framing the reversal process.

If we want to create new Rainforests, however, we need to reverse that process. We have to intentionally create systems that usually occur organically. The reverse might be described this way:

Behaviors › Attitudes › Beliefs

We build Rainforests by shaping the outward behavior of innovators. Over time, those behaviors can create changes in attitude, and eventually, the changes in attitude can lead to changes in beliefs. We cannot simply start with the Rules of the Rainforest. *We need to start with the behaviors that embody the Rules.*

We can think of building Rainforests as a version of *cognitive behavioral therapy.* Cognitive behavioral therapy (CBT) is a validated way to change human behavior through a process of real world interaction, helping people link actions, thoughts and feelings. The clinical track record of CBT is strong, and it is used today for treating a variety of mental conditions.[24]

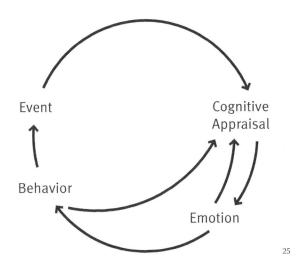

25

---

24 Aaron T. Beck, "The Current State of Cognitive Therapy: A 40-Year Retrospective," *Archives of General Psychiatry,* Vol. 62, 953-959 (2005), 953-954.

25 Wright, Jesse H., M.R. Basco, and M.E. Thase, *Learning Cognitive-Behavior Therapy: An Illustrated Guide* (Washington: American Psychiatric Publishing, 2006), 5.

CBT works by correcting what psychologists call *cognitive distortion.* Cognitive distortion happens when we interpret actions of others through biased lenses, as we described in Chapter 4. This distorted processing of information is an obstacle when we build Rainforests because it creates significant social transaction costs. CBT helps people confront cognitive distortions, challenges them to consider alternative views, and helps them adopt new behaviors (*cognitive restructuring*). We cannot make people change their feelings, but we can provide them with a way to interpret facts differently and then change their actions. CBT reinforces certain behaviors through a process of "collaborative empiricism," in which people are coached to evaluate their behaviors and emotions objectively, test out actions in real situations, and make revisions iteratively, just as scientists test hypotheses with experiments.[26] Over time, the brain's patterns of behavior can be rewired through self-awareness and real-world validation of certain behaviors as opposed to other behaviors. Thus, CBT helps people learn actions that achieve more positive outcomes in their social interactions.

The CBT model is useful for thinking about how we can build Rainforests. Evidence shows that CBT can be applied to groups, perhaps even more effectively than with individuals.[27] To do so, leaders can develop hands-on programs where people are actually "doing innovation" (such as building startup companies) with diverse partners. In these programs, the goal is to create environments of trust where people learn behaviors from role models and peers, and then help them test those behaviors in real life, based on social feedback and the application of social norms. The process might be depicted like this:

---

26 Peter J. Bieling, Randi E. McCabe, and Martin M. Antony, *Cognitive-Behavioral Therapy in Groups* (New York: Guilford Press, 2006), 46; and Jesse H. Wright, "Cognitive Behavior Therapy: Basic Principles and Recent Advances," *FOCUS (Psychiatry Online)*, Spring 2006, Vol. IV, No. 2 (pp. 173-178), http://focus.psychiatryonline.org/data/Journals/FOCUS/2634/173.pdf.

27 John R. White, Arthur S. Freeman (editors), *Cognitive-Behavioral Group Therapy for Specific Problems and Populations* (Washington: American Psychological Association, 2000), xi. "We have seen over and over that a group's capacity for adaptive response usually exceeds the ability of those same individuals to undertake adaptation while by themselves."

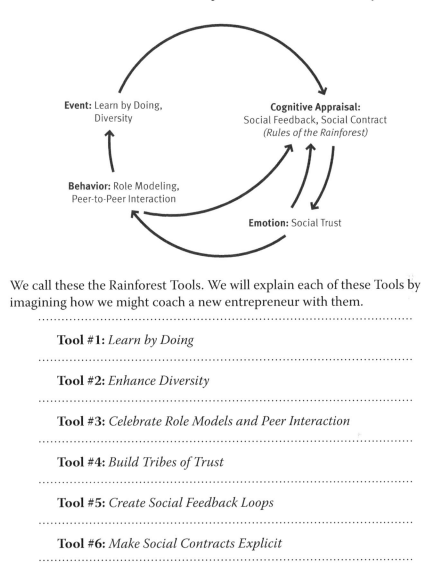

We call these the Rainforest Tools. We will explain each of these Tools by imagining how we might coach a new entrepreneur with them.

....

Tool #1: *Learn by Doing*

....

Tool #2: *Enhance Diversity*

....

Tool #3: *Celebrate Role Models and Peer Interaction*

....

Tool #4: *Build Tribes of Trust*

....

Tool #5: *Create Social Feedback Loops*

....

Tool #6: *Make Social Contracts Explicit*

....

Tool #1: Learn by Doing

Imagine a scientist who wants to turn his new biomedical invention into a real product that saves lives, but he is terrified of businesspeople. A conventional way to assist him might be to place him in a classroom to learn how entrepreneurs commercialize medical devices or, worse, make him read a book about it.

In our experience, the best way is to actually have him do the real work of commercializing his device, not just thinking or reading about it. This work can be painful, uncomfortable, distressing, and even tear-inducing, but we can coach or mentor him through it. There are many ways to run coaching or mentoring programs, but the basic theme is consistent: learning is done through real-world interactions, what psychologists call *in vivo* learning and the execution of *tasks*. This is the only way that people truly change. Startup coach Janet Crawford, who specializes in behavioral science, describes the psychological process she sees in entrepreneurs she works with:

> We are paradoxically wired to fear change and to find discovery pleasurable. Deep learning comes from experience. People can't be told things and have them coded into behavioral patterns. There is no fundamental rewiring when there is no insight.[28]

We create Rainforest culture by doing, not by lecturing. Only people who are "doing" can be coached to discover new ways of thinking for themselves.

Therefore, we might tell our scientific inventor that in order to qualify for a small seed investment, he needs to engage with potential customers or channel partners to develop useful product specifications for his biomedical product. The scientist may not realize that his task—bridging the distance between disparate social groups—is the first step in a broader transformation. At first, he may only see that his actions lead to better product specifications. Such actions, however, can eventually lead to shifts in attitudes and beliefs, as he starts to experience firsthand how certain behaviors yield better results.

In our work, we have witnessed how this process is a form of psychological transformation for many people. A scientist can become distrustful, fearful, angry, and uncertain. Rohit Shukla observes this among his new entrepreneurs: "There is such a paranoia that develops in the beginning among them." [29] Deep emotion is part of the process of entering a Rainforest. There is no substitute for real-time, real-life interactive programs that coach people through the process of building a real company or commercializing a real technology.

---

28 Crawford, interview.
29 Rohit Shukla, telephone interview with author, April 18, 2011.

Tool #2: Enhance Diversity

Once we have engaged our biomedical scientist in the real work of innovation, how do we instigate conversations between him and potential customers or channel partners? What makes people from different backgrounds "bump into" each other?

In order to generate social friction and encourage serendipity, we must increase diverse interactions. But how do we actually increase diversity in places where populations are segregated, homogeneous, or do not mix well? What do we do in societies where tribalism separates individuals and diminishes their ability to trust each other? These are fundamental challenges in many places around the world.

Keystones. First, there must be keystones—whether individuals or institutions—who serve as the agents that catalyze diverse interactions. For example, since our scientist wants to commercialize a biomedical device, a keystone's mission should be to create an environment where that entrepreneur can connect with important partners, which might include the right people at Johnson & Johnson, General Electric, or any of the other major device manufacturers for his product. Keystones break down *vertical* social silos and enable valuable *horizontal* interactions to happen. In the same way that organizations like CONNECT or Larta Institute reach across social barriers to forge human connections—or the way that Larry Bock or Bill Otterson glued people together—keystones are the critical links between far-flung corners of a Rainforest.

If there are no recognized keystones in a community to start with, we need to anoint them or build them. We have facilitated the building of keystone organizations in numerous markets, including recently in Colombia where we helped launch CONNECT Bogotá in August 2011. In doing so, we do not merely assemble the "right" resumes. Keystone individuals must exhibit the cultural behaviors we want to see replicated throughout a network. Keystone organizations should gather individuals from a diverse range of social networks, integrate them, and get them committed to the community's goals. When developing such organizations, we encourage "matching"—everybody involved must commit something of value, whether it is money, time, or expertise. Matching contributions foster a sense of "co-creation," and everyone shares ownership because they build it together. Consequently, no faction is perceived to dominate the organization, and everyone is engaged in meaningful tasks that best leverage their unique contributions and capabilities.

Networking. Keystones should create environments that encourage unpredictable and serendipitous interactions between people. We have discussed the importance of "spontaneous sociability" and the value of "water coolers" where people congregate. Steve Jobs designed the offices of Pixar to encourage such encounters and unplanned collaborations.[30] Similarly, networking is ubiquitous in Rainforests. Rainforests tend to have high rates of networking activities because people find value in opening doors to serendipitous conversations and relationships.[31] Over the years, we have participated in a wide range of such activities, from the Venice Interactive Community that helped spark the first wave of digital media startups in Los Angeles in the late 1990s, to the IT Club in Yerevan that today is connecting innovators in the Armenian startup community.

Rohit Shukla, CEO of Larta Institute, emphasizes the value of real-world interaction in his work with startup entrepreneurs:

> The notion that you can actually teach this stuff in a classroom needs to be exploded. Companies do not have time to go through a linear process of learning. Every day, they must be constantly asking, "What is the state of the market, who can I get to, what are my global linkages?" This is impossible to apply in the context of a curricular program. So much of it is non-linear, so much is of the moment, a mixture of inspiration and contact and connectivity in the context of learning by doing...Why is the supply chain question not asked of small tech companies? Where exactly do you fit into the existing product lines or services? The only way to know that is to get under the skin of the industry to figure out where exactly it fits.[32]

Serendipitous networking is essential because, in the real world, it is impossible for a central agent to do everything. No agent can possibly have enough information and time to broker all the potentially useful connections in a Rainforest. For example, leaders frequently promote institutional collaborations, such as between scientific and business entities, but they rarely work as promised. A typical such collaboration might look like this on paper:

---

30 Walter Isaacson, *Steve Jobs* (New York: Simon & Schuster, 2011), 431.

31 Saxenian, *Regional Advantage*, 46-47, 130. Annalee Saxenian has written about the value of networking activities in the early years of Silicon Valley, including the role of "forums for learning and information exchange" and the importance of numerous business associations, like Santa Clara County Manufacturing Group (SCCMG), Western Electronics Manufacturers Association (WEMA), and Semiconductor Equipment and Materials Institute (SEMI).

32 Rohit Shukla, interview.

This collaboration is doomed from the start. Leaders routinely make the error of thinking that drawing lines between organizational boxes is the same as actually connecting real people between the organizations. They fail to look through the macro "paper" structures to see the micro individuals within. After all, it is the individuals—not the leaders—who will actually do the work and deal with the real challenges. *Real-life linkages are human-to-human, not group-to-group.*

It is one thing to forge a partnership between a university and a corporation in which the Chancellor of one and the CEO of the other shake hands and pledge their best-intentioned commitments to work together developing new innovations. It is another thing entirely for a university inventor, tucked away in a basement laboratory or grinding away on research grant applications, to "bump into" a product developer in a major corporation, who is spending much of his time battling the corporate bureaucracy on other matters.

The only practical way to test a technology's potential is through one-on-one, real-world interactions between makers and users, providers and customers, or inventors and distributors. While new technologies can sometimes become the basis for highly successful startups, they are usually better integrated into existing business channels. Even more often, they are not commercially viable at all. We want to know those types of answers as quickly as possible in the Rainforest. Networking programs that are "intentionally serendipitous"—that focus on bringing together people who might be located deep within their respective organizational charts—can be immensely valuable. Our goal should be to achieve these hard-to-create, but valuable, connections:

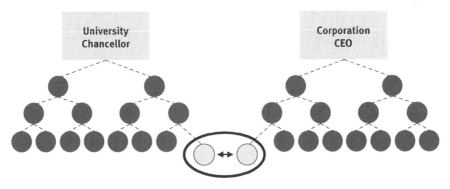

It is also important to recognize the "invisible diversity" in a region. When we talk about diversity, we are not just talking about geographical distance. We seek to overcome a wide range of social barriers that prevent people from working together, including people living next door to each other. Two people may both be Armenian engineers living in Yerevan, but they might belong to extremely different social circles. One might be an expert in electronics and the other in medical devices; one might work in a university and the other in a multinational corporation; they might be a generations apart or belong to different churches. If they are not interacting, the value of their potential relationship remains latent, and the Rainforest loses.

Diaspora. One of the most powerful tools for generating diversity is diaspora. We do not just mean ethnic diaspora, such as Jewish or Chinese people spread around the world. We mean diaspora in the broadest sense, as in boundary-crossers—people who have left one group to join another. This might include immigrants, emigrants, university alumni, former co-workers, or former collaborators.

People who are boundary-crossers can simultaneously serve as role models, cultural translators, and trusted channels for cross-boundary relationships. They can translate between the social norms of different cultures. They can "speak" the cultural language of people both inside and outside a network. Wherever we have worked, people who are active in diaspora networks have always served as leaders to build Rainforests in their native communities.

Global Connections. Today more than ever, innovators must connect across global geographic boundaries. A social media startup company in Cape Town today would be foolish not to think about how its work complements or competes with Google, Facebook, Twitter, or any number of other potential partners or competitors. The same applies for a biotech startup in Bogota, a wireless company in Ljubljana, a mobile design company in Kaohsiung, or a textile firm in Rwanda. Little startups are on the same playing field as major multinational corporations today.

Keystones and diaspora can help their communities create these valuable bridges to the rest of the world. Global linkages to the right talent, the right market information, the right corporate partners, the right technology—these are no longer optional for startups. Today, entrepreneurs anywhere can access real-time market intelligence, business insight, strategic partners, and human talent worldwide—resources that were previously available only to a select few. Many of the special advantages that enabled startups in places like Silicon Valley to grow and thrive in the past are now available to all entrepreneurs.

Tool #3: Celebrate Role Models and Peer Interaction

Our scientist is now actively engaged in discussions with key partners for his biomedical invention. What does he say in these discussions? How does he behave?

Role models are powerful tools for learning new behaviors. The cultural transformation of a Rainforest is accelerated by role models who can inspire others to emulate them. Social scientists have discovered that networks actually have a "tipping point" where the opinions of a consistent and inflexible minority—as little as 10% of a population—can shift the opinions of the entire majority.[33]

Role models come in all shapes and sizes. For instance, Fadi Ghandour, the CEO of Aramex, is not your conventional corporate executive. He certainly has credibility in the business world—Aramex, based in Amman, was the first company in the Middle East to be listed on the NASDAQ. But more importantly for the Rainforest, Fadi has become one of the most influential role models for entrepreneurs throughout the Middle East.

Fadi frequently mentors young Arabs, urging them to take the path less traveled, inspiring them to take chances, and even funding their startups as an angel investor. He sees role models transforming the culture of the Arab world:

> Role models are important in the Middle East, where the tendency is to have the feeling that you are unable to change things in society, that the system is so much more powerful than you, that you are unable to make it without pulling strings. A role model is a "can do" example. It shows that it can be done. Maktoob [the Arab Web portal acquired by Yahoo! in 2009 for $164 million] is the ultimate role model story in the region. I cannot tell you how important Maktoob was for young entrepreneurs. These people didn't believe... When Yahoo! comes in, that's a massive result for two young entrepreneurs who started from scratch. Every entrepreneur said, it can be done. If these guys do it, I can do it. [34]

---

33 J. Xie, et al., "Social Consensus Through the Influence of Committed Minorities," *Physical Review* 84(2011): 011130, doi: 10.1103/PhysRevE.84.011130.

34 Fadi Ghandour, telephone interview with author, August 26, 2011. For more information, see also "Aramex's Fadi Ghandour Unfolds His Roadmap for Budding Entrepreneurs in the Middle East," Arabic Knowledge @ Wharton, May 4, 2010, http://knowledge.wharton.upenn.edu/arabic/article.cfm?articleId=2446; "Yahoo," dubaibeat.com, August 25, 2009, http://www.dubaibeat.com/2009/08/25/yahoo_acquired_middle_east_int.php.

Fadi has become known for delivering inspiring speeches in which he motivates Arab entrepreneurs by proclaiming "Ya la!"—which means something like "Come on, let's go!" in Arabic.

Deming also wrote about the importance of role models. He believed that transformed individuals can "set an example" and "continually teach other people." [35] Role models should not only be examples of business success; they must also be examples of normative behavior. When transforming culture, Deming argued that it was essential for role models to "help pull people away from their current practice and beliefs, and move them into the new philosophy without a feeling of guilt about the past."[36] Role models should be optimists who inspire others to emulate not only their actions, but their attitudes and beliefs as well.

Role models help people dream of what is possible. As one example, how many countless young entrepreneurs around the world were inspired by the video of YouTube co-founders Chad Hurley and Steve Chen, at the respective ages of 29 and 28, giddily announcing their company's acquisition by Google for over $1.3 billion?[37] A common phenomenon of university-based startup companies in the United States is what is sometimes jokingly called the *Porsche Principle*. This principle holds that one of the greatest motivators for professors or graduate students on campus to start new companies is when one of their colleagues drives up in a new Porsche after selling their startup. Janet Crawford sees this effect in her coaching work: "Confidence is contagious." [38]

Role modeling can happen quietly or loudly, overtly or secretively, in a public speech or in a private dinner. The moments are invisible to us; they serve as a form of free transaction in the Rainforest, as ideas and behaviors are passed from one person to another. The most powerful role models are often peers. One peer can unknowingly change the expectations and behaviors of another, which creates a form of "costless" economic value. Role models and peer learning can help dissipate social friction in a Rainforest with little investment of labor or capital.

Role models can be useful practically when building companies. They can teach skills, because successful innovation is a craft that is honed and is best learned from experienced craftspeople. They can also provide emotional support, because the only people who can fully appreciate the experience

---

35 Deming, *The New Economics,* 93. See also Edgar Schein, *Organizational Culture and Leadership* (New York: John Wiley & Sons, 2010), Kindle edition, which discusses how leaders transmit norms, values, procedures, and assumptions in companies.

36 Ibid.

37 "A Message from Chad and Steve," YouTube video, 1:37, the YouTube founders talk about the Google acquisition, posted by "YouTube," October 9, 2006, http://www.youtube.com/watch?v=QCVxQ_3Ejkg.

38 Crawford, interview.

of being an entrepreneur are other entrepreneurs. Thus, in our practice, we find the most powerful way to change the behavior of someone is to have them spend time and listen to someone else whom they want to emulate. We often kick off a mentoring process by inviting participants to listen to the shared wisdom of other entrepreneurs who were in their shoes just a few years before.

Our brains are flexible, and we are wired to learn by emulating. As author Tom Peters humorously quips, "Innovation is easy…Hang out with weird, and thou shalt become more weird. Hang out with dull, and thou shalt become more dull."[39] Neuroscience research shows that the reward system in the brain's striatum is activated by following the behavior of others who have achieved success.[40] Additional scientific research validates the idea that culture is learned by imitating people we feel are similar to us[41] or whom we admire as socially dominant.[42]

The mechanism in our brains that causes this phenomenon is called the *mirror neuron system.* [43] It is the mechanism by which the human brain learns by copying the behavior of others. In fact, based on recent observations about how the brain works, many scientists now feel that the mental boundary between "self" and "others" is actually not so clear.[44] As scientist John Cacioppo of the University of Chicago has said, "It sounds like an oxymoron. But it's not. In fact, the idea that the center of our psychological universe, and even our physiological experience, is 'me'—this just fundamentally misrepresents us as a species." [45]

---

39 "Innovation Is Actually Easy!" YouTube video, 2:52, lecture by Tom Peters, posted by "BetterLifeCoaches," February 20, 2007, http://www.youtube.com/watch?v=8AGTpu_i8sc.

40 Schultz, "Reward, Decision-Making," 55 (see chap. 4, part I, n. 25).

41 Elizabeth A. Reynolds et al., "Answering the 'Other' Question in Cultural Neuroscience: Theory and Data on How Culture Gets Into the Brain," Poster presented at the 2010 Social and Affective Neuroscience Conference, Chicago, IL, October 29-31, 2010, http://www.socialaffectiveneuro.org/docs/SANS_program_2010.pdf.

42 Jonathan B. Freeman et al., "Culture Shapes a Mesolimbic Response to Signals of Dominance and Subordination that Associates with Behavior," *NeuroImage* 47 (2009): 353-359, doi:10.1016/j.neuroimage.2009.04.038.

43 Giacomo Rizzolatti and Laila Craighero, "The Mirror-Neuron System," *Annual Review of Neuroscience* 27 (2004): 174, 10.1146/annurev.neuro.27.070203.144230; Valeria Gazzola and Christian Keysers, "The Observation and Execution of Actions Share Motor and Somatosensory Voxels in All Tested Subjects: Single-Subject Analyses of Unsmoothed fMRI Data," *Cereb Cortex* 19 (2009): 1252, doi: 10.1093/cercor/bhn181.

44 Jamil Zaki and Kevin Ochsner, "You, Me, and My Brain: Self and Other Representations in Social Cognitive Neuroscience," in *Social Neuroscience: Toward Understanding the Underpinnings of the Social Mind,* ed. Alexander B. Todorov et al. (Oxford: Oxford University Press, 2011), chap. 2. The authors ask, "Does dissolving boundaries between ourselves and others actually help us to navigate the social world?"

45 Joshua Wolf Shenk, "Two Is the Magic Number, A New Science of Creativity," *Slate,* September 14, 2010, http://www.slate.com/id/2267004/.

We can help nurture Rainforests by showcasing successful role models and creating peer support networks that validate and reinforce this new, non-traditional value system. These efforts can be embodied in activities as simple as monthly coffee shop gatherings, or as sophisticated as community newsfeeds or online social networks that connect people to learn from each other.

Tool #4: Build Tribes of Trust

Our biomedical scientist is now fully engaged and inspired in productizing his new device, but he still doesn't trust businesspeople the way he needs to. To overcome this type of mentality, we must help build new tribes based on trust.

Psychologists studying group cognitive behavioral therapy have validated the importance of social cohesion based on trust, support, and altruism in driving behavioral outcomes.[46] People "learn by doing" only in trusting, nurturing environments, but trust is not created by people saying "trust me." It is created by people actually "doing work" together, building trust through real-life collaboration.

We cannot change an entire society at once, but we can start by developing small Rainforests around highly influential, respected, and trusted keystones. In our work in Latin America, for instance, we have been able to help launch new organizations by convening core, respected groups of such leaders. To change a system, we must always start with one person or a small group of people who can serve in that role. The values of that group should reflect the Rules of the Rainforest. They cannot just talk about trust and higher motivations; they must live them daily in their behaviors.

Social network scientists are proving that trust can be multiplied, and at a low cost. Researchers James Fowler and Nicholas Christakis at the University of California at San Diego have measured how "cooperative behavior cascades in human social networks." In one experiment with volunteers, they actually quantified how one person contributing to a public good influenced others in the group, leading eventually to a *tripling* of the total contribution from the whole group. Social capital can multiply itself dramatically under the right circumstances and the right leaders.[47]

---

46 Bieling, et al, *Cognitive-Behavioral Therapy in Groups*, Ch. 1, Kindle edition.

47 James H. Fowler and Nicholas A. Christakis, "Cooperative Behavior Cascades in Human Social Networks," *PNAS* 107 (2010), 7, doi: 10.1073/pnas.0913149107.

A good example of this can be found in the CONNECT Springboard program. It is not just that people mentor startup companies in Springboard—it is the way they do it. Springboard starts with the assumption that it is easier to give someone advice than it is to get them to act on it. That's why every mentor in Springboard is assigned to a company team for several months, in a process intended to build trust between the mentors and the team. If entrepreneurs trust the mentors, they are more likely to take their advice. They are also more likely to trust other people in the Rainforest encircling them. We see similar mechanisms at work in the programs of organizations like Larta Institute, TechWadi, and Endeavor— they mentor startups in a process that creates multiplying bonds of trust among the people involved.

Trust is also created through transference. We all know this is true in real life—A and B might not ordinarily be friends, but the fact that C introduced them can make them friends. The "halo effect" can be powerful when building Rainforests. Larta Institute leverages this halo effect when mentoring entrepreneurs who have received funding from the National Institutes of Health. At the beginning of each program year, the program staff at the NIH sends out a letter to their portfolio of companies, inviting them to participate in the Larta program. Sometimes, over a hundred companies are inspired to join. The value that Larta provides is only partially based on the fact that they are matching qualified entrepreneurs with mentors and advisors. There is an even greater, invisible value in the circle of trust being created as the halo passes from NIH to Larta. The result is a virtual Rainforest that involves hundreds of people in a trust-based network.

People can be rewired to join new tribes, and we are seeing this happen on a global scale. Entrepreneurs and innovators increasingly behave like they are members of a global tribe of innovators. Groups like TechWadi, for instance, are building mentoring connections between entrepreneurs in Egypt and mentors in Silicon Valley, creating a virtual Rainforest founded on cross-border relationships halfway around the world. There is the unmistakable sense in such groups that the innovators participating are members of a new type of global family.

Tool #5: Create Social Feedback Loops

Our heroic scientist has come a long way. He has completed a deal to manufacture and distribute his biomedical device to thousands of patients. Suddenly, his company hits a delay, and he is now vulnerable to his investors, who could drag him to sell his company at a price that leaves him with next to nothing. What prevents predatory behavior from destroying Rainforests?

The Rules of the Rainforest are continually reinforced and re-interpreted through social feedback. Leaders can enhance this process by supporting social feedback mechanisms that reward good behavior and penalize bad behavior in a transparent manner. A good analogy is the star rating system that buyers use to review sellers of goods on eBay. The eBay feedback system enhances the positive behaviors of honesty, service, timeliness, fairness, and trust. How can we replicate that dynamic in the Rainforest?

Human beings for millennia have relied on social gossip as something like an invisible star rating system. When people deviate from what the group considers fair, the system penalizes the offenders. As Stanford social network researcher Matthew Jackson notes, "The term 'gossip' sounds pejorative. But it is extremely valuable in social settings. You know that if you perform badly, people will hear about it."[48] Scientists have shown how members of a group will spend irrationally high resources to engage in "altruistic punishment" against violators of social norms.[49] We are wired to enforce the unwritten rules of our societies, even if it costs us.

We can observe this occurring, for instance, in electronic newsletters that are delivered throughout the venture capital community.[50] A venture firm's reputation directly affects its ability to get into the most desirable deals. There are three major daily newsletters in the American venture business— Private Equity Hub, VentureWire, and Fortune Finance (edited by Dan Primack)—which provide a steady stream of social feedback for the industry,

---

48 Matthew Jackson, personal interview with author. See also, Matthew O. Jackson, *Social and Economic Networks* (Princeton: Princeton University Press, 2010), Kindle edition. In discussing the value of social sanctioning, Jackson notes the work of J.S. Coleman. "Coleman emphasizes the role of closure, which roughly corresponds to high clustering, in the enforcement of social norms. He points out that closure allows agents to coordinate their sanctioning of individuals who deviate from a social norm and thus can help enforce prescribed behavior. Coleman also notes that closure helps in terms of spreading information about reputation from one neighbor of an individual to another." See James S. Coleman, "Social Capital in the Creation of Human Capital," *American Journal of Sociology* 94 (1988): 105-107, http://onemvweb.com/sources/sources/social_capital.pdf.

49 Tim Johnson, Christopher T. Dawes, James H. Fowler, Richard McElreath and Oleg Smirnov, "The Role of Egalitarian Motives in Altruistic Punishment," *Economics Letters* 102 (2009): 194, http://jhfowler.ucsd.edu/role_of_egalitarian_motives.pdf. The team is able to "demonstrate empirically a link between egalitarian motives and altruistic punishment."

50 Saxenian, *Regional Advantage*, 116. The role of gossip for sharing valuable information in the early years of Silicon Valley, and the lack of such gossip in Boston, was described by Annalee Saxenian.

including castigations of venture firms that mistreat their entrepreneurs. Another source—the website www.TheFunded.com—enables entrepreneurs to provide candid, anonymous eBay-like ratings and reviews of investors. These ratings matter so much to investors that some of them have even launched behind-the-scenes campaigns to urge their entrepreneurs to provide feedback to bump-up their scores.

An example of the Rainforest's interpretative dynamic is the valuation of stock in Silicon Valley startups. What is considered a "fair" valuation is constantly evolving to fit changing circumstances. This is not just for the shares purchased by an investor. It also includes the "fair" amount of shares to be allocated to various employees, advisors, board directors, founders, and other key people in a startup company. Does a leading advisor deserve options for 0.25% of a company's stock or 0.50%? Does a vice president of product development deserve 1% or 2%? The answer varies depending on countless, constantly shifting factors. The numbers are often tracked and published by various organizations, which encourages a process of generating better numbers through "collective intelligence."

Such types of social feedback mechanisms—whether networks for information sharing, forums for social peer interaction, online postings, or blogs—can lower social barriers, encourage transparency, and facilitate communication among parties. Another example of this process is the way that startup legal documents have evolved in the U.S. Over several decades, through millions of interactions, the system has evolved a set of fairly common documents for term sheets, convertible notes, seed investments, venture investments, and even intellectual property licensing. There are standard versions of these "model deal documents" that have been publicly published by various groups—including law firms, associations, angel groups, and venture firms—with the purpose of lowering barriers to transactions. They seek to create a fair, fast middle-ground for all parties at low cost.

Tool #6: Make Social Contracts Explicit

Our imaginary scientist has survived numerous ups and downs, and his biomedical product is now ready to launch. What happens after our mentoring work with him is finished? How can he continue to inculcate the culture of the Rainforest in his work?

To foster this process, we implement actual Social Contracts. Whereas social contracts in our ordinary lives are implied and invisible, we seek to make Social Contracts for the Rainforest manifest and visible. These contracts are physical documents that attempt to manifest the Rules of the Rainforest, as applied to local circumstances. They are like written constitutions for innovation ecosystems: they provide maps for people to navigate the informal rules of their new communities. As in cognitive behavioral therapy, Social Contracts work by making people more self-aware and conscious of their choices for action.

We can ask entrepreneurs, fund managers, mentors, and others who want to participate in building a Rainforest to sign such a physical contract. We can even make it a requirement for receiving incubation services, a grant, or capital. To sign, they must use a good old-fashioned pen. By signing, they are agreeing to abide by the norms that are necessary for growing a vibrant innovation ecosystem. The actual wording varies from place to place, as it should. Here is one example of what a Social Contract might look like:

The Rainforest Social Contract

I am joining a global community of people who share a common faith in the culture of innovation and entrepreneurship. I am open to meeting anyone in this community.

I understand that I will receive valuable help from others for free or at a very low cost.

I agree to "pay forward" whatever positive benefits I receive. For every introduction I get, I will provide an introduction to another person. For every hour of advice I receive, I will give an hour of advice to someone else. For every risk someone takes with me, I will take a risk with a different person.

I will give trust to others before expecting to receive trust in return. I will treat everyone fairly. I will take advantage of no one.

I will bring people together, as none of us is as smart as all of us.

I will dream, experiment, iterate, and persist. I understand that mistakes and failure are acceptable ways of testing new ideas.

I will open myself to learning from others. I will help nurture learning in others.

Each person is a role model for everyone else. I will live these ideals as a member of the community.

Agreed to and signed by:

Mr. or Ms. Entrepreneur

The Rules of the Rainforest function invisibly in Silicon Valley, but invisible is not necessarily better. We believe that codifying the Rules—writing them down in Social Contracts—is a way to seed or accelerate the creation of these norms.

Neither Chicken nor Egg

Rainforests are built on soft culture as much as—if not more than—hard assets. The Rainforest Recipe provides a way to map and build Rainforest culture where little might have existed before. By paying attention to both the hardware and the software, we can nurture an entire ecosystem that supports the serendipitous process of innovation.

The Rainforest Recipe works because it helps liberate people to collaborate. It seeks to overcome their tendencies to push each other apart. Interestingly, we can find powerful analogies in the natural world. As astrophysicist Erich Jantsch writes:

> The natural dynamics of simple dissipative structures teach the optimistic principle of which we tend to despair in the human world: the more freedom in self-organization, the more order. [51]

Nature organizes itself more efficiently when atoms, cells, and species are freer to interact with one another. Similarly, in the Rainforest we see this surprising result: freedom creates order. Bringing down social barriers is like removing chains and allowing people to organize in valuable ways. Thus, the Rainforest Recipe provides a framework to help human systems copy the self-organizing behavior of natural systems. The Rainforest Tools provide specific actions we can take to encourage that process.

So now we have an answer to an ancient universal question, posed earlier in this book. When we seek to build a Rainforest, which comes first, the chicken or the egg?

The answer is neither. It is the *nest* which allows serendipitous innovation to emerge.

---

51 Erich Jantsch, *The Self-Organizing Universe: Scientific and Human Implications of the Emerging Paradigm of Evolution* (Oxford: Pergamon Press, 1980), 40.

Chapter Seven: Capital in the Rainforest

"Big V, Little C"

"If you want to make money, do private equity.
If you want to have fun, do venture capital."

— **Alan Patricof, providing unexpected advice**
to co-author Victor Hwang at breakfast on
June 6, 2008

Going West

"I felt like I had travelled in a time machine," Phil Wickham recalls.[1]

He was already an experienced venture capitalist when he moved from Boston to Silicon Valley in 1996. An associate at OneLiberty Ventures in Boston, Phil had already heard plenty of pitches from entrepreneurs. He had, in his career, witnessed or participated, perhaps hundreds of times, in the ritual dance between startup companies and venture firms. He had also been a successful entrepreneur, building and selling a business in Japan.

Even so, he was unprepared for the culture shock he experienced moving to the West Coast. Most people would imagine that the Boston technology corridor known as "Route 128" had a great deal in common with the high-tech community in Silicon Valley. The contrast between the two regions, however, was far more profound than Phil had expected.

On the East Coast, money was power. Money called the shots. You see this behavior on Wall Street. You see it everywhere in fact. In most places in the world, the presumption in business is that money dominates and sets the rules. But the West Coast was different. "In Boston, it was the entrepreneurs who dressed nicely and showed up on time to impress the investors," Phil remembers. "In Silicon Valley, it was the opposite."[2]

Why this difference? Where did it come from? The role of money on the West Coast had followed a different path. Forged in the egalitarian culture of the American frontier—where what you could do mattered more than what you owned or where you came from—capital was just one component in the complex tapestry of the economic landscape. Money did not confer inherent entitlement or hierarchy, as it might elsewhere. Money was considered a tool.

The venture capital industry that evolved on the West Coast inherited that belief. As Phil observes, "Look at what venture capital really is. It's just a service industry to entrepreneurs. The entrepreneurs in Silicon Valley have figured out that they are the real gems and that the money itself is just a commodity. They have a 'buying' mentality." [3]

---

1 Phil Wickham, personal interview with author, May 9, 2011.

2 Ibid. See also Saxenian, *Regional Advantage*, 65 (see chap. 2, n. 24). She quotes Gordon Bell, DEC's Vice President of Engineering during the 1960s and 1970s: "There is no real venture capital in Massachusetts. The venture capital community is a bunch of very conservative bankers. They are radically different from the venture capitalists in Silicon Valley who have all been operational people in companies."

3 Ibid.

Despite all the fanfare, the Silicon Valley venture capital model is based on the recognition that its success is derived from the success of its entrepreneurs. This is not to say that venture capitalists are humble—in fact, more often, they are just the opposite. But, in the practice of venture capital as a business, the most successful VCs learned particular behaviors that help them maximize their long-term success. Successful venture capitalists have learned that they frequently need to check their egos at the door, and focus on helping their entrepreneurs and startups. Phil continues, "What an entrepreneur needs from a venture capitalist is a flow of insights, opportunities, and resources. The capital needs will evolve as a company grows, so venture capitalists cannot start with the presumption that they know the business better than the entrepreneur."

Phil would continue for several more years in the venture capital business until, in 2008, he made a radical change in his career. He accepted a job as CEO of the Center for Venture Education, a nonprofit organization dedicated to training the next generation of leaders in the venture capital ecosystem. The Center runs the Kauffman Fellows Program, which helps develop emerging venture capitalists and others that nurture innovation. By 2011, across 40 countries, 580 fellows and mentors in the Society of Kauffman Fellows had made $6 billion in venture capital investments, supporting the growth of hundreds of new enterprises, $15 billion in annual revenues, and the creation of 50,000 jobs.[4] Some would argue that it has become the closest thing there is today to an established social network in the venture capital ecosystem. Both of us—Victor and Greg—are fortunate to be members of this Fellowship.

Phil has focused the program on a mission to mobilize capital to innovators, regardless of where they are in the nation and the world, regardless of the stage of the enterprise. "There is a science to capital formation that has been developed by the great venture capitalists in America," he observes. "Venture capital only thrives when it is based on trust, and trust is powered by transparency and connectivity. Our goal now is to help codify that science and disseminate it so that it is not limited to just a few cottage funds anymore."[5]

A surprising revelation from the Silicon Valley school of thought is that venture capital is not primarily about the capital at all. As one of the founders of the industry, Arthur Rock, puts it, "Writing a check is easy...

---

4 "Society of Kauffman Fellows," accessed August 30, 2011, http://www.kauffmanfellows.org/home.aspx.

5 Wickham, interview.

yeah, it doesn't take much ink."[6] This is not an obvious conclusion to outsiders. The world has been conditioned to the idea that money is usually both the problem and the solution for most ills. Investor Kevin Kinsella of Avalon Ventures sees it another way. The difference, he says, between good venture capitalists and bad venture capitalists is that the good ones think of venture capital with a "Big V and a Little C."[7] In other words, the venture— that is, the startup—is always more important than the capital.

Although capital is a basic factor of economic production generally, capital in the Rainforest is fundamentally different from other forms of capital. In trying to cultivate a Rainforest, we need to address a significant uphill challenge: how do you create a community that does not operate with a conventional "Big C, Little V" attitude?

Building Rainforests requires recognizing the unique qualities of this distinctive form of capital, and fostering the right incentives accordingly. What are those particular qualities and incentives? What is the recipe for capital in the Rainforest? The answers are not obvious, as demonstrated by countless governments and corporations that have attempted and failed to create successful, sustainable investment programs. Let us explore another layer in the mystery of Rainforests: the nature of venture capital.

The Continuum of Capital

The way that most people think about capital in Rainforests is actually quite narrow. When executives or leaders want to spur innovation, they tend to focus on the two mystical words—"venture capital"—almost as if they had magic powers. But perhaps surprisingly, the issue is not just about venture capital, as it is strictly defined.

When we seek to build Rainforests, what we are really referring to is the entire range of *innovation capital*. Innovation capital is the complete "continuum of capital" that is required from the beginning of the innovation process, even before an actual company is formed. The continuum starts when ideas and inventions are just being spawned, and extends to all the capital needs of a company over its lifetime. This is a philosophy that Phil Wickham has pursued, as the Kauffman Fellows Program increasingly includes people from across that continuum, fulfilling its original mission set forth in 1993.

---

6 *Something Ventured* (unpublished dialogue list, March 28, 2011), Word file. *Something Ventured*, a documentary about the birth of the venture capital industry was conceived by Paul Holland, a Silicon Valley venture capitalist. Paul, a general partner with Foundation Capital, produced the film along with Molly Davis of Rainmaker Communications. The film was directed by Emmy-Award-winning filmmakers Dan Geller and Dayna Goldfine. We thank Molly Davis for providing us the transcript of the documentary.

7 Bock, interview (see chap. 3, n. 2).

Capital is not just an engineering problem; it is more importantly a biological problem. We have helped foster innovation capital in places as far flung as Taiwan, Armenia, Kazakhstan, Mexico, Colombia, and the Palestinian Territories—far away from the comforts of California. In every place and each unique situation, the biggest problem was never in the formal fund structure itself. Structuring of capital is usually fairly straightforward. We could describe the basic framework of almost any venture capital fund on a single page or two, if needed. But how do you design a fund so that it fits productively within a community of people in an emerging Rainforest? To use a biological analogy, how do you fit a new species of carnivorous animal into a highly complex ecosystem without destroying it? How can this species be positive-sum instead of zero-sum?

When we think of the Anti-Google story in Chapter 2, and imagine what *might* have happened, we can see how different types of capital are useful to grow technology startups at different points in the cycle: to fund the basic research for ProFusion's meta-search technology (research grants, professors' salaries, laboratory equipment, etc.), for the development of a working prototype to validate technical feasibility (provided to ProFusion by a public university), for the iterative conversations with customers to validate market feasibility, for the early building of the business itself, and then for scaling up the business to reach sustainable levels of revenue. Each of these capital stages has a distinct risk profile and requires different resources to support entrepreneurs.

The Continuum of Capital in the Rainforest

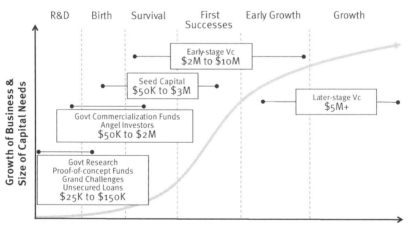

Stage of Business & Stage of Capital Needs

As you can see from the diagram above, different forms of capital are necessary as a company moves from left to right. Just as different types of nutrients are needed to grow weeds in a natural rainforest, an innovation

Rainforest needs a full range of innovation capital. In the early stages of a new company, even a few thousand dollars can mean life or death. It can represent the missed payroll that keeps a startup's first employees from giving up, the price of a plane flight to meet a key distributor, the cost of making the first product, or the difference between a cheap-looking website and one that convinces a customer to buy the first product. It does not take much money to make a huge difference in the beginning.

Therefore, the problem with innovation capital is not money. Money is everywhere. Instead, the key is how capital is aggregated and structured at each stage, and the behaviors of the people who control it. To build Rainforests, capital must be designed in ways that are different from conventional methods of managing money. A Rainforest cannot be developed on the back of money alone.

We will not go into every possible issue regarding innovation capital because many other writers have covered the general subject.[8] Therefore, let us closely examine just two critical issues: the mysterious scarcity of early innovation capital and the recipe for building a venture fund. These topics provide a useful lens with which to view and understand how innovation capital is integrated into the Rainforest as a whole.

The Mystery of the Missing Capital

If most of the consumer retail banks in America were limited to a single geographic area, do you think people would be upset? Of course they would. They would be furious. But this is essentially what the landscape for venture capital looks like today, especially for seed-stage and early-stage risk capital. About half of it is in Silicon Valley, and California as a whole has even more of it.[9] There is apparently a lot of "missing capital" elsewhere in America and indeed in the rest of the world.

Why is this so? Conventional business wisdom says if there is money to be made, then people will find a way to make it. Neoclassical economics says that capital flows efficiently in the marketplace. If these assumptions are true, why is there not more seed-stage and early-stage risk capital everywhere? It would seem that there are vast fortunes to be made, so there ought to be more investors willing to take that risk and to seek that reward, right?

---

8 See for general information, Josh Lerner, *Venture Capital and Private Equity: A Casebook* (Hoboken, NJ: Wiley, 2000); Thomas Meyer and Pierre-Yves Mathonet, *Beyond the J Curve: Managing a Portfolio of Venture Capital and Private Equity Funds* (New York: John Wiley & Sons, 2005).

9 "PricewaterhouseCoopers National Venture Capital Association MoneyTree Report," PricewaterhouseCoopers, accessed August 30, 2011, https://www.pwcmoneytree.com/MTPublic/ns/index.jsp.

To solve this mystery, we must examine the risks inherent in the earliest stages of a company. Imagine yourself as an aspiring high-tech entrepreneur at the true beginning of the process. You do not know if your underlying technology even works in the real world, or what your commercial product will ultimately look like. You do not know who your first customer will be, if indeed there will be any customers at all. You are probably making little or no salary. Your colleagues, employees, and other partners may also be making little or no salary in this endeavor, and it is possible any of them might quit at any time. You do not know if you will be able to find any investors, much less know if you will be able to find the right investors to support you two years down the road at a critical juncture. In short, it is a huge amount of risk.

Now, put yourself in the shoes of an investor hearing about this opportunity. One way to calculate the odds of the enterprise succeeding is to multiply the odds of passing all the critical hurdles. Here is a typical calculation that might happen inside the mind of an early-stage venture capitalist:

$$\% \text{ Chance of Success} =$$

$$\begin{array}{ccccccc} \text{Technology} & & \text{Product} & & \text{Customers} & & \text{Manufacturing} \\ \text{Works} & \times & \text{Works} & \times & \text{Buy} & \times & \text{Works} \end{array}$$

$$\begin{array}{ccccc} & \text{Business Model} & & \text{Enough} & & \text{Team Can Handle} \\ \times & \text{Works} & \times & \text{Capital} & \times & \text{This Whole Thing} \end{array}$$

When you calculate the probability of clearing all of these hurdles, the odds of an early-stage business opportunity ever making money tend to be remarkably low. And remember that no one ever really knows the "real" odds of success, which makes the true risks even harder to assess. For a startup company developing a new pharmaceutical drug that requires government regulatory approval (yet another hurdle), the odds are even lower.

We often encounter scientists around the world who will say something like, "Why won't you invest in my company? I have a discovery that can provide clean energy for millions of people. If it works, this company can be worth billions of dollars!" Once we had a group of entrepreneurs with an interesting scientific discovery tell us that their company was already worth $6 billion! An investor's response, especially when a new opportunity is still ¬n early phase of development, is evident from the equation above. There g, long way to go.

This also explains why the private markets do not invest more capital in the early stages of innovation. On the left side of the capital continuum, the risks outweigh the benefits to such an extent that private market mechanisms are usually unable to sustain themselves. The risks are not rewarded by the returns. This conclusion may be a shock to many people schooled in traditional economics, as a basic tenet of modern portfolio theory is that higher risk is compensated by higher return. Economists call this the *risk premium*—the reward enjoyed by investors who are willing to accept the risk and volatility of investing much earlier. Stock brokers generally agree, for example, that investing in small cap public companies yields higher returns over time than investing in large cap public companies.[10] So why does this risk-reward equation not extend to the earliest stages of company formation? Shouldn't the private market take care of this on its own? Why should public subsidies for R&D and scientific commercialization be necessary at all?

It is because, in the earliest stages, the risk-reward equation breaks down. Based on our practical experience investing in startups, this is what we see happening in reality:

Breakdown of the Risk Premium in the Continuum of Capital

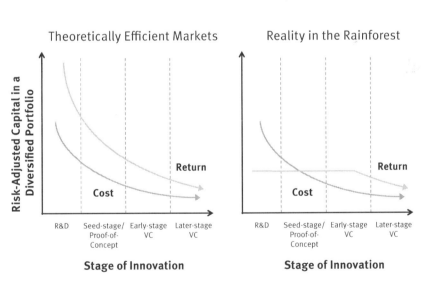

<hr />

10 Eugene F. Fama and Kenneth R. French, "The Cross-Section of Expected Stock Returns," *The Journal of Finance* 47 (1992): 427, doi:10.2307/2329112; Rof W. Banz, "The Relationship Between Return and Market Value of Common Stocks," *Journal of Financial Economics* 9 (1981): 3-4, http://perrittmutualfunds.com/media/Banz_Small_Firm_Effects.pdf.

On the left is what we might predict if the markets for innovation capital worked perfectly efficiently to create an expected risk premium: investors who invest earlier should be rewarded for their risk. The diagram on the right, however, reflects the real world. You can see that some investing might be correlated with higher returns, but there is a curious flattening point. The risk premium does not just diminish as one invests earlier—it completely vanishes.

Why the difference between theory and reality? Shouldn't supply and demand just balance out eventually? There are several explanations commonly cited for this riddle. The most widespread explanation given by people in the venture capital industry is that it is simply too expensive and time-consuming to work with really nascent companies. The costs of finding a good opportunity, performing due diligence, structuring a deal, and helping grow a later-stage company are at least the same as—or even greater—for a seed-stage or early-stage company. Thus, it makes sense for investors to move into later and later stages of investing. The real-world transaction costs of doing seed-stage or early-stage investments can eliminate many of their theoretical benefits.

Another accepted reason for this divergence between theory and reality is that putting together funds is extremely time-consuming and difficult. Venture capitalists, especially emerging fund managers, often spend well over a year raising new funds. The costs of aggregating and structuring seed-stage and early-stage capital funds often outweigh the benefits. If you are going to spend over a year of your life raising money without getting paid for it, you might as well invest large amounts of money at a time and get the biggest leverage possible to make it worthwhile. Thus, few venture capitalists are willing to invest relatively small amounts in companies that are still proving their underlying technology or developing their first product. It is too hard to organize a venture fund only to "waste it" on such small deals.

Making More by Owning Less

Both of these reasons are valid, but we believe that they are only part of the story. There is another fundamental reason for this breakdown in the risk-reward system. It is one deeply rooted in the nature of the Rainforest, and has been largely under-appreciated.

Perhaps we can explain using an odd analogy. When you are squeezing an orange to get the juice, there is a point you reach when you simply cannot extract any more juice, no matter how hard you try. Investing in early-stage companies hits a similar limit. At some point, an investor cannot get more financial return out of a company, no matter how early in the risk curve he or she invests.

For example, say a founding team in a brand new startup has a big idea to develop a new type of database technology for the Web. They have developed a basic prototype of the software architecture. They are thinking about approaching several customers, but they need capital to productize the software, pay for more computing equipment, travel to meet customers, maybe pay for marketing expenses, and numerous other startup costs. They approach a potential investor for their first seed capital. The investor has a choice: he could invest now, possibly invest later, or not invest at all. The founding team owns 100% of the stock today, but they are naturally concerned about giving up too much ownership of the company. In fact, if they owned less than 50% of the company at such an early stage, they would start to feel like they were just working for someone else, not for themselves, and they would probably start to lose motivation to work that extra hour, take that extra trip, or make that extra customer call.

The investor knows the same thing from past experience—when he owns more than roughly 50% of a seed-stage company like this, the team can become demotivated and the chance of success quickly diminishes. He cannot own more without hurting the investment's chance of success. So he has a choice. He could invest now, owning 50% of a company that has no product and no market validation. Or, he could wait a year and then invest basically the same amount to own 50% in the same company—but then maybe with real products and real customers.

In theory, as a company matures, the valuation should increase, and the same amount of stock should cost more to purchase. In practice, however, we know this theory breaks down in the earliest stages of startups. An additional share of stock purchased by an investor can be offset by additional disincentive for entrepreneurs, which lowers the odds of success for everyone. There is an invisible cost to owning more stock in an early-stage company. The most stock a venture capital investor can own is a "fair" amount, as perceived by the entrepreneurial team. After that, *each dollar more invested is undercutting the value of the prior dollar invested.* At some point, you cannot squeeze any more juice out of the orange. So, the investor has a great incentive to wait. Earlier risk does not yield a commensurate reward. In later stages, after the total value of a company has grown, even a smaller relative percentage can be enough to motivate a team, so the problem diminishes. Higher risk in early-stage venture capital is not rewarded the way one would expect in the bond markets or the public stock markets.

Thus, practice does not correspond to theory. If venture capital followed a pure supply-demand equation, as free markets usually follow, most investors could probably take 90% of the stock of most seed-stage or early-stage startup companies they funded. There is far more demand for early risk capital than there is supply. We frequently see this in our work in the Middle East, East Asia, and South America, where the common presumption is that investors will own almost the entire company if they provide early capital. The result in those regions is that awfully little seed-stage and early-stage investing actually happens. When it does happen, the entrepreneurs are often not incentivized to "go the extra mile" to fight for a company's success and end up treating it like a "regular job." Such an approach does not build sustainable Rainforests, nor does it make for profitable venture capital investing.

In a healthy Rainforest, there must be a balance of interests among the participants. Finding that point of balance is critical to the Rainforest, because it is where the stereotypically adversarial relationship between entrepreneur and investor can be transformed from zero-sum to positive-sum. However, two competing interests—an investor's desire for financial return and an entrepreneur's need to be fully incentivized—are constantly working to upset this balance. It means that at some point, investing earlier in a company does not yield the expected risk premium. Where the line goes flat is where investors cannot extract more value from a deal.

As Brad Jones of Redpoint Ventures says, "At the end of the day, you don't want to get the best price you can get. You want a fair price. If you take so much that you remove the motivation of the entrepreneur, well, you get what you pay for."[11] There is a limit to how much of a young company an investor should own because a startup cannot be just a job for an entrepreneur; an investor wants the entrepreneur to treat it as an all-consuming passion. *Experienced venture capitalists have discovered, ironically, that one can often make more money by owning less.* What Warren Buffett once said about stock investing—"It's far better to buy a wonderful company at a fair price than a fair company at a wonderful price"—applies to startup companies too.

Fairness goes beyond just price. It includes all the terms in the transaction. Venture capitalist Jeff Bussgang of Flybridge Capital Partners wrote, "As one of my partners is fond of saying, 'A good price doesn't help a bad investment.' That is why VCs tend to emphasize 'clean terms,' which are entrepreneur-friendly, rather than focus on complex bells and whistles to protect any downside."[12] A venture capitalist's goal, after a deal is done, is to have an entrepreneur wake up 100% motivated the next morning, and every morning thereafter.

---

11 Brad Jones, telephone interview with author, July 28, 2011.

12 Jeff Bussgang, "Can VCs Be Value Investors," *peHUB* (blog), October 6, 2010, http://www.pehub.com/84474/can-vcs-be-value-investors/.

In fact, a main reason that VCs might consider investing earlier, when it does happen, is not to extract more return from a particular deal. Instead, they are often trying to get the jump on their competitors in the VC industry. Venture capitalists often get in early when they are afraid of losing out on the next big thing, not usually because they feel that early risk is directly rewarded. Investing earlier in a deal, when it happens, must be counter-balanced by the strong potential of a massively disproportionate payout at the end. Otherwise, it is simply not worth the risk.

Fixing the Gap

So we confront another big mystery of the Rainforest. With the risk premium shrinking the earlier one invests, what makes it worthwhile for investors to play at all? How can one possibly create entire Rainforests of sustainable capital?

Looking at the Rainforest through the lens of capital, we can observe how trust and normative behavior affect systemic financial returns. When actors in the Rainforest behave in a way that significantly lowers the costs of doing business together, it shifts the entire curve. Lowered transaction costs due to trust and social norms make high-risk seed-stage and early-stage venture capital investing more profitable. We can see this effect in the diagram below:

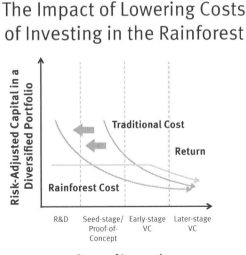

Since profit exists where *return* is higher than *cost* in the diagram above, shifting the cost curve to the left means that profitable investing can happen in earlier stages. As a result, investors can invest more sustainably in younger companies. Furthermore, such a shift increases the profitability of *all* stages of investing in the continuum. One can literally make more money when people get along better.

Seed-stage and early-stage capital is rare not because there aren't enough great opportunities. It is rare because of the limitations inherent in the process of enterprise creation, capital aggregation, deal structuring, and human motivation. However, there are still great companies to be built. That is why there has always been a need for *subsidized capital* to fill the gap. Subsidized capital can come from a government or a corporate sponsor, but its purpose is the same—to create a financial bridge for innovation, so that opportunities can move from the left side of the diagram to the point at which the risk-reward equation finally enables the profit mechanism to take over sustainably (i.e., where the two lines cross).

Subsidized capital plays a huge role in American innovation, but that role is underpublicized. Irwin Jacobs, the co-founder of Qualcomm, credits the existence of his company to a little known grant program called Small Business Innovation Research, or SBIR.[13] Each year, the government quietly invests about $2.5 billion in thousands of startup companies that are seeking to bring new scientific inventions from the laboratory to the marketplace. SBIR is specifically designed to address the gap between the starting point of an idea and the point at which private funders can profitably invest in its commercial potential. The process is not perfect, but without the support of SBIR, most of these companies probably would have died before they even had a chance. One study calculated that SBIR accounts for about one-quarter of all the innovations ranked among the R&D 100 Award winners each year.[14] In fact, as a testament to the general importance of subsidized capital, only 11 of the U.S. entities that produced award-winning innovations in the year studied were not beneficiaries of any federal funding at all.[15]

There are many difficulties in creating subsidized capital. For one, it can skew incentives and create dependency. People respond to incentives, and scientists and entrepreneurs are no different. If a grant program tells people to build a business a certain way, they will do it. If it incentivizes them to keep pursuing more grants, or to achieve engineering targets instead of securing real-life customers, they will do that too. Subsidized capital only works when it is integrated into the continuum of capital in the Rainforest,

13 "SBIR Reauthorization 2011 Dr. Irwin Mark Jacobs (Qualcomm)," YouTube video, 5:43, testimony of Dr. Irwin Jacobs, Co-Founder, Qualcomm, posted by "sbirinsider," February 23, 2011, http://www.youtube.com/watch?v=5X88LSV8kqs.

14 Fred Block and Matthew R. Keller, "Where Do Innovations Come From? Transformations in the U.S. National Innovation System, 1970-2006," *The Information Technology & Innovation Foundation* (2008), http://www.itif.org/files/Where_do_innovations_come_from.pdf.

15 Ibid.

not existing separately from it. Grants for the commercialization of cutting-edge science work best when they link grantees to the rest of the Rainforest, encouraging them to meet new people, hear new ideas, take new risks, and learn new behaviors. The hardest but most important role of subsidized capital, therefore, is to integrate newcomers into the ways of the Rainforest.

How to Build a Venture Fund

Given that capital is so important to the Rainforest, how do we construct it? There are two ways to build a venture fund. One takes as little as thirty minutes to learn. The other can take twenty years or more. It is a common mistake for investors to take the short course, and then mistakenly believe that they have taken the long course instead.

The short course is to learn the formal legal structuring and financial processes of a typical venture fund. If you were interested, any venture capitalist with a few years of experience could probably describe a run-of-the-mill limited partnership structure, the division of management fees and carried interest, the concept of diversified portfolio theory, the meaning of internal rates of return, the decision process on an investment committee, the voting rights of sitting on a startup board, and the way that investments are ultimately liquidated. That would be fairly easy, but it would be like giving you the hardware for an iPhone without the software. The device would have all the correct parts, but it would not function.

The more difficult and time-consuming course is to learn the human behavioral dynamics that happen in and around venture funds. The way that investors interact with other people in the Rainforest is at least as critical to their success as the formal structures and assets of a fund. Human relationships tie the success of a fund to the health of the Rainforest, because a fund depends symbiotically on resources from the social networks around it. Venture capitalists are continually grappling with questions such as:

- How do you treat others in situations where mistakes and failures happen almost daily?

- How do you build a reputation for trust, candor, and integrity when millions of dollars are at stake?

- What type of value can you provide an entrepreneur who probably knows far more about the business than you do?

- How do you actively listen to an entrepreneur, and then see beyond their words to the true prospects of a company?

- How do you know when a CEO is not fit to run a company anymore?

- How do you help a tiny company build life-or-death relationships with huge, powerful customers or strategic partners?

These are not just speculative questions. They are at the heart of daily life in the venture capital business. How a venture capitalist answers these questions can determine whether or not he or she succeeds in the business.

This perspective is not obvious to most people. Recently, we accepted an assignment to design a new venture fund for a nation in Asia. With the eyes of a government ministry and the World Bank watching, we felt a great deal of pressure to get it right, but the sponsors of the fund just wanted to get it launched, and kept pressuring us to hurry up. Indeed, they had already spent years getting to that point, so their primary goal was just to have a fund in existence. From a political standpoint, it would be a victory. They said to us, "Let's just close the money and get things started. The rest will follow." Their assumption was that raising the capital and structuring the legal formalities of the fund properly was the goal of the battle. The running of the fund was a separate thing and could be dealt with later, almost as an after-thought.

The truth, however, was exactly the opposite. Raising and structuring a fund, as hard as it might seem, is only about 5% of the battle. You cannot execute a fund successfully without thinking about the other 95% at its creation. We spent several months working with our hosts to custom-design a venture fund that would maximize the chances of long-term success by fostering a Rainforest around itself. To do so, we focused heavily on grooming fund managers, building global relationships to assist the growth of portfolio companies, and nurturing a culture that could grow and sustain the entire Rainforest around the fund.

The systemic role of venture capital—when done well—is to help orchestrate the vibrancy of the surrounding Rainforest. Venture capital, therefore, is not about writing a bunch of small checks. Nor is it about selecting winning stocks, like a mutual fund manager or stock broker. Venture capital is about creating value where none existed before. This value is grown only after the money is invested—in close collaboration with the entrepreneurs. As Todd Kimmel of Mayfield Fund observes, "Too many people think venture capital is simply about picking and choosing winners. It's more than that. It's about partnering and building relationships."[16] Similarly, John Doerr, one of the most famous venture capitalists today, says, "Others might say, people, people, people—but I'm most interested in the team as a whole—its

---

16 Todd Kimmel, personal discussion with author, May 18, 2011.

mix of experience and personalities, its chemistry."[17] A venture capitalist, by investing, ends up buying his or her way onto that team, for better or worse. Therefore, a venture capitalist's unspoken job description is to make that team chemistry even better, or certainly not make it any worse.

The difficulty of doing the job well becomes apparent when one realizes that venture capital is actually six jobs in one. The diagram below shows the typical life cycle of the venture capital process: [18]

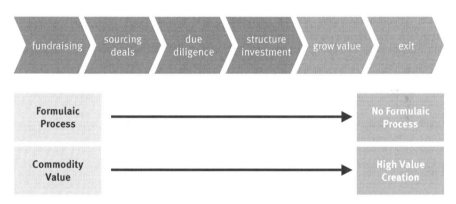

Note that each of these six jobs has its analogues in other highly-specialized professions—fundraiser, market analyst, auditor, lawyer, executive, and investment banker. People can build entire careers playing any one of these roles, but venture capital merges all these areas of expertise and requires a basic level of fluency in each. There is no easy way to outsource any of these functions completely, and you can't skip any of them either. The only phase in which one actually "makes" real-world value—i.e., the fifth of the six phases above—cannot occur without successfully navigating the first four phases. To make it even more complicated, the formula that works for one company is likely to be different from the formula that works for the next company.

17 Michael S. Malone, "John Doerr's Startup Manual," *Fast Company,* February 28, 1997, http://www.fastcompany.com/magazine/07/082doerr.html

18 Holly Davidson (of JamesBeck Global Partners), in discussion with the authors, circa 2006.

Throughout this entire process, venture capitalists must wear multiple hats. They are constantly dealing with incentives pulling them in three separate directions.

Multiple Incentives in Venture Capital

Venture capital requires practitioners to manage their daily actions at the intersection of these three roles, which are frequently in tension with one another:

- **Portfolio management** (with a *fiduciary obligation* to maximize financial return on behalf of their own investors)

- **Operational development** (*building companies* in close partnership with entrepreneurs, or at least not hindering the creation of value)

- **Community development** (participating as supportive *citizens of the Rainforest*, living by its social norms, aiding connectivity in the system, and developing new relationships with emerging talent)

When a region seeks to create a venture capital industry, we have found that the most common error is to focus on the first of the three roles above—the fiduciary role—to the detriment of the other two. True, fund managers have an obligation to maximize return on investment: it is data-driven, it is measurable, and it is also required by the law. Not doing so usually constitutes a breach of fiduciary obligation and—in the U.S. and in many places in the world—is a punishable offense.

However, focusing on the fiduciary role to the exclusion of the other two is a recipe for failure when building a Rainforest. Venture capital in emerging markets often fails because its practitioners do not recognize or are unable to balance these three competing roles at the same time.

Mutualism

In the tropical Amazonian rainforests, locals say that evil spirits haunt certain mysterious places. They call these places the "Devil's Garden," where large patches of rainforest are completely dominated by a single type of tree, and no other plants are able to grow. The largest known Devil's Garden contains 328 trees, covers over 1,300 square meters, and is around 800 years old.[19] Far from being a supernatural occurrence, however, scientists recently discovered that this phenomenon happens when a specific species of ant—the lemon ant—nests inside a tree called a *Duroia hirsuta*.[20] The lemon ants feed on the tree and create a natural herbicide that kills every other type of plant in the area. The ants receive protection and nutrients from the trees; the trees reproduce easily with their competition eliminated by the ants spreading the poison. The symbiotic results can be strong.

There is a biological analogy to the relationship between entrepreneurs and venture capitalists in the Rainforest. Biologists call this type of relationship *mutualism*. In mutualism, both organisms derive benefit from the relationship. The Devil's Garden is but one example. Think of the microorganisms in your intestines, called gut flora. Your body depends on about 100 trillion (10^{14}) such microorganisms digesting your food on your behalf this very moment.[21] Both you and your gut flora benefit from this mutualistic relationship. Indeed, neither you nor your gut flora could live without the other.

Mutualism can be extremely powerful, but when the balance is upset, it can be extremely destructive. Think of the indigestion you experience when your gut flora are either too few or too many. The mutualism between entrepreneurs and venture capitalists requires a similarly tricky balance. Done well, companies can flourish. Done poorly, they cannot get out of bed.

Therefore, pure financial managers are rarely the best venture capitalists, as they are often trained only to measure risk and maximize financial return, and not to find that mutualistic balance. A common error in emerging economies is that bankers or stock analysts are often considered the most qualified people to run new venture capital funds. It is true, they may have some expertise in general financial management, but good venture capitalists are positive-sum builders of companies—not zero-sum money

19 Alison Ross, "Devilish Ants Control the Garden," *BBC News,* September 21, 2005 http://news.bbc.co.uk/2/hi/science/nature/4269544.stm.

20 Megan E. Frederickson and Deborah M. Gordon, "The Devil to Pay: A Cost of Mutualism with *Myrmelachista Schumanni* Ants in 'Devil's Gardens' is Increased Herbivory on *Duroia Hirsuta* Trees," *Proceedings of the Royal Society* B 274 (2007): 1117, 10.1098/rspb.2006.0415; Megan E. Frederickson, Michael J. Greene and Deborah M. Gordon, "Ecology: 'Devil's Gardens' Bedevilled by Ants," Abstract, *Nature* 437 (2005): 495-496, doi:10.1038/437495a.

21 Bengt Björkstén et al., "Allergy Development and the Intestinal Microflora During the First Year of Life," *The Journal of Allergy and Clinical Immunology* 108 (2001): 516, doi:10.1067/mai.2001.118130.

managers. Venture capital is not about extracting value out of companies, like an oil pump might extract oil. It is about creating long-term value in close relationships, not exploitation or maximizing short-term gain.

Venture capital done wrong can ruin entrepreneurs and even destroy a local venture economy, like a parasitic species introduced into a natural ecosystem. We have seen numerous regions around the world where the lack of a thriving venture capital system can be attributed to the way that investors behaved and treated entrepreneurs and others in the network. In some places, venture capitalists have intentionally blocked out other venture firms—to the detriment of the entire system. In other places, they have taken predatory advantage of entrepreneurs, often at their most vulnerable points. The negative ripple effects in the system from these types of behaviors are long lasting. One bad apple can spoil the whole orchard when building Rainforests.

The behavior of venture capitalists matters because they often have life-or-death power over startup companies. They can influence the hiring or firing of a CEO, withhold future capital, or affect critical decisions needed to sustain the company. They also exercise "soft power" that comes from their ability to persuade people involved in the enterprise. Character counts, as they are often in the challenging position of simultaneously being both competitors and collaborators with their entrepreneurs, co-investors, and corporate partners. Personal integrity, transparency, candor, and sincerity are more than nice qualities for investors in a Rainforest; they are an essential part of the recipe.

The most fundamental role of venture capitalists is to control how equity is allocated in a company and to align incentives of key parties productively. Without everyone involved in a startup feeling like they are getting a mutually fair deal, and being fully motivated to move in the same direction, the fragile bonds that hold a startup together can easily fall apart. As Phil Wickham describes:

> You're trying to build the best organization you can, to solve the most acute problem you can, to address the biggest market you can. The only way to do that is through trust. How do you do that without trust? If you set up the incentive structure right, then that culture will drive the behavior of the team. If you think of it like a crew race, you cannot possibly design conflict into that kind of structure. You want to be competing against the guys who are rowing in different directions, not the ones rowing together. You cannot enforce a startup structure through hierarchy or legal recourse; you are competing against people who aren't wasting their time on those issues. While you're arguing about internal issues, the other companies are rushing to the finish line.

Venture capital done well is a form of biological mutualism—it reinforces the fragile bonds that hold people together in a nascent enterprise. Venture capital done poorly can break those bonds apart quickly.

In practice, many venture capitalists do not exercise their influence responsibly, often because they lack a complete understanding of their role in the innovation ecosystem. It is like giving a teenager the keys to Dad's Ferrari after a basic driver education course. The entrepreneurs are the ones who suffer because they usually have no idea how well a venture capitalist can drive before getting in the car. Once the Ferrari gets going, however, there is no jumping out. Phil continues, "Arguably, venture capital is the most important service provider in the system. But unlike other service providers, you can't fire your investor. You are marrying them."

There are many types of venture capitalists, but perhaps the one trait that is common among the most successful ones is the ability to understand the needs of entrepreneurs. One example comes from a story that George Doriot, the founder of American Research & Development Corporation (considered the first venture capital firm in the world), used to tell his students at Harvard Business School. Venture capitalist Tom Perkins, who was a former student, recalls, "He would talk about working with entrepreneurs, and when times got tough, as they always will. And he made that point that he would invite the entrepreneur over to his home. They'd have dinner. And then he'd just sit him down in his library, and play phonograph records of French marching music, you know, just to deal with the psychological wounds, you know."[22]

Some people, like venture capitalist Brian Dovey of Domain Ventures, call it *empathy*. As Brian recalls:

> Good VCs can come from most every walk of life. In my late 40s, when I was becoming a venture capitalist, I went around to many VCs and asked them to give me advice on how to do it. Every one of them had a different answer—the answer that played to their own backgrounds. But there was one thing they had in common. All of them had empathy for the entrepreneur. They knew how difficult it was. They were in sync with the entrepreneur. The entrepreneur was not the enemy, not someone to be pushed hard or beaten, but someone to be respected, even forgiven for some things that would go wrong.[23]

Another venture capitalist, Matt Harris of Village Ventures, puts it simply, "People who are not experienced VCs often do not realize how fragile these entities are. You need to respect the difficulty of what entrepreneurs are doing."[24]

---

22 *Something Ventured.*

23 Brian Dovey, telephone interview with author, July 28, 2011.

24 Matt Harris, telephone discussion with authors, June 13, 2011.

The Rainforest Capital Recipe

Successful venture capital requires generating financial returns while simultaneously serving as good citizens in the Rainforest and good coaches to entrepreneurs. Given the complexity of this task, how can one develop venture capital as part of an innovation ecosystem? We call this the Rainforest Capital Recipe:

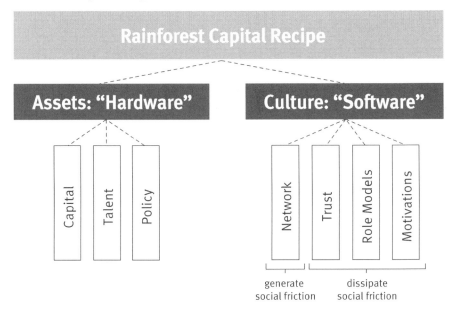

Like the Rainforest Recipe in Chapter 6, the Rainforest Capital Recipe has two sections, one focused on the hardware of capital and the other on its software. The following are some of the critical hardware issues we typically address:

- **Capital Infrastructure**. How strong is the base of "limited partners" in a community, whether they are institutional, individual, governmental, or corporate? (Limited partners are the original sources of capital that invest in venture funds.) Are they capable, sophisticated, and willing to tolerate some portfolio risk? Are they willing to co-invest in new fund formation to help grow a venture capital industry over the long term? Are the sources sufficient so that, taken together, the industry can invest throughout the entire continuum of capital? Are they willing to take calibrated risks on new fund managers developing new vehicles for new market niches? Are investors that are seeking to fill the seed-stage and early-stage "gap"—such as governmental institutions and development banks—willing to invest in grants and/or equity, not just debt?

- **Talent Infrastructure**. How strong is the pool of talent interested in and capable of venture fund management? How strong are the practical skills and experiences of such people in building startup companies, developing new products, and creating personal networks in the Rainforest community? What are the human leadership qualities of these people?

- **Policy Infrastructure**. How does the law define fiduciary obligations to investors? Do tax incentives guide investing toward or away from early-stage, privately-held startups? Are investors able to use a broad toolkit of financial vehicles (e.g., convertible debt and preferred stock) or corporate entities (such as corporations, limited partnerships, limited liability companies, other pass-through entities, or joint stock companies) to address different investing circumstances? How low are the liquidity barriers (i.e., for a company to be acquired or make an initial public offering of its stock)? What types of subsidized capital help fill gaps in the continuum of capital?

On the software side of the recipe, we typically ask questions like these:

- **Network**. Does a highly-networked community exist or can it be built? Is the fund actively connected to the global marketplace? How strong are the connections between local fund managers and key people (e.g., co-investors, partners, customers, executives, entrepreneurs, researchers, academics, lawyers, bankers, accountants, and other professionals) who are critical to the success of startup companies? Communities that are captive to a single venture fund (or handful of funds) will foster weak ecosystems, so do investors appreciate that a diversity of venture capital resources is preferable to a monopoly situation?

  Funds cannot be islands. Modern venture capital requires real-time knowledge of global technology market trends and access to global sources of capital, talent, expertise, and business partnerships.[25] Robust networks can help *raise the quality of deals* because fund managers can calibrate investment opportunities against global standards. These networks can help their companies by enhancing global access to *additional sources of capital*, including co-investors,

---

25 Josh Lerner, "Geography, Venture Capital, and Public Policy" (policy brief, Rappaport Institute/ Taubman Center, Harvard Kennedy School, John F. Kennedy School of Government, Cambridge, 2010), http://www.hks.harvard.edu/var/ezp_site/storage/fckeditor/file/pdfs/centers-programs/centers/ taubman/PB_final_lerner_vc.pdf. "Surprisingly, much of the VC outperformance in these venture capital centers arises from their non-local investments. This finding is counterintuitive, since venture capitalists might be expected to be the most involved and add the most value to the geographically closest companies." Lerner speculates about supply-demand arbitrage for capital and higher hurdle rates for investing as potential explanations. We hypothesize that the advantage might be traced to the fact that venture firms are brought into non-local deals specifically for the value added by their global linkages.

follow-on investors, and institutional partners. They can also *increase the odds of successful acquisitions or public offerings* for their startups by connecting startup companies to potential acquirers early, or by accessing public markets in other countries.

- **Trust**. Venture capital depends on human relationships more than transactional structures. Do fund managers build deep and trusting relationships throughout the community? Can they develop such relationships in other markets to create valuable linkages? Does a fund have the credibility to leverage trusted and respected channels to open new relationships? Do investors have the ability to speak honestly and openly with entrepreneurs and others without destroying value or creating adversarial relationships?

- **Role Models**. Venture capital is learned through apprenticeship. There is a common saying in the industry that it takes $20 million to train a venture capitalist. Are emerging fund managers able to benefit from the experience, advice, ethics, networks, and track records of successful mentors? Do role models act according to the Rules of the Rainforest, and are they able to pass their behaviors on to fund managers? Do investors learn to focus on long-term, sustainable success rather than short-term advantage?

- **Motivations**. Are investors motivated beyond the lure of money? Do they practice the Rules of the Rainforest? Are they able to appreciate the importance of the extra-rational motivations that drive entrepreneurs and others?

Most venture funds sponsored by governments or corporations—no matter how well-intentioned—don't generate lasting impact because they fail to treat venture capital as a biological system, not just an engineering problem. The Rainforest Capital Recipe accounts for the importance of both of these aspects: culture and structure must be integrated together. Therefore, creating capital in a Rainforest is similar to creating the rest of the Rainforest—we need to "engineer" biological systems.

Ass vs. Class

"BEWARE OF ASSHOLE VCs!"

So read the sensational headline of a blog entry[26] by Seth Levine, a venture capitalist at the Foundry Group. Seth tells the story of a startup that was forced by its venture capitalists to close down so that the VCs could hedge their risks and take a short-term payout, rather than let the entrepreneurs continue trying to build the company. As a result, the entrepreneurs were left with little reward for their efforts. Seth proclaims his "golden rule of venture: "MANY VCs ARE ASSHOLES." And he continues by saying, "The irony here from my perspective is that it actually wasn't even a very smart economic move by the investors involved (ASSHOLE VCs aren't always that smart)."

Given the large amount of money at stake, the temptation in the venture capital business to do the "wrong" thing—to seek a short-term advantage, crush an entrepreneur, or take a moral shortcut—is omnipresent. The critical lesson—for a government, a corporation, or any community trying to build a Rainforest—is that one cannot ignore the macro effects of these types of micro behaviors. To create the right kind of macro-system, one must intentionally nurture the "right" set of micro-behaviors, and involve people who have the character to live up to those standards. The world does not need more asshole venture capitalists.

To understand the American venture capital industry of today, it helps to understand the industry's roots. The beginning of this chapter starts with an off-the-cuff remark that legendary venture capitalist Alan Patricof made to one of us at breakfast a few years ago. It was a sharp but true observation. Venture capital is definitely not the easiest way for someone to make money. Doing private equity—also known as leveraged buyouts—is far easier. If one is going to do venture capital, one should do it for reasons that go beyond simple financial gain.

From its beginnings, venture capital has been tied to the same non-economic motivations that also drive entrepreneurs to build companies. This is a surprising fact for many people who look at the industry from afar. The thrill of competition, the novelty of discovery, the joy of creation, the satisfaction that comes from helping other people, or any number of other extra-rational motivations—they are woven into the fabric of venture capital. After all, the term "venture capital" was originally derived from

---

26 Seth Levine, "Beware of Asshole VCs," *Seth Levine's* VC Adventure (blog), July 28, 2011, http://www.sethlevine.com/wp/.

wealthy businessman Jock Whitney's idea that this money was intended as "private adventure capital."[27]

The roots of Silicon Valley venture capital were founded on this sense of adventure. Although we no longer think of venture capital as an entrepreneurial enterprise, it was that way not long ago. The early venture capitalists in the Valley were a lot like cowboys. Many of them had frontier-style mindsets. Much of the industry as we know it today started in the 1950s and 1960s from a small, informal group of young, not-so-wealthy individual investors in San Francisco. As Bill Edwards, one of the original members of the group, recalls, "None of us had enough money to do an investment by ourselves, so we had to have help."[28] The entire venture capital industry in Silicon Valley raised only $10 million in 1975.[29] Surprisingly, this multi-billion industry that has transformed the world was barely in existence just a few decades ago.

Molly Davis, the executive producer of the documentary *Something Ventured*, observed the behavior of the early venture capitalists who were interviewed in her film: "They're working really hard, they're very bright, they're working together, and they're collaborating. And there's a lot of fun involved in achieving things together as a group. So, I don't think you can underestimate how much fun the people… had doing what they did. I think they're extremely proud, but when they talk about these stories, they're laughing, they're smiling. There's just this excitement and energy about building something."[30]

The pioneers of venture capital were forced to work closely together, not unlike the pioneers on the American frontier a century before. As Don Valentine of Sequoia Capital remembered, "Funds in those days were tiny, and in order for us to start a company, we had to very collegially work together."[31] Despite all the competitive pressures, they had no choice but to participate as collaborative members of a tight community in order to succeed. A "gentlemen's culture" existed during the industry's first decades, and open conflicts such as lawsuits between Silicon Valley venture firms were almost unheard of.

---

27 Steve Blank, "The Secret History of Silicon Valley," *Steve Blank* (blog), October 26, 2009, http://steveblank.com/2009/10/26/the-secret-history-of-silicon-valley-11-the-rise-of-%E2%80%9Crisk-capital%E2%80%9D-part-1/.

28 *Something Ventured.*

29 Andrew Pollack, "Venture Capital Loses Its Vigor," *The New York Times,* October 8, 1989, http://www.nytimes.com/1989/10/08/business/venture-capital-loses-its-vigor.html?src=pm. The article cites data from *Venture Economics.*

30 SXSW Interview- Molly Davis, *Something Ventured,* YouTube video, 4:05, Campaign for Free Enterprise interview with Molly Davis, posted by "Freeenterprise," March 16, 2011, http://www.youtube.com/watch?v=fe2jjoaDMLk.

31 *Something Ventured.*

The behavioral culture of venture capital, therefore, is critical in Rainforests. History shows that the Silicon Valley venture industry was built by people who were motivated by more than just a desire to maximize profit at the expense of their relationships or their integrity. Fund managers that succumb to the temptation to be "assholes" do more than harm a single company—they can prevent Rainforests from springing to life.

Money ≠ Venture Capital

As we have argued, money is not the same as venture capital. When most people invest money to buy shares in a publicly-traded company, their relationship with that company tends to be extremely limited. At most, they might attend a shareholder meeting or check a box to vote on an occasional resolution. When capital is invested by a venture fund, however, it is just the beginning of a complex and symbiotic relationship.

Venture capitalists must be actively involved not only in the fortunes of their portfolio companies, but in the fate of their entire innovation communities. An invasive species may thrive temporarily in a new environment, but if it destroys the habitat, it is ultimately doomed. Similarly, a venture capitalist may benefit temporarily by maximizing short-term gains, but in so doing, they ruin their chances for long-term success. This is why some funds can stimulate the creation of entire Rainforests, while others seem to be toxic to the ecosystems around them. The role of venture capital, done well, is to balance interests and create mutualism among parties. In addition to serving their investors and their own personal interests, venture capitalists should be incentivized to respect the needs of their companies, their communities, and even their competitors. The recipe for venture capital in Rainforests requires the design of new structures that reflect these incentives.

We can summarize some basic lessons for capital formation in Rainforests:

> **Lesson #1:** *Rainforests need different forms of capital to serve different stages of innovation growth.*

> **Lesson #2:** *Capital markets are inherently inefficient at early stages of innovation.*

> **Lesson #3:** *Rainforests bridge the market gap for early-stage innovation by using subsidized capital and by fostering social norms and trust to lower transaction costs.*

> **Lesson #4:** *Venture capitalists must treat deals not as one-time transactions with individual startups, but as repeat transactions with the entire community.*

> **Lesson #5:** *Fund managers must fulfill their informal obligations to entrepreneurs and the Rainforest, not just their formal fiduciary obligations.*

> **Lesson #6:** *Venture capitalists should structure investments in symbiotic ways that keep entrepreneurs 100% incentivized to make companies succeed.*

Our Rainforest Capital Recipe can grow innovation capital in new places. It seeks to incentivize fund managers—through a framework of normative rules, personal motivations, incentives, and mentoring structures—to behave in ways that support the creation and long-term sustainability of Rainforests. As Phil Wickham puts it, a fund that does not learn the real, underlying lessons of the American venture capital industry is not building a Rainforest. "They are just building a terrarium."[32]

---

32 Wickham, interview.

Chapter Eight: How Do You Measure a Rainforest?

Taking the Heartbeat of Innovation

There are the rushing waves...
mountains of molecules,
each stupidly minding its own business...
trillions apart
...yet forming white surf in unison.

— **Richard P. Feynman, "The Value of Science," address
to the National Academy of Sciences (1955)**[1]

---

1   Richard P. Feynman, "The Value of Science" (address, National Academy of Sciences, Autumn, 1955), http://www.ma.utexas.edu/users/mwilliams/feynman.pdf.

Skype to Skype over Skype

In your pocket or purse right now perhaps is a phone. We still call it that name, but the word "phone" is really inadequate to the task anymore. It is really not so much a phone anymore as it is a totally integrated communications device, allowing you to communicate over the WiFi in a coffee shop, a Bluetooth network with your car or headset, or the wide area networks that your cell phone company provides. A lot is happening in that device now mislabeled as a "phone."

One of the reasons we have been able to pack so many complicated systems into a phone is because of people like Wen Tsay and his team on the small island nation of Taiwan. Wen launched his startup company, AirDio Wireless, to take those numerous communication technologies and shrink them down to a single package—one centimeter by one centimeter—that could fit inside a small device. His team has been on the cutting edge of what is called "system-in-a-package" technology.

But technologies in isolation do not make a company, as we have shown in this book. AirDio had to be part of a Rainforest. One story in particular from the Rainforest surrounding AirDio stands out. When AirDio wanted to grow, they looked for capital. By the time they were done, remarkably enough, they were able to bring in a highly unusual angel investor—one of the founders of Skype, who was based in Estonia about 5,000 miles away. How did this happen?

To overcome the geographic, social, and other barriers that hindered AirDio's search for capital, the parties worked through a series of human bridges. The bridge started with the investment firm of Toivo Annus, a Skype co-founder, who reached out to the organization CONNECT Estonia to help him contact startups in Asia. People at CONNECT Estonia reached out to us, and asked us to help Toivo. The bridge continued, as we made contact with the team at CONNECT Taiwan, which was run by the Taiwan government's Institute for Information Industry. CONNECT Taiwan completed the bridge by putting Toivo and Wen directly in touch with each other. The two people talked numerous times—over Skype, naturally—and a deal was eventually reached.

At this point, neoclassical economic theory has little more to add. A classically-trained economist might observe that Toivo and Wen had arbitraged market inefficiencies to create a mutually-beneficial investment transaction. We would simply have to wait and see if their transaction paid off over time. It was like picking a winning stock. In the real world of innovation, however, their story had just begun.

After the deal was in place, Wen discovered that he was now connected to an entirely new and powerful social network. He was suddenly immersed in a group of over fifty startup CEOs around the world, all of whom ran companies in Toivo's investment portfolio. He saw how these people could access valuable advice, assistance, connections, or partnerships through this virtual network. According to Wen:

> One CEO would send an email asking for help. Another CEO would give advice on how to survive the recession and cut expenses. There was a lot of sharing. It was valuable because it is hard for a CEO to make decisions on his own. One CEO said he needed a technology, and was there anyone familiar with this technology?... The group had wide knowledge about different kinds of technology. They knew a lot of people globally and could introduce you to other investors and other people to build connections.[2]

More than simply getting money, Wen benefited from relationships that transcended huge social and geographic barriers. We called this a "social tesseract" in Chapter 2, and likened it to the land bridges that connect isolated regions to form integrated ecosystems. It is exactly what the Anti-Google needed, and what Larry Bock actually did.

We have already demonstrated the enormous value in building social networks that connect people from opposite ends of the earth, or opposite sides of town, but this suggests another layer to the mystery of innovation. If we want to create Rainforests and then measure their effects, we must account for the millions of invisible, intangible interactions like the ones among Wen, Toivo, and this virtual group of CEOs. From high above the treetops in the Rainforest, how can we possibly observe such microscopic interactions? Traditional economic tools fail to capture the value of these relationships.

There is no "Gross Innovation Product" that governments publish to reflect the volume of such interactions in a system, although such a tool would be extraordinarily useful. No one reports their new business collaborations to a central data bureau. No one measures the value of an interesting idea that circulates between Estonia and Taiwan. No one calculates the level of trust between two innovators, nor the trust in a virtual group of entrepreneurs. When it comes to watching the amount of innovation happening in a system, we are essentially flying blind, too high above the Rainforest to see what really matters.

However, our leaders—from CEOs and Prime Ministers, to product managers and civil servants—are desperate for better vision. This is a problem. We need new tools to observe the Rainforest.

2 Wen Tsay, telephone interview with author, August 9, 2011.

The Goldilocks Microscope

Remember the conversation on the tumultuous airplane ride at the beginning of the book? We posed a big question that we still have not fully answered: *how do we measure the waves of the ocean*? How do we account for the ways people come together to exchange ideas and build companies? How do we map the dynamic relationships that drive innovation?

Innovation cannot be seen by looking at the whole ocean. That is too macroscopic a perspective. Innovation originates from people interacting, like individual atoms, one relationship at a time. Some of these interactions turn into waves, and some of those waves eventually lift the entire ocean. However, it would be impossible to identify and measure every facet of every single wave.

On the other hand, is it possible to devise a model that describes the overall *rhythms of the waves* in an ocean without having to measure every wave? Can we find a useful way to capture the patterns of interactions among people? To measure the Rainforest accurately, we must find a "Goldilocks" microscope: a tool that sees at a magnification level appropriate to the scale of the Rainforest. We are in a situation like the girl, Goldilocks, who wanted her porridge "just right"—neither too hot, nor too cold. Similarly, we are in between two extremes—atoms (humans) on the one hand, oceans (human society) on the other—and we want to assess the waves (collaborative networks) that are in the middle. If we had a "just right" Goldilocks microscope, we could better observe the innovation activity happening in a system. As economists use indexes like Gross Domestic Product to measure the health of macroeconomic systems, can we try to create something like a Gross Innovation Product to measure the health of Rainforests?

A Node-by-Node Rainforest

We can always create a Goldilocks microscope the hard way. Following the footsteps of the Incas—who built stunning structures near the Amazonian rainforests one stone at a time—we could similarly construct a model by linking together social networks one person at a time. It might look something like this social network diagram, which shows how emails flow within an organization:[3]

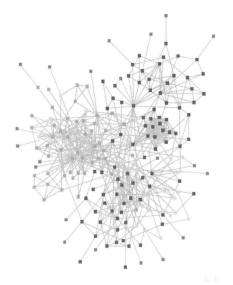

For example, we could draw the story of AirDio by depicting Wen Tsay and Toivo Annus as nodes that were initially four "degrees of separation" from each other. We could link every step of the path that led to their connection, from one person to the next. Finally, once Toivo invested in AirDio, we could draw a direct line of connection between Toivo and Wen. We could then represent how Wen was able to access Toivo's network of entrepreneurs by showing how members of that network were just one more link away.

The node-based social network model explains the Toivo-Wen transaction the same way a chemist might describe the interaction of atoms or molecules—through distinct and clearly-drawn dots and lines. It is like a mechanical, piece-by-piece schematic diagram. Can this model help us measure the health of a Rainforest? Let's think about what such a model might look like for describing an entire Rainforest.

---

3 "Data Mining Email to Discover Social Networks and Emergent Communities," orgnet.com, accessed August 30, 2011, http://www.orgnet.com/email.html. Reprinted courtesy of Valdis Krebs (2008). Diagram depicts flow of email on a business project.

In theory, we could construct a massive version of the social network model like the diagram above. We could draw upon cutting-edge software to help us. We would try to calculate every single economic exchange happening in the system. An exchange might be something as intangible as a referral via email, a suggested way to test a device, or an idea overheard in a coffee shop. An exchange might also be something as tangible as a venture investment where cash is transacted, a joint research project, or the purchase of market research data. If we could capture all of that, we would have a thorough map of everything valuable happening in a Rainforest.

However, such a model would be extraordinarily complex. A Rainforest can involve countless people, each with their own particular set of motives, life experiences, interests, values, and eccentricities. As Stanford social network professor Matthew Jackson says, "The great challenge in modeling behavioral aspects is that we do not want to assume that people conform."[4] Real life is very, very messy.[5]

This would be further complicated by the fact that we need to create, not one, but *two* overlapping models to describe a Rainforest comprehensively. The first model would describe the normative behavior of people in a system—the level of trust between each pair of parties, each party's adherence to its community's Rules, and the extra-rational motivations of each person in the system. Professor Jackson's work, for instance, includes cutting-edge mathematical models that show how cultural behaviors can be spread by keystones in a system.[6] His equations could help us calculate how norms revert over time in the absence of keystones.[7] They could also help calculate how people tend to create "normative islands," where there are higher concentrations of certain cultural behaviors, such as the Israeli startup community. This normative network model would measure precisely how norms and trust are spread in a Rainforest, describing for instance the way that Toivo and Wen leveraged a series of trust-based relationships to build their own connection.

The second model, overlaid on the first model, would seek to measure every single transaction in a system. In the Rainforest, every possible linkage between any two people can open the door to a potential transaction. Thus, we would "test" every single link to see if a connection could be forged

---

4 Jackson, interview (see chap. 6, n. 48).

5 Jackson, *Social and Economic Networks,* 54-56 (see chap. 6, n. 48). Even the scale-free models that appear to explain traffic on the Web are not as complete as they appear—they require "hybrid models" that blend different approaches together.

6 Matthew O. Jackson and Leeat Yariv, "Social Networks and the Diffusion of Economic Behavior," *Yale Economic Review* 3 (2006): 45, http://www.stanford.edu/~jacksonm/yer-netbehavior.pdf.

7 Daron Acemoglu and Matthew O. Jackson, "History, Expectations, and Leadership in the Evolution of Cooperation" (NBER Working Paper No.17066, National Bureau of Economic Research, Cambridge, 2011), http://www.nber.org/papers/w17066.pdf.

between two people, based on the frequency of their interactions and on a complex cost-benefit equation. The cost side would be adjusted for the social barriers caused by geography, distrust, culture, language, and social groups. The benefit side would be adjusted for the level of extra-rational motivations among the parties. This transaction network would measure precisely every single exchange of value. The greater the social distance between parties, the greater the potential value to be exchanged, but the harder it would be to consummate an exchange. [8] To describe the AirDio story, for instance, we would examine every referral link and make a series of cost-benefit calculations—was it worth it for each person to pass the referral to the next person?

If we could overlay these two models, in theory, we could obtain our Gross Innovation Product. The economic value created in an entire Rainforest would be the sum total of every single economic exchange through every single link in the system. Even a simple email referral from one person to another would be counted.

This type of model would yield a huge amount of detailed information about a system. However, building such a purely atomistic model would be incredibly difficult. How do you actually measure such fuzzy concepts as trust, social norms, or human motivations? What are the true benefits and costs of something as simple as an email referral from one person to another? The model seems useful in theory but impossibly difficult to execute in practice.

Perhaps there is another way. When we have exceedingly messy particles, as in a real-world Rainforest, looking at countless particles and interactions one at a time is simply too difficult. Let's consider approaching the problem from a different angle. To discover the right type of Goldilocks microscope, we turn to the biological world for a possible solution.

The Secret Life of Mushrooms

In 2006, a breakthrough idea came from an unlikely source. Sheep breeder Karen Tesson had taken a break from her profession to pursue a Ph.D. at the University of Bath. For her research, she decided to explore an unusual subject—the intersection of ecology and psychology—and she speculated

8 Peter Csermely, *Weak Links: The Universal Key to the Stability of Networks and Complex Systems* (Dordrecht; New York: Springer, 2009), 1-4, http://www.weaklink.sote.hu/weakbook.html. This reflects the work of social scientist Mark Granovetter, who observed that the weakest social links are also the ones that have the most potential impact on the entire network. These weak links are like the glue of a community.

in her doctoral dissertation that there might be a radical new way to model social networks. She based it on the fungus.[9]

Do you ever wonder why mushrooms are so hard to kill? They certainly thrive everywhere. At Victor's home in the hills of Silicon Valley, there is one great mulberry tree in a courtyard that has mushrooms growing in the base of its trunk. No matter how often one tries to wipe them out, the mushrooms always find a way to come back, like zombies in a horror movie. Battling those mushrooms remains an ongoing test of will between Man and Nature, one that Nature will ultimately win. Experts estimate that up to one-quarter of the world's biomass is of fungal origin, made up of 1.5 million species.[10] At first blush, mushrooms may seem to have little to do with innovation ecosystems. Yet the biological reason mushrooms are so resilient can give us profound insight into ways we can measure the health of innovation systems. As we will show, Rainforests have a lot to do with mushrooms.

Fungi are among the most robust biological systems on Earth. Mushrooms are just the fruiting body of the true culprit underneath—like the tip of an iceberg. Underneath mushrooms is the important stuff—the vegetable part of the fungus called the *mycelium*, deeply embedded in the ground. A mycelium does not have a "body" per se. It is made entirely of hyphae, which are long, thin tubes filled with liquid that act like a complex web of veins.

11

9 Karen Jane Tesson, "An Interdisciplinary Study of Network Organization in Biological and Human Social Systems" (PhD diss., University of Bath, 2006), 32, http://www.jackwhitehead.com/teesonphd/007c6.pdf.

10 Abigail C. Leeder, Javier Palma-Guerrero and N. Louise Glass, "The Social Network: Deciphering Fungal Language," *Abstract, Nature Reviews Microbiology 9 (2011)*, doi:10.1038/nrmicro258.

11 Photo reprinted courtesy of Shane Mulholland, http://www.foragedandfoundorganics.com/mycofiltration_services (accessed September 2, 2011).

The unique structure of the mycelium makes a fungus one of the most durable plants in the world. Why is a mycelium so extraordinarily durable, given that other plants have roots too? The answer is called *anastomosis*. Anastomosis happens when the ends of the hyphae networks become fused together, like this:

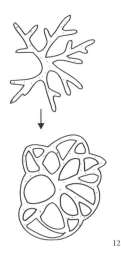

12

Anastomosis creates a fully connected circulatory system in the fungus. It is highly resilient. When a fungus attains anastomosis, you can cut off part of the system, but the rest of it stays alive. The circulation of vital fluids is always able to reach any part of the network, no matter which part is damaged. In addition, the mycelium has the ability to absorb nutrients from anywhere in the network and distribute them to the rest of the system. For example, if part of the network touches a rotting log, the nutrients from the log do not just benefit the part of the fungus that is touching the log—the nutrients circulate throughout the full network.

There are other trees and plants that have structures similar to those of fungi. One example is the largest single organism in the world. If you went for a walk in a particular forest of aspen trees in south-central Utah, you would be standing on it. Its name is Pando. It weighs over 6,000,000 kilograms, covers 107 acres, and is estimated to be over 80,000 years old. This entire aspen forest is actually a single organism with a dense, interconnected root network. It is similar to the way that a fungal mycelium works—but instead of mushrooms on top, we get aspen trees.

---

12 Tesson, "An Interdisciplinary Study," 125. Diagram adapted from A.D.M. Rayner, et al., "Self-integration—an emerging concept from the fungal mycelium," in N.A.R. Gow, G.D. Robson and G.M. Gadd, (eds.), *The Fungal Colony.* Cambridge: Cambridge University Press (1999).

In fact, the human circulatory system is a partial example of such a "round trip" network. You can lose a limb or digit—say, a finger—but with the right care, the rest of the body is able to maintain full circulation and eventually recovers.

So what do mushrooms, aspen trees, and fingers have to do with innovation? If a particular system is robust in nature, then might it also be robust for human society? How can Nature's designs serve as a basis to measure the health of human Rainforests?

The Flow-Form Model

Whereas node-based social network models are reductionist (by looking at isolated fragments of the whole system), Karen Tesson felt that it would be useful to have a model that could describe the vast complexity of an entire biological system. Why should we "delineate artificial boundaries" such as individual nodes in these models? For instance, if we were analyzing a football crowd of 100,000, why would we look at just three football fans in isolation, when the behavior of those three fans is likely influenced by the other 99,997 screaming fans in the stadium?

In place of the social network model, Tesson suggested a new model based on the concept of anastomosis. She called it the "flow-form model." It is premised on the idea that *flow* is a better representation of what happens in biological systems than *links*. The flow-form model depicts the connections in a social network as the movement of fluids in tubes, as in a mycelium network. As Tesson describes:

> The "flow-form model" contrasts at a profound level with
> conventional models of communicative networks, which
> are often presented as systems of interconnected *nodes*,
> and it offers a radically different way of conceptualizing
> how a networked structure could behave. The flow-form
> model therefore represents a shift away from the node-
> centered thinking of conventional network theory, towards
> an understanding of networks as representations of
> communicative *flow.* "[13]

We believe that the flow-form model serves as a useful tool to describe the Rainforest. It is like a Goldilocks microscope, located at the halfway point between observing individual atoms and observing the entire ocean. In other words, at the transition point between the atomistic models on one end, and the thermodynamic models on the other, we can think of the

---

13 Ibid., 32-33.

Rainforest as a network of fluid-filled arteries.[14] We can see the "waves" of human interaction moving through those arteries.

The nutrients within the arteries of Rainforests are the basic ingredients of innovation—ideas, talent, and capital. In studying biological diversity, some scientists have argued that natural ecosystems can be explained as "energy transduction systems"—that is, the species richness in an ecosystem derives from the evolution of organisms as they become more and more efficient in using the food web.[15] Plants or animals that utilize the available nutrients in biological ecosystems most efficiently are those that survive. We believe it is useful to extend this biological concept to innovation Rainforests, too. Ideas, talent, and capital form a "food web" that provides sustenance to people as they organize themselves into new collaborations, such as startup companies. Startups draw these resources—like plants drawing nutrients through their roots—and attempt to utilize them in the most efficient ways possible.

The velocity of fluid flowing in a network correlates to the ability of people to communicate with each other. When a system possesses strong diversity, trust, normative rules, and extra-rational motivations, then the arteries open wide to allow the fast flow of ideas, talent, and capital. When a system does not, then the arteries constrict, and the resources slow down or stop their flow entirely. For example, if a scientist who has invented a therapy for cancer does not trust nor engage with businesspeople necessary to commercialize it, his invention cannot obtain the necessary nutrients through the arteries around him and will die. *The lack of a Rainforest culture is like freezing the food web.*

---

14 See for example Robert Herman and Ilya Prigogine, "A Two-Fluid Approach to Town Traffic," *Science* 204 (1979): 149, doi:10.1126/science.204.4389.148. Ilya Prigogine won the Nobel Prize for his theories in irreversible thermodynamics. Prigogine and colleague demonstrated that human traffic patterns on city streets could be described by fluid-based models. "The average speed of the moving vehicles is assumed to be proportional to the fraction of the vehicles that are moving raised to a power that reflects the 'goodness' of the traffic." Such a model might be helpful in devising a formula to calculate the flow of knowledge, talent, and capital in a Rainforest.

15 Peter Würtz and Arto Annila, "Roots of Diversity Relations," *Journal of Biophysics*, Volume 2008 (2008), Article ID 654672, doi:10.1155/2008/654672, http://www.hindawi.com/journals/jbp/2008/654672/.

Below is a table that summarizes how the flow-form model compares to the alternative models for measuring the health of economic systems

	Individuals-Startup	Rainforest	Nation-State-World
Physical analogy	Atoms/Molecules	Waves	Oceans
Discipline of study	Social network analysis	Flow-form model (anastomosis)	Neoclassical macroeconomic models
Mathematical basis	Node-based network	Fluid-based network	Fluids (thermodynamic)
Method of action	Cost-benefit transactions between nodes	Communication between nodes	"invisible hand" (efficient movement of resources)
Predictability of results	Generally random	Probabilistic	Deterministic
Positive variables	Benefits of transaction (influenced by extra-rational motivations)	Velocity of ideas, capital, talent, and other resources in circulation (increased by diversity, trust, norms, extra-rational motivations)	Basic factors of economic production (labor, land, capital; possibly technology, human capital, and entrepreneurship)
Negative variables	Costs of transaction (influenced by trust, norms)	Constriction of arteries (caused by social barriers of geography, distrust, culture, language, inefficient social networks)	Inefficient productivity, inefficient resource allocation
Direction of analysis	Bottom up (build up relationships node-by-node)	Top down (every relationship is possible, but constrictions in flow create inefficiencies in the system)	High-level view

Economic activity looks atomic when examined at the microscopic level, but it appears like a fluid when examined at the macroscopic level. The flow-form model is a way to represent the middle point where the micro and macro intersect. Instead of creating a complex set of overlapping models to describe the workings of real-world ecosystems, we can use a flow-form model.

The flow-form model helps explain much of what we observe in real Rainforests. The model reflects the non-quantifiable nature of small but important acts, like idea-sharing, mentoring, lending validation, and making referrals. Someone contributing time—say, a successful entrepreneur giving a free idea or a piece of advice to a newcomer—is a legitimate form of value creation in the Rainforest. The flow of that little idea from one person to another, happening during a tiny fragment of time, has the potential to transform the entire system.

In contrast, the social network model and the macroeconomic model do not easily account for such non-measurable events. Economic transactions in those models tend to focus on measurable exchanges of goods, services, or other value between nodes. But in the Rainforest, ideas, talent, and capital can flow from one person to the next without a discrete or formal "transaction" per se. Tesson describes the flow-form model similarly:

> It suggests that rather than treating communication as a process of transition between discrete *states*, we could consider communication to be the result of fluid transformations.... Rather than suggesting that flow-form networks are merely diagrams of the forces to which they have been exposed... they are actually the physical manifestations of the interaction between contents and contexts.[16]

In Rainforests, the movement of ideas, talent, and capital—the "contents"— is dependent on the relative openness or tightness of the arteries—the "contexts". Communication between people is the heart of flow within the system.[17] For example, the series of global referrals that were made to connect Wen Tsay and Toivo Annus "flowed" because the arteries were wide and fast. Although the exchange happened through a chain of people, it would seem strange to think of those referrals as discrete economic transactions in any traditional sense. Even seemingly inconsequential tidbits of advice in the Rainforest can be of extraordinary value. Recall in the story of the Anti-Google how a single off-hand remark from Tim Draper eventually led to the acquisition of the Gauches' second startup company.

---

16 Ibid., 115, 136.

17 See also Steven S. Wildman, "Communication and Economics: Two Imperial Disciplines and Too Little Collaboration," *Journal of Communication* 58 (2008): 693–694, doi: 10.1111/j.1460-2466.2008.00409.x. Wildman notes the idea that economics and communications are the two "imperial disciplines", often at odds with one another.

The manner in which intangible value is exchanged in a Rainforest follows
its own set of laws, not captured by traditional economic models. It is
similar to a notion that has become attributed to writer George Bernard
Shaw, which goes:

> If I have an apple and you have an apple and we exchange
> apples—then you have an apple and I have an apple. But if I
> have the idea that the apple is red and you have the idea that
> the apple is small and we exchange ideas, then you have two
> ideas and I have two ideas. It is quite obvious, therefore, that
> *the laws governing thoughts or ideas are different from the laws
> governing things.*[18]

Thus, the flow-form model gives us a powerful way to think of the overall
health of an entire Rainforest because it reflects the way things actually
work. The faster the velocity of nutrients within a system, the healthier
the entire system.[19] We can think of ideas, talent, and capital like particles
that are limited by the speed at which they flow. If a new idea is injected
somewhere in the network—say, a revolutionary method to convert waste
to energy at lower cost—we want that idea to have the ability to circulate
within the whole system, to get where it is needed, whether that destination
ends up being an entrepreneur, a corporation which can license the
technology, or a researcher who can incorporate the idea in her own work.
Talent and capital are similar—if they can quickly get where they need to go,
then the Rainforest as a whole benefits.

The fast referral network that connected Wen and Toivo was beneficial
for the whole system. When Toivo reached out to the system with an
opportunity, the system responded from halfway around the world to open
the flow of ideas, talent, and capital between him and Wen. Additionally,
thousands of other entrepreneurs and investors have quietly made their own
connections through these same networks. The power of flow-form systems
is that they are "highly responsive to their environmental contexts."[20] As
people develop new ideas to adapt to the changing market, the arteries are
open to them, too.

---

18 A variation of this quote is commonly attributed to George Bernard Shaw, but it may be apocryphal.
  The earliest citable source we could find is *Phi Kappa Phi Journal,* Volumes 32-34 (Honor Society of Phi
  Kappa Phi, March 1952), Google books (italics added).

19 See for comparison Ian P. McCarthy et al., "A Multidimensional Conceptualization of Environmental
  Velocity," *Academy of Management Review* 35, (2010): 604-626, http://thomaslawrence.files.wordpress.
  com/2008/08/mccarthy-et-al-2010-a-multidimensional-conceptualization-of-environmen.pdf. Other
  researchers have noted the possible use of velocity to measure economic activity. However, such
  approaches tend to view velocity in macroeconomic terms (such as the speed of changes in supply,
  demand, or other broad indicators). Our approach argues, instead, that we should measure the velocity
  of the basic factors of economic production as they course through social networks. The former is like
  watching the velocity of oceans rising; the latter is like watching the velocity of new waves forming.

20 Tesson, "An Interdisciplinary Study," 32

The flow-form model also helps to better explain the outliers. The investment by Toivo's firm in AirDio—an Estonian investor in a Taiwanese startup—was an outlier by any typical measure. According to the traditional social network model, it would be a highly unlikely event and not easily predicted or measured. However, Rainforests thrive on the outliers. Outliers are like weeds—they are the critical, unexpected connections that can lead to explosive economic results. Connecting these weak links—or what Professor Peter Csermely calls the "creative links"—generates great value for the system.[21] The flow-form model is powerful because it assumes, by definition, that any relationship *might* happen in an interconnected system. In fact, it is the absence of such outliers that indicates the weakness of an innovation ecosystem. When we build Rainforests, we want *more* outlier relationships to happen by encouraging more open flow of nutrients in the system.

Thus, the flow-form model works in the opposite direction of the social network model. It moves top down, rather than bottom up. We can picture the ideal flow-form model as a complete network in which all connections are possible, but face the risk of being constrained (top down), rather than a model in which connections are constructed like Incan pyramid bricks, one at a time (bottom up). Mathematically, the flow-form model starts with a complete graph of all possible relationships and then works backwards. The question we ask is, "Why is the glass still half empty?" not "How did the glass become half full?" Any relationship is a genuine possibility in the top-down model, not just the ones that derive from the prior assumptions of the network. In other words, there is no such thing as a weak link per se, only links that are hindered by social barriers that constrict the arteries. *The flow-form model assumes that all links can potentially be opened given enough diversity, trust, rules, and extra-rational motivations.* The model helps us "run the film backwards" and find more ways to generate more valuable outliers, which become the weeds that determine the vibrancy of Rainforests.

Surprisingly, the flow-form model may even explain the neoclassical macroeconomic model. When our microscope is observing a Rainforest up close, we cannot ignore the varying diameters of the arteries. Those variations matter a great deal. However, as our perspective lifts higher and higher, and our magnification decreases, those variations matter less. From high above, we can overlook the variations, just as we would ignore tiny ripples of varying pressure or temperature when viewing an entire ocean. To make "good enough" observations at the macroscopic scale, macroeconomists can assume that a system has uniformly open arteries

---

21 Csermely, *Weak Links*, preface VII.

moving resources around—like an "invisible hand"—and still have a useful model. In this way, the flow-form model serves as a bridge between the micro and the macro.

'Shroom Boom

Arguably, the flow-form model helps explain many observable phenomena we see in the world. Financial crises in the Eurozone today, for instance, ripple immediately throughout the entire global system. Protests in Tunisia and Egypt spread quickly through the Arab world, and within a year they appear to inspire similar uprisings in Tel Aviv, London, and throughout the U.S. *The Internet is causing the anastomosis of human society.*

It is as if the long root structures of humanity, which started in various disparate civilizations around the world, are starting to connect together again at their ends. People are being connected who would never have been connected before. The potential for huge transformations in the world is obvious to everyone. Perhaps Silicon Valley was just one of the first points of fusion of these human networks.

Anastomosis in the human race, however, can be dangerous. There is significant risk because unlike the fungal mycelium networks or the aspen forest, the human race is not a single organism. *Humans often have allergic reactions to one another.* We are wired to distrust easily or to trust with great difficulty. The flow-form model had little utility when there were so many blocked arteries due to geography. Now, with geographical barriers lowering, we are dealing with the social distances between people more and more often. People are increasingly shoulder-to-shoulder, yet still miles apart. The Rainforest might be considered a type of anti-allergy medication for human civilization.

But anastomosis is not free. While people can thrive when connected in a trusting environment—as in the AirDio story—it takes energy to overcome that distance and build that trust in the first place. Just as a fungus must expend nutrients to fuse the ends of hyphae together, a society must invest resources to connect distant points in social networks. Governments and nonprofit organizations in Taiwan and Estonia were actively involved in creating the institutions that helped build a new "artery" between Wen and Toivo.

Indeed, such investments are often worthwhile. We can see what anastomosis looks like in Silicon Valley, a system with wide arteries and a rapid flow of ideas, talent, and capital. In the diagrams below, there is more than a passing resemblance between the real social networks of Silicon

Valley (among the founders of the semiconductor industry) on the left and the diagram of a real mycelial network experiencing anastomosis on the right:[22]

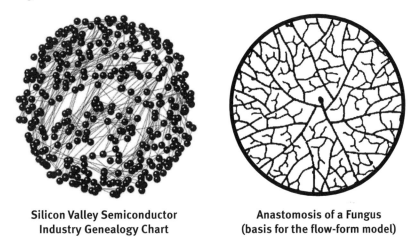

Silicon Valley Semiconductor Industry Genealogy Chart　　　　**Anastomosis of a Fungus (basis for the flow-form model)**

Judith Cone, who advises the Chancellor of the University of North Carolina on innovation and entrepreneurship, describes how the social network maps of various regions in the United States look when compared against one another:

> When we did social network maps comparing regions, the maps looked really different. In Silicon Valley, the pure density of that map is amazing, and Boston is second…What is the connectivity of those dots? And who makes up the dots? Silicon Valley has lots of dots that are highly connected. And the actors are the real deal—lots of players who have built companies and have investable dollars as angel investors. If you are an entrepreneur, you have everything working for you in that social environment. Our local map had very few dots that were not that connected.[23]

The flow-form model reflects what Judith observes: the fast flow of interconnected relationships, expert knowledge, and capital in real-life Rainforests. However, we believe that the flow-form model can be developed much further. Mathematical equations based on this model—perhaps drawing from tools created by biologists, physicists, psychologists, and sociologists—could provide useful ways to describe the behavior of social

---

22 SEMI Semiconductor Industry Genealogy Chart. First conceived by Dan Hoefler, later maintained by SEMI. Cited in Emilio J. Castilla, et al, "Social Networks in Silicon Valley," *The Silicon Valley Edge* (Stanford: Stanford University Press, 2000), 228. Hyphal fusion diagram adapted from the original at A.H.R. Buller, *Researches on Fungi,* vol. 5. (London: Longman, 1933).

23 Judith Cone, telephone interview with author, August 2, 2004.

networks in Rainforests and how to improve the flow of resources within them. We challenge the next generation of scholars to develop these new tools.

Biology has given us a model—anastomosis—that describes what an efficient system might look like. We can summarize some key lessons:

....

> **Lesson #1:** *Node-based social network models cannot easily capture the complexity of entire Rainforests.*

....

> **Lesson #2:** *The biological flow-form model—based on the concept of anastomosis—is a useful way to measure the health of a Rainforest.*

....

> **Lesson #3:** *The flow of nutrients—as measured by the velocity of ideas, talent, and capital moving in a network—helps grow weeds.*

....

> **Lesson #4:** *Flow is clogged by constricted arteries that occur when social barriers exist between people.*

....

> **Lesson #5:** *Flow in arteries can be opened by communication between people, which is increased by the "software" of the Rainforest Recipe.*

....

> **Lesson #6:** *The flow-form model is consistent with the neoclassical macroeconomic model. They just operate at different magnifications.*

....

The flow-form model also reinforces the most important lesson from Silicon Valley. It is not that technology startups are the economic salvation of society. *The real lesson is that human connectivity is the most important underlying characteristic.* Silicon Valley is just one example of what such a robust biological system might look like. Therefore, rather than creating more clones of the Valley, leaders should focus on the creation of systems that foster diversity, trust, normative rules, and extra-rational motivations. These systems do not necessarily have to involve the latest Web startups or the next "next big thing." Anastomosis can come in a variety of shapes and sizes.

Measuring the Waves

Many traditional measures for economic development tend to focus on static aspects—like measuring someone's temperature or weight. They are snapshots in time. What is more important is to measure the dynamism of the system over time—like measuring someone's pulse. The flow-form model gives us a tool to take the "heartbeat" of innovation, rather than its "temperature."

Although we cannot possibly calculate the actual velocity of every particle of knowledge, talent, or capital in a system, we can utilize proxies that help us measure the openness or constriction of the arteries in a system. We can apply the Rainforest Recipe framework to do this. The left side—the hardware—helps determine the *shape* of the system, while the right side— the software—helps determine the *dynamism* of the system. Here are a few examples of the "hardware" metrics we might assess:

- **People Infrastructure.** Examples: Where are the engineers and other technologists, and what is their ability to absorb technological knowledge from elsewhere? Who are the leaders with the potential to become keystones that can connect disparate ends of the social network?

- **Professional Infrastructure.** Example: What professional organizations and other affiliations cross traditional social barriers, and how can they leverage that ability to facilitate connections between people?

- **Physical infrastructure.** Example: How effectively does the communications infrastructure enable online communication across social barriers—whether by email, cellular phone, Skype, Facebook, or other social networking tools?

- **Policy infrastructure.** Example: How flexible is a system in allowing organizational structures (both formal and informal) that reduce transaction costs for individuals to combine and recombine with people across social boundaries?[24]

---

24 We propose that policymakers consider the creation of a new legal form of company entity—a *provisional corporation*—to provide formal protection to people in the exploratory process of forming a new startup. The cost for registering this type of entity should be free. Thus, it would reflect the real-world process of creative reassembly in which individuals come together at the beginning of the startup cycle. The current barriers to formal company registration are not insignificant: forming a company can cost hundreds of dollars and generate daunting paperwork. Alternatively, entrepreneurs who choose not to register as a company are treated, by default, as either sole proprietors (with personal liability) or partners (with joint and several liability, which means that the actions of one person can create full liability for the others). A provisional corporation could allow startup founders to begin work together— allowing them to apply for grants, license intellectual property from universities, pitch for investors, etc.—without risking liability. Their provisional status would have to be disclosed to all counterparties, and they could be given a specified timeframe in which to convert their provisional status to full status.

On the "software" side, we measure the extent of anastomosis, the velocity of the flow, and the constriction of the arteries:

- **Diversity: What is the extent of anastomosis in a system?** Examples: How active are the "water coolers" where people gather serendipitously, and how diverse are the people around them? How frequently do people attend networking events that break down social and professional hierarchies? How quickly do first meetings turn into real partnering? How active are diaspora (or other barrier-crossing people) in the system? How actively do keystones reach throughout the system to "glue" distant parties together?

- **Extra-Rational Motivations: How strong is the force pushing fluid through the arteries (i.e., the attempted velocity)?** Examples: What is the pace of serial entrepreneurship and mentoring? What is the speed of the "free stuff" in the system, including information, advice, donations, and civic participation?

- **General Social Trust: How open or constrained are the arteries generally?** Examples: What is the pace of funding of public-private partnerships? What is the pace of foundation and endowment creation? How quickly are collaborative research agreements created?

- **Rules of the Rainforest:** How open or constrained are the arteries in different areas of a system?

  » **Break Rules and Dream.** Examples: How many submissions are received at startup business plan competitions over time? What is the level of interest in entrepreneurship each year? How frequently are there identifiable success stories that people wish to emulate?

  » **Open Doors and Listen.** Examples: Are people open to civil discourse, or are they argumentative? How quickly are ideas shared online with others? How often are women and minorities active participants in startup creation?

  » **Trust and Be Trusted.** Examples: How quickly are transactions consummated? Are public debates and discussions open and transparent?

  » **Experiment and Iterate Together.** Examples: How quickly do relationships turn into joint projects? How easily do startup teams form and grow? How often do large companies or customers talk with small startups and how collaborative are those relationships?

» **Seek Fairness, Not Advantage.** Examples: How entrepreneur-friendly are valuations for angel or venture investments? How often are stock options used to incentivize employees? How quickly are deals consummated without complex lawyering?

» **Err, Fail, and Persist.** Examples: How quickly do failed entrepreneurs try again? Do entrepreneurs and others respond to feedback constructively or with passive-aggressive behavior? How active is the peer and mentor support network for struggling entrepreneurs?

» **Pay It Forward.** Examples: Do successful entrepreneurs disappear, or do they engage with new startups soon afterwards? How rapid is the culture of philanthropic activity among successful entrepreneurs?

• **Interpretation of the Rules: How well do the arteries heal themselves to stay open over time?** Examples: How rapid are the social feedback mechanisms for enforcing normative behavior? How influential are the keystones in promoting the Rules and encouraging transparent communication across social barriers?

So, can we eventually design something like a Gross Innovation Product? Probably. We are already working on it. Computer technology is increasingly more effective at analyzing vast amounts of information, and hearing extremely faint "signals in the noise." One example comes from scientists Juan Camilo Bohorquez, Sean Gourley, and their colleagues, who wrote a paper on the mathematics of war and insurgency, covering conflicts from Iraq to Sierra Leone and mapping global terrorism. The team was able to aggregate and process countless tidbits of computer data, including public statistics, newspapers, blogs, and other media sources. They created a database of over 54,000 unique events covering 9 different wars.[25] The information revealed that highly complex human systems are guided by underlying mathematical properties, as combatants grouped and regrouped in varying combinations. As Gourley stated in an interview:

> ... the interesting part of our research is not that it is simply "harder" to kill more people in an attack, but that it is *precisely* harder to kill more people in an attack. Indeed, our research shows that when alpha equals 2.5 it is 316 times harder for insurgents to kill 100 people in an attack than it is for them to kill 10 people in an attack...[I]t is the power-law distribution with exponent -2.5 that, to the first order, defines *precisely* this concept of "harder.[26]

As the researchers observed, there are parallels between a military insurgency and a startup company competing against large incumbents. Winning in these systems is a game of probabilities, not of certainties.

As computing power increases, we may be able to watch this creative reassembly—the process of people breaking apart and recombining—in real time, with increasing specificity and detail. As we discover and refine the underlying mathematical models that describe human systems, we may even be able to see the Rainforest "breathing" someday.

Quantum Finale

According to quantum theory, the plane we flew on at the beginning of this book crashed. At least, one of the planes did, if you believe in the "many-worlds interpretation" of quantum physics. However, in the parallel universe we are lucky enough to be in right now, the plane landed just fine, the vodka eventually wore off, and we were able to write this book you are reading.

---

25 Juan Camilo Bohorquez et al., "Common Ecology Quantifies Human Insurgency," *Nature* 462 (2009): 2, doi:10.1038/nature08631.
  http://mathematicsofwar.com/wp-content/uploads/2009/12/WarEcologyNature-2.pdf.

26 Sean Gourley, "Sean Gourley on the Mathematics of War," filmed February 2009, TED video, 07:22, Sean Gourley on the strong mathematical relationship linking the fatality and frequency of attacks, posted May 2009, http://www.ted.com/talks/sean_gourley_on_the_mathematics_of_war.html.

Quantum theory—for all its oddities regarding alternate realities—matters for the Rainforest because it explains the behavior of particles in a fluid. When we observe people in a place like Silicon Valley, sometimes they behave like atoms bouncing randomly and sometimes they behave like oceans moving together. The flow-form model is a hybrid of the two, describing the streams of fluid in which we pass ideas, capital, and talent to each other. The notion that quantum theory underlies the Rainforest is not that far-fetched. Although chemistry thinks of bonds between atoms as forces, quantum theory thinks of bonds between atoms as relationships. The forces that attract or repulse atoms are studied using quantum theory. These interactions are never based on certainties, but rather on probabilities. Sometimes atoms attract; sometimes they repulse. Sometimes planes crash; sometimes they don't.

This is the same in the Rainforest. Sometimes entrepreneurs get along; sometimes they can't stand each other. There are infinite ways a conversation can happen between two people at any given time. We just never know. Factors like diversity, trust, normative rules, and extra-rational motivations greatly increase the odds of positive results, but they never guarantee it. *Designing Rainforests is about enhancing the quantum probabilities of innovation, not attempting to engineer perfection.*

In searching for the secret recipe of Rainforests, we see that humans are just biological beings, and human society is just another biological system. We are all simply ingredients in a biological soup, doing our best to live, learn, laugh, love, and innovate together. How elegant that the physics in a droplet of water or the biology of a simple mushroom might reveal to us patterns in our own interactions with one another. We are fortunate to have a front row seat to this journey, as we unlock the value that is hidden in our relationships with our fellow human beings. There is mysterious beauty in the design of the Rainforest.

Chapter Nine: Conclusion

The Future of the Rainforest

Well you may dance the night away
and laugh among the stars,
And you may spill the milk away
and cry among the bars.
And you may wake the rafters
and break the heart of stone,
But you've got to go to sleep alone.

— **Jimmie Dale Gilmore, West Texas country singer,**
"Go to Sleep Alone"[1]

---

1 Lyrics reprinted courtesy of Hal Leonard Corporation.

The Last Frontier

Some considered it impossible, but there it was. Posters with spectacular lettering proclaimed a "GREAT EVENT" on May 10, 1869. One writer called it "a great national work, transcending, in its magnitude, and in its results, anything yet attempted by man."[2] It was the first of its kind in the world.

The completion of the First Transcontinental Railroad, linking East Coast and West Coast, transformed America. On "The Wonderland Route" through the West[3], the trip from New York to San Francisco that used to take a life-risking six months could now be done by ordinary people in six days. But despite the ease of travel, the spirit of the frontier continued among the new individuals crossing the Great American Desert. The advertisements for the journey would continue to play to the "aura of adventure" and the opportunity to build great fortune in these western lands.[4]

Over the next two decades, the United States would experience the fastest economic growth in its history—the Gilded Age, as Mark Twain called it. The transcontinental railroad was arguably the key.[5] Productivity per person grew annually by 4.5% during the 1870s and 3.8% during the 1880s.[6] By the turn of the century, America had become the greatest economy on Earth.

The railroad was the great "social tesseract" of its time. The day after the "golden spike" was driven to complete the rail line at Promontory Summit, Utah, the first train left California for the East Coast with a shipment of fine tea from Japan.[7] It was just a hint of things to come. Suddenly, goods could be shipped rapidly, news and ideas could be shared quickly, and people could skip the dangerous frontier trails or the overseas route around South America. "New York is no longer an antipode [to San Francisco], but a neighbor," one person observed.[8]

---

2 Stephen E. Ambrose, *Nothing Like It In the World: The Men Who Built the Transcontinental Railroad, 1863-1869* (New York: Simon & Schuster, 2000), 26.

3 Ryan Johnson, "Those were the Days… that Tried Men's Mettle: Tourism, Western Masculinity, and the Transcontinental Railroad, 1865-1880", *Perspectives* 36 (2009):44-45, http://www.calstatela.edu/centers/perspectives/volume36/Johnson.pdf). Cites advertisement picture in Ezra Bowen, ed., *The Old West: The Railroaders.* (Virginia: Time-Life Books, 1973), 138.

4 Ibid.

5 There is debate about the extent of the railroad's role in the Gilded Age, but the evidence strongly indicates that the railroad had a powerful role in American economic growth. For contrasting views, see David H. Bain, *Empire Express: Building the First Transcontinental Railroad* (New York: Viking-Penguin, 1999); Richard White, *Railroaded: The Transcontinentals and the Making of Modern America* (New York: W. W. Norton & Company, 2011).

6 U.S. Bureau of the Census, *Historical Statistics of the United States* (1976).

7 "The Impact of the Transcontinental Railroad," PBS.org, accessed August 30, 2011, http://www.pbs.org/wgbh/americanexperience/features/general-article/tcrr-impact/.

8 "Through to the Pacific: A Series of Letters Published in the *New York Tribune,* May-June, 1869, by Albert D. Richardson," Central Pacific Railroad Photographic History Museum, CPRR.org, accessed August 30, 2011, http://cprr.org/Museum/Through_to_the_Pacific/Through_to_the_Pacific.html.

However, the railroad was not a naturally-occurring social tesseract. It was financed by the U.S. Congress through a 30-year bond measure passed in the middle of the American Civil War. The first Pacific Railroad Act was signed by Abraham Lincoln in 1862. The railroad was a public good financed by public money. With the entire nation at risk, the national government had the foresight to invest in one of the most difficult and expensive projects of its time. Connecting distant corners of the national economy was worth the price. It was active capitalism, not passive capitalism.

As we have discussed, linking disparate economic network**s** creates an *n-squared* effect in the number of potential transactions between all the parties in an ecosystem. Just as nature conservationists try to maintain "land bridges" to create contiguous parkland, we find that creating human bridges does the same for an economic system. The railroad was the bridge that forged a contiguous economy across the length of the United States. The advent of the steamboat in the 1830s did the same thing for the Midwestern states, integrating the economies of the northern and the southern states along the Mississippi.

Whether we look at the railroad or the steamboat, we see the obvious economic benefits when people are able to overcome geographic barriers. Once we overcome geography, however, we are still left with the vast invisible distance between two people in a coffee shop. *The last great frontier to cross is the one that divides two souls.*

The Rainforest overcomes human-to-human barriers just as the transcontinental railroad overcame geographic barriers. The magic of the Rainforest is the way it lowers social barriers between people sitting right next to each other. That is the "secret sauce" of Silicon Valley. It is not the talents of the people, the physical buildings, or even the capital flowing—although all of those are important ingredients. It is the ecosystem with its special culture of human behavior to optimize creative reassembly that fosters innovation.

For the Rainforest to work effectively, we need the Rules of the Rainforest, the unwritten norms of behavior that help close divisions between people. The Rainforest Recipe we have provided in this book is a formula for leaders who seek to disseminate the Rules and enable the creation of Rainforests.

More than Metaphor

Visitors to Silicon Valley often wonder how to build something like it back home, just as an engineer might seek to build a skyscraper. But the answer is not about engineering. It is about biology. To understand Silicon Valley, we must think of its people as a living biological system, not the sum of its individual components. We have named this biological system the Rainforest. We could also have called it the Reef, the Cloud Forest, or any other rich biological system that allows new species to emerge, resources to circulate, and atoms to recombine. (Much as we appreciate the anatomy of mushrooms, however, we did shoot down the idea of calling it the Fungus.)

Biological systems emerge from evolution, not engineering, and evolution comes from experimenting, iterating, tinkering. Mutation and natural selection—through a process of trial and error—ultimately lead to thriving species in a complex ecosystem. Peter Csermely, in his book on the value of weak links in social networks, explores this idea:

> François Jacob [Nobel laureate in Medicine in 1965] pictured evolution as a *tinkerer,* "who does not know exactly what he is going to produce, but uses whatever he finds around" and "gives his materials unexpected functions to produce a new object." Indeed, evolution does not optimize the system in advance, making a blueprint, but assembles interactions until they become good for the task.[9]

The Rainforest helps innovators "tinker" together in the same way that atoms "tinker" together in natural biological systems. Tinkering is how Rainforests discover more valuable recipes for combining and recombining ideas, talent, and capital together. Therefore, the Rainforest is more than just a metaphor.[10] We seek to create human systems that encourage evolutionary tinkering.

....

The Big Picture*: Rainforests thrive because of normative culture that accelerates the evolution of human organizations into ever-increasing patterns of efficiency and productivity.*

....

9　Csermely, *Weak Links,* 97 (see chap. 8, n. 8) (italics added). Citing Maynard-Smith and Szathmary, 1995.

10 See also Beinhocker, *The Origin of Wealth,* 187 (see introduction, n. 3). The view we describe is also followed by complexity economists. For example Beinhocker, who states: "One of the strongest claims of Complexity Economics is that this language [of evolution] is no mere metaphor—organizations, markets, and economies are not just like evolutionary systems; they truly, literally are evolutionary systems."

We have traveled a long journey in this book, and we are grateful that you have purchased a ticket for this transglobal ride with us. Like passport stamps that mark the stops on such a journey, here is a summary of what we have seen on this adventure:

1. Innovation comes not from the basic ingredients of economic production, but from the way that people interrelate to combine and share ideas, talent, and capital. A community that facilitates such relationships is a biological system we call a Rainforest. Its animating process is creative reassembly.

2. Certain individuals and organizations we call "keystones" have the special ability to integrate disparate people, influencing them to act in ways that impact the entire system. They glue people together in the Rainforest.

3. People do not connect easily. Social barriers—based on geography, social networks, language, culture, and distrust—create transaction costs that prevent people from finding each other and working together. Human beings are wired to distrust one another.

4. A system can overcome barriers to human collaboration when people are motivated by extra-rational motivations, and when transactions are less costly due to social norms we call the Rules of the Rainforest.

5. The Rainforest Recipe demonstrates how such systems are constructed, based on diversity, trust, motivations, and norms. Diversity is enhanced by mixing people from different social groups. Cultural behavior is learned through the Rainforest Tools: real-world practice, role modeling, peer-to-peer interaction, social feedback loops, networks of trust, and making norms explicit through social contracts.

6. Capital must be designed as a service integrated into the Rainforest, not as an end in itself. It must be part of the social fabric, not distinct from it.

7. We measure the health of a Rainforest by watching the waves, not just the atoms or the overall ocean. The flow-form model—based on robust biological systems—emphasizes the velocity of ideas, capital, and talent flowing in a system. Lowering social barriers is like opening arteries to accelerate their flow.

Fighting Pussies, Saving the World

Author Michael Malone calls it the "Pussification of Silicon Valley." [11] He is not alone in this sentiment. Is Silicon Valley going soft? Is the legacy of the frontier fading, as Frederick Jackson Turner feared over a century ago?

There was a time in the Valley—not that far in the past—when your word was your bond, conventional wisdom was your enemy, and everyone's top job was to build killer companies.[12] As Malone observes, the Valley is increasingly becoming populated with people "who will compromise everything—pleasure, physical excitement, love, and friendship—in the hope of living a long, healthy, and hopelessly uneventful life. Silicon Valley used to pulverize such pussies, now it lionizes them."[13]

As the Valley matures, some feel that it is losing its old-school edge. Some wonder if the code of behavior may be fraying, too.

> ... when an honest-to-goodness retro-hard guy, such as T. J. Rodgers, appears on the scene and starts popping off opinions that used to be the received view in Silicon Valley—like supporting entrepreneurs, trusting innovation, keeping the government off our backs—he's greeted about as warmly as an accused child molester.[14]

A silent transformation may be happening in Silicon Valley, changing it from a place where people dare to "make an opportunity" into a place where people just want to "find a job." The evolution of venture capital into an "asset class"—not simply a tool to serve entrepreneurs and build great companies—has strengthened the incentives for investors to take short-term gains and treat innovation as a zero-sum game. As one person said, "Return On Investment is now the new God."[15]

Whether the Valley is going soft we cannot know for certain. As every industry matures, it is perhaps inevitable that culture evolves and the hard edges get dulled. If that is so, then what is the future of Silicon Valley?

---

11 Michael S. Malone, *The Valley of Heart's Delight: A Silicon Valley Notebook: 1963-2001* (New York: John Wiley & Sons, 2002), 145.

12 See for example Saxenian, *Regional Advantage,* 111 (see chap. 2, n. 24). People have been speculating about cultural change in the Valley for a long time: "By the 1980s Silicon Valley was no longer the tightly knit community of technological pioneers that it had been in earlier decades. No longer did everyone in the region 'know everyone else'... But the culture of relative openness, the fast pace of business activity, and the cooperative practices that distinguished the region remained intact."

13 Malone, *The Valley,* 146.

14 Ibid., 147.

15 Ibid., 150.

As we have discussed, human systems are dissipative. Trust and norms tend to revert over time. It takes effort to maintain their strength. The biggest danger to the future of Silicon Valley is not global competition, the current slowdown in venture fund formation, or even America's macroeconomic weakness. It is the erosion of the culture of the Rainforest. The future of Silicon Valley will depend on the power of its keystones—and the new keystones that may emerge—to maintain the trust, the norms, the motivations, and the positive social feedback processes that have made it what it is.

Thankfully, the Valley benefits from a constant infusion of new blood: people who self-select to join the club and adopt its norms. The region is like a self-renewing keystone institution unto itself. As many of its insightful leaders have said, "Silicon Valley is not a place. It is a state of mind."

The rest of the world is charging ahead, with or without the Valley. For economic growth, *innovation is no longer a nice-to-have; it has become a must-have.* Companies and regions all over the world are trying hard to create innovative systems, attempting to replicate the DNA of Silicon Valley in new places. Innovation is not just a tool of business anymore. It is now a business itself, and a cutthroat one at that.

The upside opportunity for Silicon Valley is vastly larger than most people realize—and the downside risk is much steeper. The Valley has the potential to be to global innovation in the 21st century what New York City has been to finance and media in the 20th century, what Amsterdam was to trade in the 17th century, and what Northern Italy was to finance, trade, and the arts in the 15th century. Despite all the Valley's brains, know-how, and connections, its greatest value is usually overlooked. *The core value proposition of Silicon Valley in the coming decades will be its role as the cultural center of gravity, the enforcer of norms, and the connector of resources in the global Rainforest.* The history of the world shows that every great region, every great market, every great set of business practices only provides temporary advantage. If the Valley does not rise to the challenge, it risks becoming increasingly irrelevant as the rest of the world's innovation economies emerge.

If we look at the rest of America and the world, we can make one certain prediction: in the efforts to grow Rainforests in new markets, all approaches that do not focus on cultural transformation are doomed to fail. Leaders—from CEOs and Prime Ministers on down—should focus more on the recipe, not just the ingredients, of innovation. We call upon a new generation of leaders to develop initiatives that nurture the growth of entire Rainforests, not just the funding of isolated deserts. Leaders must evolve as well. It is not enough to encourage innovation among a small cluster of people who live close together, and who think and act alike. Globalization has destroyed that notion. *Innovators today must engage with the world.*

Free markets fail because people are imperfect, but that is where the greatest potential for value creation lies. The key to unlock that value is the Rules of the Rainforest. Like a fractal equation, the Rules provide a simple behavioral formula that, repeated over and over again, can create a massive impact on society-at-large. The micro can transform the macro. Rather than building innovation as engineers build skyscrapers, we should cultivate Rainforests as naturalists think of biological systems. We should emulate the way that evolution allows atoms to "tinker," eventually creating new weeds and nurturing them to grow.

The Rainforest concept does not come naturally to many leaders. With elections around the corner or quarterly earnings to be announced, leaders most often strive to define and control outcomes. Innovation, however, is serendipitous. Leaders in the Rainforest must learn to *engineer serendipity, not outcomes.* Their primary weapons in this fight are the bridging of social barriers, the building of trust, and the adoption of the Rules. These are not slogans that win elections or lead to fast promotions, but they are vital for success in the long run.

We are proposing a new *active capitalism.* Capitalism is not about simply reciting the mantra of "less government." Capitalism is about decentralizing decision-making and empowering individuals to connect, collaborate, experiment, and create commercial value on their own. Congress did exactly this when it funded the First Transcontinental Railroad about 150 years ago. It is perfectly consistent with capitalism that we invest in bridging divides between people to lower their transaction costs for doing business with one another.

The Rainforest is not mere business theory. It provides a new paradigm for policies and strategies that transcend the left and right divides of the political spectrum. The mechanisms of the Rainforest touch the heart of capitalism—making markets more efficient, enabling the factors of economic production to mix more efficiently, reducing transaction costs to create private value, and giving individuals the freedom to pursue their dreams. And they validate our faith in innovation as a way to elevate the welfare of humankind.

Epilogue

The Mysticism of Innovation

"We're in a free fall into the future. We don't
know where we are going...And all you have to
do to transform your hell into a paradise is to
turn your fall into a voluntary act. It's a very
interesting shift in perspective, and that's all
it is. Joyful participation in the sorrows, and
everything changes."

—**Joseph Campbell,** *Sukhavati: A Mythic Journey*[1]

---

1 *Sukhavati: A Mythic Journey* (Mystic Fire Video, 1998), Netflix.

Dualism

You have not really done yoga until you have done it in a foreign language.

After a hard day of Extreme Venture Capital, we like to explore the places we visit. Sometimes, we take long walks. Other times, we take a ride on a bus, train, boat, or taxi to help us see out-of-the-way sights. In between our normal visits to startup offices, incubators, laboratories, ministries, and office buildings, we are fortunate that our work also takes us to castles, reefs, pyramids, skyscrapers, towers, slums, mansions, lakes, bars, boutiques, museums, mountains, churches, temples, mosques, and many other little-visited corners in dozens of countries. Occasionally, we go to yoga studios.

For amateurs like us, doing yoga in English is an essential crutch. You can always rely on the instructor to tell you what to do. The instructor says "extended side-angle pose"—and that is what you do. You don't have to think for yourself. You just do as you are told. If you are a yoga pro, you might be able to understand the Sanskrit name of that pose, *Utthita Parsvakonasana*. But we are far from yoga pros.

When the crutch of your native language is gone, you are left with yourself and your own thoughts. As a candle flickers, the sound of a bell dings in slow cycles, a soft voice speaks in a tongue that you no longer understand, and you can start to lose yourself. The boundaries between you and the rest of the room begin to dissolve, and sometimes—when everything works out just right—the boundary with the rest of the universe can dissolve too.

At those moments, one can see through the trappings of society. One realizes that chaos, not order, is actually the norm in the universe. Our work, our startups, our civilization—they are but transitory moments in time. A company is just an event. One can feel the flow.

The legendary professor Mihalyi Csikszentmihalyi, formerly at the University of Chicago, developed the psychological concept of "flow" to describe a state when "the ego falls away" and one feels immersed in the outer world, not worried about hunger or the passage of time.[2] You sometimes feel this when you are engaged in an activity that you love. Perhaps it comes when you are painting, reading, gardening, playing sports, or going for a walk in your neighborhood. When you finish, you cannot believe how you lost track of the time. You were in the flow. Similarly, Karen Tesson felt that the name "flow-form model" reflected the way that an object in such a system is a "contextualized being, intrinsically communicating with their environments, and with the others it encounters there." [3]

---

2   For additional information, see Martin E. P. Seligman and Mihalyi Csikszentmihalyi, "Positive Psychology: An Introduction," *American Psychologist*, 55(2000): 5-14.

3   Tesson, "An Interdisciplinary Study," 134.

To explain how to create "flow" in the Rainforest, we have taken you on long journey. We have deconstructed complicated human systems, we have decoded the human brain, we have extracted social norms that optimize human collaboration, and we have devised complex recipes to generate innovation despite our human wiring. Whew! That seems like an awful lot of work. Could not human beings have evolved into something a little easier to deal with?

Suppose that everyone in the world took all their ideas, insights, and experiences, threw them into a giant vat and mixed them together. Every idea for an innovative product, every piece of information about customers' desires, every hard-earned experience that informs what it takes to make and sell innovative products—imagine that you could take them all, from throughout the entire world, and stir them together in one giant cauldron. But unlike Carl Sagan's stew at the beginning of this book, this time there would be lightning.

The results, of course, would be staggering. With the barriers that divide people gone, we could invent everything that could ever be invented. We would have every cure that could be conceived, every tool that could be imagined, every product that could be needed.

This is a fantasy, of course. We are all bound in human bodies, each with our own peculiar interests, desires, dreams, and neuroses. Innovation would be easier if people could sit in a room and somehow magically intuit how to maximize the collective productivity of everyone there. Unfortunately, we cannot. Innovation in the real world is a messy process that is both conscious and unconscious, verbal and nonverbal. It occurs among varied groups of individuals who are at times loud or silent, honest or deceitful, argumentative or collaborative. We are not telepathically linked.

Or are we? Increasingly, scientists are finding evidence that we are more connected than we ever thought.[4] They are finding evidence that matter is "entangled" at the quantum level. People who are physically separated are able to achieve strangely high scores when they play certain cooperative games at a distance.[5] Is it possible that we are literally wired to intuit social

---

4   Amit Goswami, "Quantum Activism for Better Health and Healing," Center for Quantum Activism, March 1 2010, http://www.amitgoswami.org/quantum-activism-health-healing/. Amit Goswami, theoretical quantum physicist and former professor at the University of Oregon, argues that science explains how dualism between mind and matter can be transcended: "In quantum physics, objects are waves of possibilities for consciousness to choose from. Conscious choice converts or 'collapses' the possibility waves into unique manifest actualities. This is where choice takes place, not in the separateness of our individual ego. Since choice is nonlocal, there is no signal involved and no paradox of dualism."

5   For additional information on the field of quantum pseudo-telepathy and the concept of quantum entanglement, see for example Gilles Brassard, Anne Broadbent, and Alain Tapp, "Quantum Pseudo-Telepathy," *Foundations of Physics* 35 (2005): 1877–1907, doi: 10.1007/s10701-005-7353-4.

norms in a community, not just through trial and error? Physicists have speculated about a Holographic Principle that implies that reality is just a three-dimensional holographic projection of all the information in the universe.[6] *The Matrix* may be more real than we realized.

Innovation can be thought of this way, too. All the things that are known in the world are out there, swimming in a soup of human knowledge, whether it is a cure for liver disease, a perfectly efficient means to convert sunlight to electricity, or some way to create infinite computing capability. The pieces of the answers are all there. It is what we call reality—with humans divided by distance, distrust, and discord—that prevents the components from coming together into a greater whole. We are bound in physical forms that exchange information inefficiently.[7] We each bring our own education, experiences, and life wisdom—our minds are like vessels for storing potential energy. It is not unlike the potential stored when you raise a rock high in the air. When you release the rock, the energy is unleashed. When humans are placed in a Rainforest, their innovative potential can be unleashed as well.

Bridging the divide that separates two people is more than just physical, or even spiritual. It creates economic value that is measurable. Like a good session of yoga, the value of the Rainforest innovation culture comes from transcending the dualism of human existence.

Love

Marcus Chown was just being a loving son. When he was a graduate student at Caltech in 1982, he asked his professor, the famous physicist Richard Feynman, to send his mother a birthday message. Chown wanted his mother to be more interested in the science he was studying.[8] His mother had enjoyed seeing Feynman on a television show, so Chown thought this might do the trick.

Feynman, however, did no such thing. Instead, Feynman sent the following message to Chown's mother:

---

6 See for example Jacob D. Bekenstein, "Information in the Holographic Universe," Reality-Bending Black Holes, *Scientific American,* March 2007, special edition,
http://www.scienceandsociety.org/web/Library_files/Astrophysics-Special_Edition.pdf.

7 Margaret J. Wheatley *Leadership and the New Science: Discovering Order in a Chaotic World,* 3rd ed. (San Francisco: Berrett-Koehler Publishers, 2006), 21-22. Wheatley is an expert in management leadership and argues that people and business organizations are hindered by their inability to adapt to chaos and embrace openness, which science shows is the way that nature behaves.

8 Marcus Chown, "Physics with a Human Touch," *New Scientist,* March 10, 1988, 72-73.

Happy Birthday Mrs. Chown! Tell your son to stop trying to fill your head with science—for to fill your heart with love is enough. Richard P. Feynman (the man you watched on BBC 'Horizon').[9]

As Mrs. Chown probably realized, love and science are intimately bound in the Rainforest. Remember that love is a way of connecting two people, a transaction of a sort, but with long credit lines and flexible terms of repayment. In this sense, love is the ultimate enabler of the Rainforest. Love is hard, though, when the world seems to change so quickly. As author Haruki Murakami wrote recently: "All around us, it appears, things have been—or are being—swallowed up by chaos." [10]

Perhaps instead of fighting the chaos, we need to become more comfortable with it. Perhaps we just need a better map. The Rules of the Rainforest provide a useful map—one that shows us the way to balance the freedom of chaos and the beauty of collaboration. After all, it is the chaos of millions of humans transacting on eBay that enables that old guitar in your attic, for example, to get into the hands of a ten-year old boy who becomes the next John Lennon. It is the chaos of millions of interactions in Silicon Valley that led the co-founders of Google, Larry Page and Sergey Brin, to bump into each other at Stanford orientation the first time. Chaos may not be so bad if people have maps to help them interact in valuable ways they otherwise could not.

Innovation cannot thrive without people confronting the chaos of the world, accepting the difficulty of doing so, and savoring every part of the journey. It requires a "joyful participation" in the ups and downs, the mistakes and the failures that are inevitable—all shared with those around you. Thus, love is like a solution to chaos.

Traditional physicists say that the world tends towards disorder—they call this the "arrow of time". They say that "creating order" requires extra energy. However, innovation seems different. We can see many examples where innovation takes less energy than chaos. Do not eBay, Facebook, and Google create more order than disorder, by connecting people more efficiently than ever before?[11]

---

9 Richard Feynman and Christopher Sykes, *No Ordinary Genius: The Illustrated Richard Feynman* (New York: Norton, 1996), 161.

10 Haruki Murakami, "Reality A and Reality B", *The New York Times*, November 29, 2010, http://www.nytimes.com/2010/12/02/opinion/global/02iht-GA06-Murakami.html.

11 Beinhocker, *The Origin of Wealth*, 316 (see introduction, n. 3). Complexity economists argue that economic value is created when disorder—what scientists call entropy—is decreased. According to Beinhocker, "All wealth is created by thermodynamically irreversible, entropy-lowering processes. The act of creating wealth is an act of creating order, but not all order is wealth creating.... Wealth is thus a form of anti-entropy. It is a form of order, but not just any order—it is fit order. Patterns of economic order, in the form of products and services, compete with each other to be needed, desired, and even craved by consumers."

Isn't this similar to real rainforests and the natural world? We see such beautiful, complex order in natural systems as a result of evolution. [12] Indeed, Nobel laureate chemist Ilya Prigogine has pointed out that order evolves in natural systems *because* of time, not despite it:

> We have now learned that it is precisely through irreversible processes associated with the arrow of time that nature achieves its most delicate and complex structures. Life is possible only in a nonequilibrium universe."[13]

As in nature, the most complex structures of human civilization—our innovative creations—are derived from serendipitous "tinkering" over time.[14] Thus, creating order is no more expensive than keeping the disorder it would displace.[15]

Amazingly, the patterns underlying human systems (Rainforests), biological systems (evolution), and physical systems (irreversible thermodynamics) all appear to be driven by the same fundamental processes. It might be shocking to discover now, at the end of this book, that Rainforests obey the laws of thermodynamics too. You may recall the beginning of Chapter 1, when we discussed how the formulae used by macroeconomists are the same ones used by physicists. But there is a difference between Rainforests and macroeconomics:

....

The Very Big Picture: *Whereas macroeconomics can be explained by the mathematics that govern the movement of oceans, Rainforests can be explained by the wave equations that govern how particles self-organize into larger patterns.*

....

---

12 See Sean Carroll, "Free Energy and the Meaning of Life," *Discover Magazine* (blog), March 10, 2010, http://blogs.discovermagazine.com/cosmicvariance/2010/03/10/free-energy-and-the-meaning-of-life/.

13 Ilya Prigogine, *The End of Certainty: Time, Chaos, and the New Laws of Nature* (New York: The Free Press, 1996), 26-27.

14 Würtz and Annila, "Roots of Diversity Relations" (see chap. 8, n. 15). The authors argue that fundamental laws of biological diversity are based on the second law of thermodynamics: "the principle of increasing entropy and the theory of evolution by natural selection are in fact stating one and the same imperative." See also, G. Mutanov, *Mathematical Methods and Models in Economics* (Almaty: Kazakh University, 2011), 90. Mutanov argues that economic systems are also based on the second law of thermodynamics.

15 For additional information, see Ilya Prigogine and Isabelle Stengers, *Order Out of Chaos* (New York: Bantam, 1984); Jantsch, *The Self-Organizing Universe*, 35 (see chap. 6, n. 51). We realize that what we have stated is an oversimplification of the science of self-organization and irreversible thermodynamics. Our general point is that innovation is based on self-organizing processes that are similar to what we see in nature, since humans are biological. According to Ilya Prigogine and Isabelle Stengers, thermodynamic systems self-organize to create order out of chaos, overcoming entropy without central planning or external force. The systems are dissipative, which means that they export entropy outwards. Erich Jantsch argues that self-organizing systems are better thought of as energy processes that manifest themselves as physical forms.

In trying to understand Rainforests, we have discovered a profound consilience. Nature organizes itself in ways that apply to human systems as much as they do to physical and biological systems. Innovation systems thrive when the frictional barriers between people are lowered in society, like frozen molecules of water being melted and released from their icy lattice. At a system level, the barriers between people are what consume energy; innovation does not. With less friction than ever before, we see innovation happening faster and faster, because people are connecting more and more.

The most hopeful aspect of our work is that we get to see a wide cross-section of the world's peoples. We have a unique vantage point: we work closely with ordinary people who are trying to build extraordinary businesses. Everywhere we go, we see the universality of the human experience. We see professionals trying to build careers. We see entrepreneurs trying to create value. We see young children at play, kicking balls in courtyards and fields. We see parents pushing strollers along boardwalks. We see teenagers laughing as they run into a movie theatre. Above their heads, the canopy of the Rainforest hovers like an invisible veil. Just a little stretch of the hand, and they would touch it.

All around, the patterns of the world keep recurring over and over again, like ocean waves lapping up on a tropical beach shore. The waves have a rhythm. It is the rhythm of the Rainforest.

If you listen closely, you can hear it, too.

Postscript

One of our goals in writing this book was not just to describe the Rainforest, but to encourage its growth. Each person can make a difference in the world. Seek diversity. Create trust. Practice positive norms. Respect humanity's deepest dreams.

Please join us and become a member of the growing tribe of innovators in the global Rainforest. Support the freedom of creative reassembly. Make your commitment to the Rules of the Rainforest by signing a version of the Social Contract online at www.therainforestbook.com. Participate in gatherings to build new Rainforests, such as ours at www.innosummit.com.

Hear the rhythm of the Rainforest. Stretch your hand, touch the canopy.

Acknowledgments

To bring about this book has required the creation of its own Rainforest.

Numerous people over the years have helped us in shaping the core ideas contained in these pages. We consider them our compatriots in the conceptualization of the Rainforest: Alistair Brett, Janet Crawford, Henry Doss, Carlos Gutierrez, Ade Mabogunje, Eric Muller, Rohit Shukla, Mary Walshok, Al Watkins, and Phil Wickham.

Many people have contributed to the development of this book in countless ways, great and small, knowingly and unknowingly: Zika Abzuk, Ghassan Al-Jamal, Bob Ashley, Eric Ball, Abi Barrow, Rich Bendis, Nick Binkley, Larry Bock, Susan Brooksbank, Daryl Browne, Priya Cherian Huskins, Shekhar Chitnis, Ben Chu, Ronald Coase, Judith Cone, Tim Cooley, Brian Dovey, Tim Draper, Rosanne Dutton, Eli Eisenberg, Kay Etzler, Peter Farrell, Nina Fedoroff, Kevin Fong, Dick Foster, James Fowler, Susana Garcia-Robles, Susan Gauch, John Gauch, Fadi Ghandour, Scott Gillespie, Joanne Goodnight, Sean Gourley, Shiv Grewal, Matt Harris, Ossama Hassanein, Michael and Maria Hawes, Abeer Hazboun, Gai Hetzroni, Ben Hsiao, Sid & Doni Hubbard, Sophie Ingerslew, Ihab Jabari, Matthew Jackson, Irwin Jacobs, Pat James, Brad Jones, Malte Jung, Mark Kachur, Natasha Kapil, Hassan Kassem, Laith Kassis, Yadin Kaufman, Avinash Kaushik, Randall Kempner, Todd Kimmel, Scott Kleinberg, Rita Kopp and the late Clint Kopp, Michael Korver, Burton Lee, Camilliam Lin, Herb Lin, Gail Longmore, Emily Loughran, John Lusk, Ramos Mays, Linda Mead, Andrew Miller, Randy Mitchell, Galimkair Mutanov, Koichiro Nakamura, Saed Nashef, Tom Nastas, Mark Nelson, Cliff Numark, Tyler Orion, the late Bill Otterson, Alan Patricof, Eliot Peper, Tom Pfaff, Mark Pydynowski, Deron Quon, David Richter, Duane Roth, Sam Shen, Michie Slaughter, Dean Spatz, George Stejic, Joe Stubbs, Karen Jane Tesson, Alan Thomas, Bill Tobin, Auelbek Tokzhanov, Eric Towne, Wen Tsay, Donna Tumminello, Larry Udell, Norayr Vardanyan, Ning Wang, Michael Webber, E.O. Wilson, Bagrat Yengibaryan, and Tobyl Zhylkybayev. We are probably forgetting many people, so our apologies in advance.

Thanks to Malte Jung for providing us early access to his thesis work while still in progress. Thanks to Molly Davis for providing a transcript of the documentary *Something Ventured* (2010), directed by Dan Geller and Dayna Goldfine and executive produced by her and Paul Holland.

Thanks to all of the entrepreneurs we have ever worked with. Their faith in making the impossible possible inspires us every day. Thanks to our growing team at T2 Venture Capital—we are honored to work with the best, the brightest, and the most passionate in the field. Thanks to our investors for their trust and confidence. Thanks to all the members of the Society of Kauffman Fellows and to the staff at the Center for Venture Education for their fellowship and for what they continue to teach us every day. Thanks to all the entrepreneurs and staff involved with Larta Institute, Global CONNECT, CONNECT, and the Global CONNECT member organizations over the years for their service, friendship, and support.

Thanks to James Klein and Tiffany Hartsell, who assisted in editing, Ketaki Sood, who helped with research, and Bill Rogers, who designed the cover and layout. Thanks to our agent, Eric Lupfer, at William Morris Endeavor Agency.

From Victor: One part of this book was the easiest to write. To discover the notion of love, I needed to look no further than my family, where my "line of credit" seems inexhaustible. To my parents, C.J. and Betty, who have given me more than life's fair share of blessings, you have my eternal gratitude and devotion. I still stand in awe of the courage, the sacrifices, and the affection that you have exhibited in your lives. To my sister, Tina, it is priceless to have someone you can always depend on. I will always be there for you, as you have been for me. To my mother-in-law, Angela, your generosity to the rest of us is humbling, and I owe you my deepest possible appreciation.

To Anders and Augustine—whose eyes are still filled with limitless wonder when they look at the stars, the elephants, and zombie games—my love for you goes beyond my ability to write the words. May you always keep that joy, curiosity, and fearlessness throughout your lives.

To my wife, Christina, who cultivated a rich Rainforest around my life long before I ever realized it, you are my life's love, salvation, and light. You have nursed me when I have fallen, held me when I have cried, and cheered the loudest when I have conquered. 愛你不容易，不愛你更難.

From Greg: The Rainforest is a relevant metaphor not only for innovation systems, but also for our families and close friends. Complex, at times threatening, competitive for resources, and inexplicably bound together by our root structure for survival and sustenance. To all those people who have come into my life, and enriched it with their love, wisdom, and friendship... thank you. To my dearest friends Victor, Wendy, Scott, Anette, and to my Global CONNECT colleagues, Peter and Nathan....thank you for allowing me to bend your collective ears with crazy ideas, random thoughts, and wild stories. I know that at times you had no idea where this was all going, and yet you still encouraged me (daily) to think and dream big. I couldn't have made it without knowing you were always there.

Bibliography

Abai, *Book of Words*. Abai International Club, 2005.

Acemoglu, Daron, and Matthew O. Jackson. "History, Expectations, and Leadership in the Evolution of Cooperation." NBER Working Paper 17066, Cambridge, MA: NBER, 2011. http://www.nber.org/papers/w17066.pdf.

Acemoglu, Daron, and Matthew O. Jackson. "How Cooperation Evolves: History, Expectations, and Leadership." On VOX: Research-based policy analysis and commentary from leading economists. June 13, 2011. http://www.voxeu.org/index.php?q=node/6639.

Alger Jr., Horatio. *Ragged Dick, or, Street Life in New York with the Boot-Blacks*. New York: Modern Library, 2005.

Ambrose, Stephen E. *Nothing Like It In the World: The Men Who Built the Transcontinental Railroad*, 1863-1869. New York: Simon & Schuster, 2000.

Ariely, Dan, Uri Gneezy, George Loewenstein, and Nina Mazar. "Large Stakes and Big Mistakes." Working paper No. 05-11, Research Center for Behavioral Economics and Decision-Making, Federal Reserve Bank of Boston, Boston, 2005. http://www.bos.frb.org/economic/wp/wp2005/wp0511.pdf.

Aron, Arthur, C. C. Norman, Elaine N. Aron, C. McKenna, and R. E. Heyman. "Couples' Shared Participation in Novel and Arousing Activities and Experienced Relationship Quality." *Journal of Personality and Social Psychology* 78, no. 2 (2000): 273-284. doi: 10.1037/0022-3514.78.2.273.

Arthur, Brian. *The Nature of Technology: What It Is and How It Evolves*. Free Press and Penguin, UK, 2009.

Bada, Jeffrey L., and Antonio Lazcano. "Prebiotic Soup-Revisiting the Miller Experiment." *Science Magazine* 300 (2003): 745-746. doi: 10.1126/science.1085145.

Bading, Karen V., Janet L. Crawford, and Lisa J. Marshall. "The Living Story." Smart Work, 2000. http://www.smartworkco.com/pdf/the_living_story.pdf.

Bain, David H. *Empire Express: Building the First Transcontinental Railroad*. New York: Viking-Penguin, 1999.

Banz, Rof W. "The Relationship between Return and Market Value of Common Stocks." *Journal of Financial Economics* 9 (1981). http://perrittmutualfunds.com/media/Banz_Small_Firm_Effects.pdf.

Barabasi, Albert-Laszlo. *Linked: How Everything is Connected to Everything Else and What it Means for Business, Science*, and Everyday Life. New York: Plume, 2003.

Barnard, Chester. *Organization and Management: Selected Papers*. Cambridge: Harvard University Press, 1948.

Bateson, Gregory. *Steps To An Ecology of Mind*. Chicago: University of Chicago Press, 1972.

Beck, Aaron T. "The Current State of Cognitive Therapy: A 40-Year Retrospective." *Archives of General Psychiatry*, Vol. 62, 953-959 (2005).

Bednar, Jenna, Aaron Bramson, Andrea Jones-Rooy, and Scott Page. "Emergent Cultural Signatures and Persistent Diversity: A Model of Conformity and Consistency." *Rationality and Society* 22, no. 4 (2010): 407-444. doi: 10.1177/1043463110374501.

Beinhocker, Eric. *The Origin of Wealth: Evolution, Complexity, and the Radical Remaking of Economics*. Boston: Harvard Business School Press, 2006.

Benkler, Yochai. "Law, Policy, and Cooperation," in Balleisen, Edward, and David Moss, eds. *Government and Markets: Toward a New Theory of Regulation*. Cambridge University Press, forthcoming. http://www.benkler.org/Benkler_Law%20Policy%20Cooperation%2004.pdf.

Bernstein, Lisa. "Opting Out of the Legal System: Extralegal Contractual Relations in the Diamond Industry." 21 *Journal of Legal Studies* 115 (1992).

Bernstein, Lisa. "Private Commercial Law in the Cotton Industry: Creating Cooperation Through Rules, Norms, and Institutions." 99 *Mich. L. Rev.* 1724 (2001).

Bernstein, Lisa. "The Silicon Valley Lawyer as Transaction Cost Engineer?" 74 *University of Oregon Law Review* 239 (1995).

Bethanis, Sue, and Janet Crawford. "Pressed for Time: What Would You Do With An Extra Hour." Wise Talk, May, 2005.

Bieling, Peter J., Randi E. McCabe, and Martin M. Antony. *Cognitive-Behavioral Therapy in Groups*. New York: Guilford Press, 2006.

Björkstén, Bengt, Epp Sepp, Kaja Julge, Tiia Voor, and Marika Mikelsaar. "Allergy Development and the Intestinal Microflora During the First Year of Life." *Journal of Allergy and Clinical Immunology* 108, no. 4 (2001): 516-520. doi:10.1067/mai.2001.118130.

Blank, Steve. "Live Life With No Regrets: Remember There Is No Undo Button" (Commencement address at Philadelphia University, Philadelphia, PA, May 17, 2011).

Blank, Steve. "Secret History of Silicon Valley - Berkeley Edition.mov." YouTube video, 1:06:10. Posted by "Techistory." March 19, 2011.
http://www.youtube.com/watch?v=eajSutMIRPY&feature=player_embedded.

Block, Fred, and Matthew R. Keller. "Where Do Innovations Come From? Transformations in the U.S. National Innovation System, 1970-2006." Washington D.C.: The Information Technology and Innovation Foundation, July 1, 2008.
http://www.itif.org/files/Where_do_innovations_come_from.pdf.

Blodget, Henry. "George Soros: We Are Just Entering 'Act 2' of the Crisis, and We're Totally Screwed." *Business Insider*, June 13, 2010. http://www.businessinsider.com/george-soros-we-are-just-entering-act-2-of-the-crisis-and-were-totally-screwed-2010-6.

Bock, Larry. "A Bromide for a Good Life" (138th Commencement Address, College of Chemistry, University of California, Berkeley, CA, May 19, 2007).

Bohorquez, Juan Camilo, Sean Gourley, Alex Dixon, Michael Spagat and Neil F. Johnson. "Common Ecology Quantifies Human Insurgency." *Nature* 462 (2009): 911-914. doi:10.1038/nature08631.

Boorstin, Daniel J. *The Americans: The National Experience*. New York: Vintage Books, 1965.

Boyd, Danah Michele. "Taken Out of Context: American Teen Sociality in Networked Publics." PhD dissertation, Graduate Division of the University of California, Berkeley, Fall 2008, 293-294.

Branson, Richard. "Richard Branson: Five Secrets to Business Success." Bnet.com, September 10, 2010. http://www.bnet.com/blog/smb/richard-branson-five-secrets-to-business-success/2155.

Brassard, Gilles, Anne Broadbent, and Alain Tapp. "Quantum Pseudo-Telepathy." *Foundations of Physics* 35 (2005): 1877–1907. doi: 10.1007/s10701-005-7353-4.

Brooks, David. "The Limits of Policy." *New York Times*, May 4, 2010.
http://www.nytimes.com/2010/05/04/opinion/04brooks.html.

Brooks, David. "Nice Guys Finish First." *New York Times Reprints*, May 16, 2011.
http://www.nytimes.com/2011/05/17/opinion/17brooks.html.

Brooks, David. "The New Humanism." *New York Times Reprints*, March 7, 2011.

Buller, A.H.R. *Researches on Fungi*, vol. 5. London: Longman, 1933.

Campaign for Free Enterprise. "SXSW Interview–Molly Davis, *Something Ventured*." YouTube video,. 4:05. Posted by "Freeenterprise". March 16, 2011. http://www.youtube.com/watch?v=fe2jjoaDMLk.

"Can VCs Be Value Investors?" BuzzBox. http://www.pehub.com/84474/can-vcs-be-value-investors/.

Carrere, Sybil, and John M. Gottman. "Predicting Divorce Among Newlyweds from the First Three Minutes of a Marital Conflict Discussion." *Family Process* 38, no. 3 (1999): 293-301. doi:10.1111/j.1545-5300.1999.00293.x.

Castilla, Emilio J., Hokyu Hwang, Ellen Granovetter, and Mark S. Granovetter. *Social Networks in Silicon Valley.. In The Silicon Valley Edge*. Stanford: Stanford University Press, 2000.
http://www.mendeley.com/research/social-networks-in-silicon-valley/.

CB Insights. "Venture Capital Human Capital Report." January-June 2010.
http://www.cbinsights.com/blog/venture-capital/venture-capital-human-capital-report.

Chatterjee, Rhitu. "Xenophobia's Evolutionary Roots." *PRI's The World*, August 10, 2011.
http://www.theworld.org/2011/08/xenophobias-evolutionary-roots/.

Chown, Marcus. "Physics with a Human Touch." *New Scientist*, March 10, 1988.

Coase, Ronald. "Interview with Ronald Coase." By Tawni Ferrarini, John Nye, Alfredo Bullard, and Hugo Eyzaguirre. At the Inaugural Conference, International Society for Institutional Economics, St. Louis, Missouri, September 17, 1997. http://coase.org/coaseinterview.htm.

Coase, R. H. "The Nature of the Firm: Influence." *Journal of Law, Economics, and Organization 4, no. 1 (1988):* 33-47. http://www.jstor.org/stable/765013.

Coase, R. H. "The Nature of the Firm: Meaning." *Journal of Law, Economics, and Organization 4, no. 1 (1988): 19-32.* http://www.jstor.org/stable/765012.

Coase, R. H. "The Nature of the Firm: Origin." *Journal of Law, Economics, and Organization 4, no. 1 (1988): 3-17.* http://www.jstor.org/stable/765011.

Coase, Ronald H. "Ronald H. Coase-Prize Lecture." Nobelprize.org. December 9, 1991. http://www.nobelprize.org/nobel_prizes/economics/laureates/1991/coase-lecture.html.

Coase, Ronald. "Why Do Firms Exist?" *Economist*, December 16, 2010. http://www.economist.com/node/17730360.

Coase, Ronald H., and Ning Wang. "The Industrial Structure of Production: A Research Agenda for Innovation in an Entrepreneurial Economy." *Entrepreneurship Research Journal* 1, no. 2 (2011). doi: 10.2202/2157-5665.1026.

Cohon, Rachel. "Hume's Moral Philosophy." *In Stanford Encyclopedia of Philosophy*. Center for the Study of Language and Information, Stanford University, Fall 2010. http://plato.stanford.edu/archives/fall2010/entries/hume-moral/.

Coleman, James S. "Social Capital in the Creation of Human Capital." *American Journal of Sociology* 94 Supplement (1988): S95-S120. http://onemvweb.com/sources/sources/social_capital.pdf.

CONNECT. "CONNECT Innovation Report – Second Quarter 2009." San Diego: CONNECT, 2009.

Conniff, Richard. "Biology's Chief Provocateur Explores the Evolutionary Origins of Cooperation, Warfare, and the Tribal Mind." *Discover Magazine*, June 25, 2006. http://discovermagazine.com/2006/jun/e-o-wilson.

Crawford, Janet L. "The Brain-Friendly Organization: What Leadership Needs to Know to Allow Intelligence to Flourish." Cascadance, 2007. http://www.cascadance.com/wp-content/downloads/crawford-brain-friendly-organization-article.pdf.

Csermely, Peter. *Weak Links: The Universal Key to the Stability of Networks and Complex Systems.* Dordrecht, New York: Springer, 2009. http://www.weaklink.sote.hu/weakbook.html.

D'Angelo, Rudy A. "The Cowboy Codes." http://rudydangelo.tripod.com/cowboy_codes.htm.

Dary, David. *Cowboy Culture: A Saga of Five Centuries.* Kansas: University Press of Kansas, 1989.

Deming, W. Edwards. *The New Economics: For Industry, Government, Education.* Cambridge: MIT Press, 1994.

De Soto, Hernando. *The Mystery of Capital.* New York: Basic Books: 2000. http://mystery-capital.livejournal.com/4277.html.

Diamond, Jared M. "The Island Dilemma: Lessons of Modern Biogeographic Studies for the Design of Natural Reserves." *Biological Conservation*, Vol. 7, no. 2 (1975).

Donald, Merlin. *Origins of the Modern Mind: Three Stages in the Evolution of Culture and Cognition.* Cambridge: Harvard University Press, 1991.

Driesen, David M. and Shubha Ghosh. "Functions of Transaction Costs: Rethinking Transaction Cost Minimization in a World of Friction." 47 *Arizona Law Review* 61 (2005).

Dubaibeat.com. "Yahoo Acquired Middle East Internet Company Maktoob.com for $164 million." August 25, 2009. http://www.dubaibeat.com/2009/08/25/yahoo_acquired_middle_east_int.php.

Dutta, Soumitra, ed. "The Global Innovation Index 2011: Accelerating Growth and Development." Fontainebleau, France: INSEAD, 2011.

eBay INC. "Report Strong First Quarter 2011 Results." eBay, San Jose, CA, April 27, 2011. http://files.shareholder.com/downloads/ebay/1347843372x0x462596/0dd3fa3d-9791-4135-9f3c-30b5fb7bce7c/eBay_Q1_2011_Earnings_Release_042711_FINAL.pdf.

Eisenberger, Naomi I. "Why Rejection Hurts: What Social Neuroscience Has Revealed About the Brain's Response to Social Rejection." *The Handbook of Social Neuroscience*, edited by J. Decety and J. Cacioppo, 586-598. New York: Oxford University Press, 2011. http://web.mac.com/naomieisenberger/san/Naomi_Eisenberger_SAN_Papers_files/39-Decety-39.pdf.

Ekman, Paul, W.V. Friesen, and J.C. Hager. *Facial Action Coding System: Manual.* Consulting Psychologists Press, 1978.

Epstein, Richard A. "Confusion about Custom: Disentangling Informal Customs from Standard Contractual Provisions." 66 *University of Chicago Law Review* 3, 821-835 (Summer 1999).

Ernst, Chris, and Donna Chrobot-Mason, "Flat World, Hard Boundaries—How To Lead Across Them." *MIT Sloan Management Review*, March 23, 2011. http://sloanreview.mit.edu/.

Fama, Eugene F., and Kenneth R. French. "The Cross-Section of Expected Stock Returns."Abstract. *Journal of Finance* 47, no. 2 (1992). doi:10.2307/2329112.

Feldman, Maryann P., and Ted Douglas Zoller. "Dealmakers in Place: Social Capital Connections in Regional Entrepreneurial Economies." Paper presented at the International Schumpeter Society Conference, Aalborg University, Denmark, June 21-24, 2010.

Ferguson, Niall. *The Ascent of Money: A Financial History of the World.* New York: Penguin, 2009.

Feynman, Richard P. "The Value of Science." Address, National Academy of Sciences, Autumn, 1955. http://www.ma.utexas.edu/users/mwilliams/feynman.pdf.

Feynman, Richard, and Christopher Skyes. *No Ordinary Genius: The Illustrated Richard Feynman.* New York: Norton, 1996.

Fikes, Bradley J. "What Next For UCSD Connect? The Godfather of San Diego's Tech Incubators is Searching (Again) for a Leader." *San Diego Metropolitan Magazine,* March 2004. http://sandiegometro.archives.whsites.net/2004/mar/ucsdconnect.php.

Fitjar, Rune Dahl, and Andrés Rodríguez-Pose. "When Local Interaction Does Not Suffice: Sources of Firm Innovation in Urban Norway." Madrid: Institute Imdea, February, 2011.

Ford Jr, Lacy K. "Frontier Democracy: The Turner Thesis Revisited." *Journal of the Early Republic* 13, no. 2 (1993): 144-163. http://scholarcommons.sc.edu/.

Foster, Dick, and Sarah Kaplan. *Creative Destruction.* New York: Broadway Business, 2001.

Fowler, James H., and Nicholas A. Christakis. "Cooperative Behaviour Cascades in Human Social Networks." Proceedings of the National Academy of Sciences 107, no. 12 (2010): 5334-5338. doi: 10.1073/pnas.0913149107.

Fowler, James H., Jaime E. Settle, and Nicholas A. Christakis. "Correlated Genotypes in Friendship Networks." Proceedings of the National Academy of Sciences 108, no. 5 (2011): 1993-1997. doi: 10.1073/pnas.1011687108.

Fox, Justin. "Are Finance Professors and Their Theories to Blame for the Financial Crisis?" CFA Institute Conference Proceedings Quarterly 27, no. 2 (2010).

Frederickson, Megan E., and Deborah M. Gordon. "The Devil to Pay: A Cost of Mutualism with Myrmelachista schumanni Ants in 'Devil's Gardens' is Increased Herbivory on Duroia hirsuta Trees." Proceedings of the Royal Society B 274, no. 1613 (2007): 1117-1123. doi: 10.1098/rspb.2006.0415.

Frederickson, Megan E., Michael J. Greene, and Deborah M. Gordon. "Ecology: 'Devil's Gardens' Bedevilled by Ants." Abstract. *Nature* 437 (2005). doi:10.1038/437495a.

Freeman, Jonathan B., Nicholas O. Rule, Reginald B. Adams Jr., and Nalini Ambady. "Culture Shapes a Mesolimbic Response to Signals of Dominance and Subordination that Associates with Behavior." *NeuroImage* 47 (2009): 353-359. doi:10.1016/j.neuroimage.2009.04.038.

French, Howard, W. "E.O. Wilson's Theory of Everything." *The Atlantic,* November 2011.

Frith, Chris. "Attention to Action and Awareness of Other Minds." *Consciousness and Cognition* 11, no.4 (2002): 481-487. doi:10.1016/S1053-8100(02)00022-3.

Frith, Chris D., and Tania Singer. "The Role of Social Cognition in Decision Making." *Philosophical Transactions of The Royal Society* B 363 (2008): 3875-3886. doi: 10.1098/rstb.2008.0156 .

Fukuyama, Francis. "Social Capital, Civil Society and Development." *Third World Quarterly* 22 (2001): 8-10. http://intranet.catie.ac.cr/intranet/posgrado/Met%20Cual%20Inv%20accion/Semana%206/Fukuyama.pdf.

Fukuyama, Francis. *Trust: The Social Virtues and the Creation of Prosperity.* New York: Simon & Schuster, 1996.

Gazzola, Valeria, and Christian Keysers. "The Observation and Execution of Actions Share Motor and Somatosensory Voxels in All Tested Subjects: Single-Subject Analyses of Unsmoothed fMRI Data." *Cereb Cortex* 19, no. 6 (2009): 1239-1255. doi: 10.1093/cercor/bhn181.

Geller, Dan, and Dayna Goldfine. *Something Ventured.* Unpublished interview transcript from documentary, San Francisco, 2011. http://somethingventuredthemovie.com/.

"The Genographic Project." NationalGeographic.com. http://www.nationalgeographic.com/xpeditions/lessons/09/g912/haplogroupO.pdf

Geron, Tomio. "What Y Combinator's Paul Graham Looks For In Founders." *Forbes,* May 24, 2011. http://www.forbes.com/sites/tomiogeron/2011/05/24/what-y-combinators-paul-graham-looks-for-in-founders/.

Ghandour, Fadi. "Aramex's Fadi Ghandour Unfolds His Roadmap for Budding Entrepreneurs in the Middle East." Interview at Arabic Knowledge @ Wharton, May 4, 2010. http://knowledge.wharton.upenn.edu/arabic/article.cfm?articleId=2446.

Gibson, Campbell, and Emily Lennon. ""Foreign-Born Population by Historical Section and Subsection of the United States: 1850 to 1990." U.S. Bureau of the Census, Population Division, March 9, 1999. http://www.census.gov/population/www/documentation/twps0029/tab14.html.

Gibson, Campbell, and Emily Lennon. "Nativity of the Population, for Regions, Divisions, and States: 1850 to 1990." U.S. Bureau of the Census, Population Division, March 9, 1999. http://www.census.gov/population/www/documentation/twps0029/tab13.html.

Gillmore, C. Stewart. *Fred Terman at Stanford:: Building a Discipline, a University, and Silicon Valley*. Stanford: Stanford University Press, 2004.

Goel, Vinod K., Ekaterina Koryukin, Mohini Bhatia, and Priyanka Agarwal. "Innovation Systems: World Bank Support of Science and Technology Development." World Bank Working Paper No. 32. Washington D.C.: World Bank, April 2004.

Gottman, John M., and Robert W. Levenson. "Marital Processes Predictive of Later Dissolution Behaviour, Physiology, and Health." *Journal of Personality and Social Psychology* 63, no. 2 (1992): 221-233. http://socrates.berkeley.edu/~ucbpl/docs/41-Marital%20Processes92.pdf.

Gottman, John Mordechai, and Robert Wayne Levenson. "The Timing of Divorce: Predicting When a Couple Will Divorce Over a 14-Year Period." *Journal of Marriage and the Family* 62 (2000): 737-745. http://socrates.berkeley.edu/~ucbpl/docs/61-Timing%20of%20Divorce00.pdf.

Goswami, Amit. "Quantum Activism for Better Health and Healing." March 01, 2010. http://www.amitgoswami.org/quantum-activism-health-healing/.

Gourley, Sean. "Sean Gourley on the Mathematics of War," TED video, 07:22, February 2009. Posted May 2009. http://www.ted.com/talks/sean_gourley_on_the_mathematics_of_war.html.

Graham, Paul. "Why To Not Not Start a Startup." Essay. March, 2007. http://www.paulgraham.com/notnot.html.

Henderson, Sarah E., and Catherine J. Norris. "An fMRI Study of Anticipation: Is the Journey More Important Than the Destination?" Poster presented at Social and Affective Neuroscience Conference, Chicago, October, 2010.

Henriques, Gregg. "The Tree of Knowledge System and the Theoretical Unification of Psychology." *Review of General Psychology*, Vol. 7, No. 2 (2003), 150–182. doi: 10.1037/1089-2680.7.2.150.

Herman, Robert, and Ilya Prigogine. "A Two-Fluid Approach to Town Traffic." *Science New Series* 204, no. 4389 (1979): 148-151.

Hickey, Patrick C., David J. Jacobson, Nick D. Read, and N. Louise Glass. "Live-Cell Imaging of Vegetative Hyphal Fusion in Neurospora crassa." *Fungal Genetics and Biology* 37 (2002): 109-119.

Higgins, Monica C. *Career Imprints: Creating Leaders Across an Industry*. New York: John Wiley & Sons, 2005.

Hine, Robert V. *Community on the American Frontier: Separate, But Not Alone*. Norman: University of Oklahoma Press, 1980.

Holt, Lester. "The Facebook Obsession." CNBC video, 2:19. December 23, 2010. http://video.cnbc.com/gallery/?video=1707620781.

Hong, Lu, and Scott E. Page. "Groups of Diverse Problem Solvers Can Outperform Groups of High-Ability Problem Solvers." Proceedings of the National Academy of Sciences 101, no. 46 (2004): 16385-16389. doi: 10.1073/pnas.0403723101.

Hurley, Chad, and Steve Chen. "A Message From Chad and Steve." YouTube video. 1:37. The YouTube founders talk about the Google acquisition. Posted by "YouTube." October 9, 2006. http://www.youtube.com/watch?v=QCVxQ_3Ejkg.

Hwang, Victor W. "The Mystery of Venture Capital." *Journal of the Center for Venture Education* (2010).

Hyde, Catherine Ryan. *Pay It Forward*. New York: Simon & Schuster, 2000.

Inagaki, Tristen K., and Naomi I. Eisenberger. "Neural Underpinnings of the Provision of Social Support." Poster presented at the 2010 Social and Affective Neuroscience Conference, Chicago, IL, October, 2010. http://www.socialaffectiveneuro.org/docs/SANS_program_2010.pdf.

Isaacson, Walter, *Steve Jobs*. New York: Simon & Schuster, 2011.

Jackson, Matthew O. *Social and Economic Networks*. Kindle edition. Princeton: Princeton University Press, 2010.

Jackson, Matthew O., and Leeat Yariv. "Social Networks and the Diffusion of Economic Behaviour." *Yale Economic Review* 3, no. 2 (2006): 42-47.

Jantsch, Erich. *The Self-Organizing Universe: Scientific and Human Implications of the Emerging Paradigm of Evolution.* Oxford: Pergamon Press, 1980.

Jaworski, Joseph, Gary Jusela, and C. Otto Scharmer . "Coming from Your Inner Self, Conversation with W. Brian Arthur, Xerox PARC." Excerpt. April 16, 1999. http://web.archive.org/web/20080724094936/http://www.dialogonleadership.org/Arthur-1999.html.

Johnson, Ryan. "'Those Were the Days…That Tried Men's Mettle': Tourism, Western Masculinity, and the Transcontinental Railroad, 1865-1880." *Perspectives* 36 (2009): 39-60.

Johnson, Tim, Christopher T. Dawes, James H. Fowler, Richard McElreath, and Oleg Smirnov. "The Role of Egalitarian Motives in Altruistic Punishment." *Economics Letters* 102 (2009): 194. http://jhfowler.ucsd.edu/role_of_egalitarian_motives.pdf.

Jung, Malte Friedrich, "Engineering Team Performance and Emotion: Affective Interaction Dynamics as Indicators of Design Team Performance." PhD diss., Department Of Mechanical Engineering and the Committee on Graduate Studies, Stanford University, Stanford, August 2011.

Jung, Malte F. *SPAFF for Design Teams.* Stanford: Stanford University, October 2007.

Jung, Malte F., Jan Chong, and Larry J. Leifer. "Pair Programming Performance: An Emotional Dynamics Point of View from Marital Pair Counseling." Paper presented at the Conference on Computer Supported Cooperative Work, Hangzhou, China, March 19-23, 2011.

Kanai, Ryota, and Michael Banissy, "Are Two Heads Better Than One? It Depends." *Scientific American*, August 31, 2010. http://www.scientificamerican.com/article.cfm?id=are-two-heads-better-than.

Kane, Tim. "The Importance of Startups in Job Creation and Job Destruction." Kauffman Foundation Research Series: Firm Formation and Economic Growth, July, 2010.

Krugman, Paul R. *Geography and Trade.* Cambridge: MIT Press, 1991.

Landes, William M., and Sonia Lahr-Pastor. "Measuring Coase's Influence." Presentation at Markets, Firms and Property Rights: A Celebration of the Research of Ronald Coase, Chicago, IL, December 4-5, 2009.http://iep.gmu.edu/CoaseConference.php.

La Porta, Rafael, Florencio Lopez-de-Silanes, and Andrei Shleifer. "The Economic Consequences of Legal Origins." *Journal of Economic Literature* 2008, 46:2, 285–332.

Leeder, Abigail C., Javier Palma-Guerrero, and N. Louise Glass. "The Social Network: Deciphering Fungal Language." *Abstract. Nature Reviews Microbiology 9 (2011).* doi:10.1038/nrmicro258.

Lerner, Josh. *Boulevard of Broken Dreams: Why Public Efforts to Boost Entrepreneurship and Venture Capital Have Failed—and What to Do About It.* Princeton: Princeton University Press, 2009.

Lerner, Josh. "Geography, Venture Capital, and Public Policy." Policy paper, Harvard Business School, Harvard University, Boston, March 2010. http://www.hks.harvard.edu/.

Lerner, Josh. *Venture Capital and Private Equity: A Casebook.* Hoboken: Wiley, 2000.

Levine, Seth. "Beware of Asshole VCs." Seth Levine's VC Adventure. http://www.sethlevine.com/wp/2011/07/beware-of-asshole-vcs.

Levine, Timothy R., Hee Sun Park, and Steven A. McCornack. "Accuracy in Detecting Truth and Lies: Documenting the 'Veracity Effect'" *Communication Monographs* 66 (1999): 125-144. https://www.msu.edu/~levinet/veracity.pdf.

LoBue, Vanessa, David H. Rakison, and Judy S. DeLoache. "Threat Perception Across the Life Span Evidence for Multiple Converging Pathways." Abstract. *Current Directions in Psychological Science* 19 (2010): 375-379. doi: 10.1177/0963721410388801.

MacArthur, Robert H., and E.O. Wilson. *The Theory of Island Biogeography.* Princeton University Press (1967).

McCarthy, Ian P., Thomas B. Lawrence, Brian Wixted, and Brian R. Gordon. "A Multidimensional Conceptualization of Environmental Velocity." *Academy of Management Review* 35 (2010): 604-626. http://thomaslawrence.files.wordpress.com/2008/08/mccarthy-et-al-2010-a-multidimensional-conceptualization-of-environmen.pdf.

MacIver, Robert M. *Community.* Chicago: University of Chicago Press, 1970.

MacLeod, Hugh. "I'm Not Delusional. I'm An Entrepreneur." http://www.flickr.com/photos/calebstorkey/5393011750/in/set-72157625791768251.

Malone, Michael S. "John Doerr's Startup Manual." *Fast Company*, February 28, 1997.
    http://www.fastcompany.com/magazine/07/082doerr.html.

Malone, Michael S. *The Valley of Heart's Delight: A Silicon Valley Notebook: 1963-2001*. New York: John
    Wiley & Sons, 2002.

Mandelbrot, Benoît B. *The Fractal Geometry of Nature*. New York: W.H. Freeman, 1982.
    http://www.amazon.com/Fractal-Geometry-Nature-Benoit-Mandelbrot/dp/0716711869.

Marshall, Lisa J. "C4-Coordinated Coaching for Culture Change." Smart Work, 2000.
    http://www.insightcoaching.com/downloads/coach_culture_change.pdf.

Mehrabian, Albert, and Morton Wiener. "Decoding of Inconsistent Communications." *Journal of
    Personality and Social Psychology* 6 (1967): 109-114.

Mehrabian, Albert, and Susan R. Ferris. "Influence of Attitudes from Nonverbal Communication in Two
    Channels." *Journal of Consulting Psychology*. 31 (1967): 248-52.

Meyer, Thomas, and Pierre-Yves Mathonet. Beyond the J Curve: Managing a Portfolio of Venture Capital
    and *Private Equity Funds*. New York: John Wiley & Sons, 2005.

Mills, L. Scott, Michael E. Soule, and Daniel F. Doak. "The Keystone-Species Concept in Ecology and
    Conservation." *BioScience* 43, no. 4 (1993): 1-8.
    http://bio.research.ucsc.edu/people/doaklab/publications/1993mills_soule_doak.pdf.

Mooney, Chris. "The Science of Why We Don't Believe Science." *Mother Jones*, April 18, 2011.
    http://motherjones.com/politics/2011/03/denial-science-chris-mooney.

Mordin, Robin I. "A Celebration of the Mind and Work of Ronald Coase." *The Record Online* (Alumni
    Magazine of University of Chicago),, Spring 2010.
    http://www.law.uchicago.edu/alumni/magazine/spring10/coase.

Mullins, John W. *The New Business Road Test: What Entrepreneurs and Executives Should Do Before
    Writing a Business Plan*, 2nd ed. New York: Financial Times/Prentice Hall, 2006.

Murakami, Haruki. "Reality A and Reality B." *The New York Times*, November 29, 2010.
    http://www.nytimes.com/2010/12/02/opinion/global/02iht-GA06-Murakami.html.

Murata, Asuka, Sam Boas, Sasha Kimel, and Shinobu Kitayama. "The Effect of Social Exclusion on the
    Sensitivity to Vocal Tone: An ERP Study." Poster presented at the 2010 Social and Affective
    Neuroscience Conference, Chicago, IL, October 2010.
    http://www.socialaffectiveneuro.org/docs/SANS_program_2010.pdf.

Muro, Mark, and Bruce Katz. "The New 'Cluster Moment': How Regional Innovation Clusters Can
    Foster the Next Economy." Executive Summary, Metropolitan Policy Program. Washington
    D.C.: Brookings Institution, September, 2010. http://www.brookings.edu/~/media/Files/rc/
    papers/2010/0921_clusters_muro_katz/0921_clusters_execsum.pdf.

Murray, Alan. "The End of Management." *Wall Street Journal*, August 21, 2010.
    http://online.wsj.com/article/SB10001424052748704476104575439723695579664.html.

Mutanov, G. *Mathematical Methods and Models in Economics*. Almaty: Kazakh University, 2011).

National Science Foundation. "Science and Engineering Indicators 2010." Division of Science Resources
    Statistics, Survey of Graduate Students and Postdoctorates in Science and Engineering.
    http://www.nsf.gov/statistics/seind10/c8/c8i.htm.

"Nativity and Place of Birth of Resident Population-25 Largest Cities: 2008." U.S. Census Bureau, Statistical
    Abstract of the United States, 2011.
    http://www.census.gov/compendia/statab/2011/tables/11s0038.pdf.

North, Douglass C., and Robert Paul Thomas. *The Rise of the Western World: A New Economic History*.
    Cambridge: Cambridge University Press, 1973.

Nowak, Martin A., Corina E. Tarnita, and Edward O. Wilson. "The Evolution of Eusociality." Nature 466
    (2010). doi: 10.1038/nature09205.

Organisation for Economic Co-Operation and Development. *Society at a Glance 2011: OECD Social
    Indicators*. OECD Publishing, 2011.

"Otters Holding Hands." YouTube video, 1:41.Sea otters at the Vancouver Aquarium. Posted by
    "cynthiaholmes." March 19, 2007. http://www.youtube.com/watch?v=epUk3T2Kfno.

Parker-Pope, Tara. "Reinventing Date Night for Long-Married Couples." *New York Times*, February 12,
    2008. http://www.nytimes.com/2008/02/12/health/12well.html.

PBS. "The Impact of the Transcontinental Railroad." PBS.org, 1996-2000.
    http://www.pbs.org/wgbh/americanexperience/features/general-article/tcrr-impact/.

Perlroth, Nicole. "Forbes Q and A With Andreessen-Horowitz's Secret Agent." *Forbes*, February 4, 2011. http://www.forbes.com/sites/nicoleperlroth/2011/02/04/forbes-q-and-a-with-andreessen-horowitzs-secret-agent/.

Perry, Susan. "Good News On Age and Creativity: You May Still Have Time To Create Your Masterpiece." MinnPost.com, June 18. 2010. http://www.minnpost.com/healthblog/2010/06/18/19035/good_news_on_age_and_creativity_you_may_still_have_time_to_create_your_masterpiece.

Peters, Tom. "Innovation Is Actually Easy!" YouTube video, 2:52. Posted by "BetterLifeCoaches." February 20, 2007. http://www.youtube.com/watch?v=8AGTpu_i8sc.

Peters, Tom, and Bob Waterman. *In Search of Excellence*. New York: Harper & Row, 1982.

Pink, Dan. "Dan Pink on the Surprising Science of Motivation." Filmed July 2009. TED video. 18:40. Career analyst Dan Pink on the puzzle of motivation. Posted August 2009. http://www.ted.com/talks/dan_pink_on_motivation.html.

Pink, Daniel H. *Drive: The Surprising Truth About What Motivates Us*. New York: Penguin, 2011.

Pink, Daniel H. *A Whole New Mind: Why Right-Brainers Will Rule the Future*. US: Riverhead Books, 2006.

Pinker, Steven. *How the Mind Works*. New York: W. W. Norton, June, 1997.

Pollack, Andrew. "Venture Capital Loses Its Vigor." *The New York Times*, October 8, 1989. http://www.nytimes.com/1989/10/08/business/venture-capital-loses-its-vigor.html?src=pm.

Porter, Michael E. "Clusters and the New Economics of Competition." *Harvard Business Review* 76 (1998): 77-90. http://www.wellbeingcluster.at/magazin/00/artikel/28775/doc/d/porterstudie.pdf?ok=j.

Porter, Michael E. *The Competitive Advantage of Nations*. New York: Free Press, 1990.

Powell, Naomi. "Business Clusters 'Irrelevant' for Innovation, Study Finds." *Globe and Mail*, March 18, 2011.

"The Predators' Boneyard: A Conversation with James Kenneth Galbraith." The Straddler, 2010. http://www.thestraddler.com/20105/piece2.php.

"PricewaterhouseCoopers National Venture Capital Association MoneyTree Report." PricewaterhouseCoopers, 2010. https://www.pwcmoneytree.com/MTPublic/ns/index.jsp.

Prigogine, Ilya. *The End of Certainty: Time, Chaos, and the New Laws of Nature*. New York: Free Press, 1996.

Prigogine, Ilya, and Isabelle Stengers. *Order Out of Chaos*. New York: Bantam, 1984.

Putnam, Robert. *Making Democracy Work: Civic Traditions in Modern Italy*. Princeton, N.J.: Princeton University Press, 1993.

Rettner, Rachael. "Successful Conversations Involve Mind Melds, Study Reveals." Live Science, July 26, 2010. http://www.livescience.com/6758-successful-conversations-involve-mind-melds-study-reveals.html.

Reynolds Losin, Elizabeth A., Marco Iacoboni, Alia Martin, and Mirella Dapretto. "Answering the 'Other' Question in Cultural Neuroscience: Theory and Data on How Culture Gets Into the Brain." Poster presented at the 2010 Social and Affective Neuroscience Conference, Chicago, IL, October, 2010. http://www.socialaffectiveneuro.org/docs/SANS_program_2010.pdf.

Richardson, Albert D. "Through to the Pacific, A Series of Letters Published in the *New York Tribune*, May-June 1869." Central Pacific Railroad Photographic History Museum, 2000-2006. http://cprr.org/Museum/Through_to_the_Pacific/Through_to_the_Pacific.html.

Richtel, Matt. "In the Venture Capital World, a Helping Hand for Women and Minorities." *New York Times*, June 15, 2007. http://www.nytimes.com/2007/06/15/business/15venture.html.

Ridley, Matt. "Humans: Why They Triumphed." *Wall Street Journal*, May 22, 2010. http://online.wsj.com/article/SB10001424052748703691804575254533386933138.html.

Ridley, Matt. "Ideas Having Sex." *Reason Magazine*, July 2010. http://reason.com/archives/2010/06/14/ideas-having-sex.

Ridley, Matt. *The Optimist: How Prosperity Evolves*. New York: Harper, 2010. http://issuu.com/hcpressbooks/docs/rational_optimist.

Rizzolatti, Giacomo, and Laila Craighero. "The Mirror-Neuron System." *Annual Review of Neuroscience* 27 (2004): 169-192. doi:10.1146/annurev.neuro.27.070203.144230.

Romer, Paul M. "Economic Growth." *The Concise Encyclopedia of Economics*. http://www.econlib.org/library/Enc/EconomicGrowth.html.

Romer, Paul M. "Endogenous Technological Change." *Journal of Political Economy* 98, no. 5 (1990): S70-S102. http://artsci.wustl.edu/~econ502/Romer.pdf.

Romer, Paul M. "The Origins of Endogenous Growth." *Journal of Economic Perspectives* 8, no. 1 (1994): 3-22. http://www.iset.ge/old/upload/Romer%201994.pdf.

Ross, Alison. "Devilish Ants Control the Garden." BBC News, September 21, 2005. http://news.bbc.co.uk/2/hi/science/nature/4269544.stm.

Rotella, Katie, Jennifer A. Richeson, Jason M. Scimeca, and Joan Y. Chiao. "Neural Bases of Trust for Ingroup and Outgroup Members." Poster presented at the 2010 Social and Affective Neuroscience Conference, Chicago, IL, October 29-31, 2010. http://www.socialaffectiveneuro.org/docs/SANS_program_2010.pdf.

Rothman, Matt. "Into the Black." *Inc.*, January 1, 1993. http://www.inc.com/magazine/19930101/3340.html.

The Royal Society. *Brain Waves Module 1: Neuroscience, Society and Policy*. Frankfurt: The Royal Society, January, 2011.

Sapolsky, Robert. *Why Zebras Don't Get Ulcers: An Updated Guide to Stress, Stress Related Diseases, and Coping*. New York: W. H. Freeman, 1994.

Sapolsky, Robert, and Marcia Reynolds. "Zebras and Lions in the Workplace: An Interview with Dr. Robert Sapolsky." *The International Journal of Coaching in Organizations* 4, no. 2 (2006): 7-15. http://pcpionline.com/~files/Authors/IJCO200642715Sapolskyfinau.pdf.

Saxenian, AnnaLee. *Regional Advantage: Culture and Competition in Silicon Valley and Route 128*. Cambridge: Harvard University Press, 1996.

"SBIR Reauthorization 2011 Dr. Irwin Mark Jacobs (Qualcomm)." YouTube video. 5:43. Testimony of Dr. Irwin Jacobs, Co-Founder, Qualcomm. Posted by "sbirinsider." February 23, 2011. http://www.youtube.com/watch?v=5X88LSV8kqs.

Schein, Edgar. *Organizational Culture and Leadership*. New York: John Wiley & Sons, 2010, Kindle edition.

Schultz, Wolfram. "Reward, Decision-Making and Neuroeconomics." *Brain Waves Module 1: Neuroscience, Society and Policy*, The Royal Society, Frankfurt, January 2011.

Schumpeter, Joseph A. *Capitalism, Socialism and Democracy*, 3rd ed. New York: Harper Colophon, 1975.

Scott, James C. *Seeing Like a State: How Certain Schemes to Improve the Human Condition Have Failed*. New Haven: Yale University Press, 1999, Kindle edition.

Seligman, Martin E. P., and Mihalyi Csikszentmihalyi. "Positive Psychology: An Introduction." *American Psychologist* 55(2000): 5-14.

Senor, Dan, and Saul Singer. *Start Up Nation*. New York: Hachete Book Group, 2009.

Sherif, Muzafer, O. J. Harvey, B. Jack White, William R. Hood, and Carolyn W. Sherif. "Intergroup Conflict and Cooperation: The Robbers Cave Experiment." Classics in the History of Psychology. http://psychclassics.yorku.ca/Sherif/chap4.htm.

Sherman, Erik. "Why Silicon Valley's Love Affair With Stock Options Is Hitting the Skids." *Business Insider*, June 29, 2011. http://www.businessinsider.com/why-silicon-valleys-love-affair-with-stock-options-is-hitting-the-skids-2011-6.

Singer, Tania, and Nikolaus Steinbeis. "Differential Roles of Fairness and Compassion-Based Motivations for Cooperation, Defection, and Punishment." Annals of the New York Academy of Sciences 1167 (2009): 41-50. doi: 10.1111/j.1749-6632.2009.04733.x.

Singer, Wolf. "A Determinist View of Brain, Mind and Consciousness." *Brain Waves Module 1: Neuroscience, Society and Policy*, The Royal Society, Frankfurt, January 2011.

Smith, Adam. *The Theory of Moral Sentiments* (orig. pub. 1759), Kindle edition.

Soon, Chun Siong, Marcel Brass, Hans-Jochen Heinze, and John-Dylan Haynes. "Unconscious Determinants of Free Decisions in the Human Brain." *Nature Neuroscience* 11 (2008): 543-545. doi:10.1038/nn.2112.

"Special Edition on Astrophysics." *Scientific American*, June 12, 2007. http://www.scienceandsociety.org/web/Library_files/Astrophysics-Special_Edition.pdf.

Stallen, Mirre, Ale Smidts, and Alan Sanfe. "The Influence of Group Membership on Advice Taking." Poster presented at the 2010 Social and Affective Neuroscience Conference, Chicago, IL, October 29-31, 2010. http://www.socialaffectiveneuro.org/docs/SANS_program_2010.pdf.

Stibel, Jeff. "Entrepreneurship As Disease." HBR Blog Network, *Harvard Business Review*, September 14, 2010. http://blogs.hbr.org/cs/2010/09/entrepreneurship_as_disease.html.

Suchman, Mark C. "Constructed Ecologies: Toward an Institutional Ecology of Reproduction and Structuration in Emerging Organizational Communities." Paper presented at the Workshop on Institutional Analysis at the University of Arizona, March 29-30, 1996. http://www.ssc.wisc.edu/~suchman/publications/constructed.pdf.

Suchman, Mark C. "Dealmakers and Counselors: Law Firms as Intermediaries in the Development of Silicon Valley," in M. Kenney (ed.), *Understanding Silicon Valley: The Anatomy of an Entrepreneurial Region.* Palo Alto: Stanford University Press, 2000.

"Sukhavati: A Mythic Journey." Mystic Fire Video, Netflix, 1998.

Sunstein, Cass R. "Social Norms and Social Rules." John M. Olin Law and Economics Working Paper No. 36 (2D Series), The Law School, University of Chicago, Chicago, 1995. http://www.law.uchicago.edu/files/files/36.Sunstein.Social_0.pdf.

Tesson, Karen Jane. "An Interdisciplinary Study of Network Organization in Biological and Human Social Systems." PhD thesis, University of Bath, 2006. http://www.jackwhitehead.com/teesonphd/002c1.pdf.

Thaler, Richard H. *Quasi-Rational Economics.* New York: Russell Sage Foundation, 1994.

Tocqueville, Alexis de, and Arthur Goldhammer. *Democracy in America.* New York: Library of America, 2004.

Todorov, Alexander, Susan Fiske, Deborah Prentice, and Deborah A. Prentice, eds. *Social Neuroscience: Toward Understanding the Underpinnings of the Social Mind.* Oxford: Oxford University Press, 2011.

Xie, J., S. Sreenivasan, G. Korniss, W. Zhang, C. Lim, and B. K. Szymanski. "Social Consensus Through the Influence of Committed Minorities." *Physical Review* E 84, no. 1 (2011): 011130. doi: 10.1103/PhysRevE.84.011130.

Wadhwa, Vivek. "Career Counselor: Bill Gates or Steve Jobs?" *New York Times,* March 21, 2011. http://www.nytimes.com/roomfordebate/2011/03/20/career-counselor-bill-gates-or-steve-jobs/look-at-the-leaders-of-silicon-valley.

Wadhwa, Vivek. "Foreign-Born Entrepreneurs: An Underestimated American Resource." *Kauffman Thoughtbook,* Ewing Marion Kauffman Foundation, 2009. http://www.kauffman.org/entrepreneurship/foreign-born-entrepreneurs.aspx.

Walton, Mary. *The Deming Management Method.* U.K.: Penguin, 1986.

Watkins, Alfred, and Joshua Mandell. "Global Forum Action Plan: Science, Technology and Innovation Building Partnerships for Sustainable Development." World Bank, September 1, 2010. http://siteresources.worldbank.org/INTSTIGLOFOR/Resources/STI_GlobalForum_ActionPlan.pdf.

Weaver, Gary. "The American Cultural Tapestry." eJournal USA (June, 2006): 18-20. http://guangzhou.usembassy-china.org.cn/uploads/images/r4YPWf8G8Npaa6zJQxaKHQ/ijse0606.pdf.

Weiss, Charles, and Nicolas Jéquier, eds. *Technology, Finance, and Development.* Toronto: Lexington Books, 1984.

"Well! What a Good Idea!" *Economist,* September, 30, 2010. http://www.economist.com/node/17145208.

Wells, Spencer. *The Journey of Man: A Genetic Odyssey.* Princeton: Princeton University Press, 2002.

Wheatley, Margaret J. *Leadership and the New Science: Discovering Order In A Chaotic World.* San Francisco: Berrett-Koehler Publishers, 2006.

White, John R., and Arthur S. Freeman (editors). *Cognitive-Behavioral Group Therapy for Specific Problems and Populations.* Washington: American Psychological Association, 2000.

White, Richard. *Railroaded: The Transcontinentals and the Making of Modern America.* New York: W. W. Norton & Company, 2011.

Wildman, Steven S. "Communication and Economics: Two Imperial Disciplines and Too Little Collaboration." *Journal of Communication* 58, no. 4 (2008): 693-706. doi: 10.1111/j.1460-2466.2008.00409.x.

Wilson, Edward O. *Consilience: The Unity of Knowledge.* New York: Vintage Books, 1999.

Wilson, Edward O. *On Human Nature.* Cambridge: Harvard University Press, 1978.

Witchel, Alex. "Coffee Talk With: Howard Schultz; By Way of Canarsie, One Large Hot Cup of Business Strategy." *New York Times,* December 14, 1994. http://www.nytimes.com/1994/12/14/garden/coffee-talk-with-howard-schultz-way-canarsie-one-large-hot-cup-business-strategy.html.

Wolf Shenk, Joshua. "Two Is the Magic Number." *Slate*, September 14, 2010. http://www.slate.com/id/2267004/.

Woolley, Anita Williams, Christopher F. Chabris, Alexander Pentland, Nada Hashmi, and Thomas W. Malone. "Evidence for a Collective Intelligence Factor in the Performance of Human Groups." Sciencexpress (2010). doi: 10.1126/science.1193147.

World Bank. "Bank Lending for Industrial Technology Development Vols I and II." Report No. 12138. World Bank. Washington D.C.: June 30, 1993.

Wright, Jesse H. "Cognitive Behavior Therapy: Basic Principles and Recent Advances." *FOCUS (Psychiatry Online)*, Spring 2006, Vol. IV, No. 2 (pp. 173-178). http://focus.psychiatryonline.org/data/Journals/FOCUS/2634/173.pdf

WTO. "Free Trade Helps Reduce Poverty, Says New WTO Secretariat Study." Press release. June 13, 2000. http://www.wto.org/english/news_e/pres00_e/pr181_e.htm.

Würtz, Peter and Arto Annila. "Roots of Diversity Relations." *Journal of Biophysics*, Volume 2008 (2008), Article ID 654672, doi:10.1155/2008/654672, http://www.hindawi.com/journals/jbp/2008/654672/.

Van Bavel, Jay J. and William A. Cunningham. "Social Identity Modulates Automatic Face Perception: Group Membership Overrides the Effects of Race on Early Event-Related Potentials." Poster presented at Social and Affective Neuroscience Conference, Chicago, October, 2010. http://www.socialaffectiveneuro.org/docs/SANS_program_2010.pdf.

Zakaria, Fareed. *The Post-American World*. New York: Norton, 2008.

Zaki, Jamil, and Kevin Ochsner. "You, Me, and My Brain: Self and Other Representations in Social Cognitive Neuroscience." *Social Neuroscience: Toward Understanding the Underpinnings of the Social Mind*. ed. Alexander B. Todorov et al. Oxford: Oxford University Press, 2011. doi:10.1093/acprof:oso/9780195316872.003.0002.

Index

About the Authors

Victor W. Hwang is a venture capitalist and entrepreneur living in Silicon Valley. He is co-founder and Managing Director of T2 Venture Capital, a firm that grows startups, invests capital, and assists the development of innovation economies worldwide. T2VC's clients have included dozens of investors, governments, and corporations, including the World Bank, the U.S. Agency for International Development, and Cisco, among many others.

Victor has spent his career at the intersection of private venture and public policy. He has founded or been involved in the original teams of numerous startup companies. He is the former President of Larta Institute, which mentors hundreds of startup companies for federal agencies, such as the National Science Foundation and the National Institutes of Health. He practiced law as a corporate attorney on transactions ranging from angel and venture investments to multi-billion dollar corporate mergers and public offerings.

He received a law degree from the University of Chicago, where his professors included Elena Kagan and Cass Sunstein. He received a bachelor's degree with honors from Harvard University, where his professors included E.O. Wilson.

He has lived across America, including Boston, Chicago, Iowa, Indiana, Los Angeles, Louisiana, North Carolina, Washington, D.C., and Austin, Texas, where his roots run deep. He lives in Silicon Valley with his two boys, Anders and Augustine, and his wife, Christina.

Greg Horowitt is co-founder and Managing Director of T2 Venture Capital, where he has invested in a variety of technology and life science startup companies. He is an advisor, speaker, and consultant to organizations around the world, including the State Department, OECD, Aspen Institute, and the National Academies of Science.

Greg is the co-founder of Global CONNECT, a think tank based at the University of California, San Diego, and focused on the development and growth of innovation ecosystems. Under his leadership, Global CONNECT has grown to encompass one of the world's largest networks of innovation hubs: more than 40 programs in 20 countries. Greg was formerly the interim Managing Director of CONNECT, an organization which is generally credited with San Diego's success as a technology leader.

He served as Entrepreneur-in-Residence for SK Global, a Silicon Valley venture capital firm. He was the President and CEO of a venture-backed enterprise software company in the Valley. Before that, he was Vice President of Regional Sales for a Berkshire Hathaway company, Flying Cross by Fechheimer.

Greg holds a degree in Biochemistry, with minors in Economics and Music Performance from the University of California, San Diego.

16814822R00172

Made in the USA
San Bernardino, CA
18 November 2014